LINDA DOBSON

The Ultimate Book of Homeschooling Ideas

500+ Fun and Creative Learning Activities
for Kids Ages 3–12

 THREE RIVERS PRESS • NEW YORK

With deepest love and gratitude to John, Mike, Greg, Charlie, Mark, Major Bill and his men, Deanna, Eddie, Sara, Dianna, Louise, Lillian, Paula R., Paula H-C, Helen, Shay, Norma, Mary S., Mary McC, Lynn, Tony, Karolyn, Jennifer, Nik, Tracy, Jamie, Kyoko, Mom and Dad, Cathie, Rob, Michaele, Todd, my beautiful children, and my life's sunshine, Emily, for all your help, love, and support.

Published by Three Rivers Press, New York, New York.
Member of the Crown Publishing Group, a division of Random House, Inc., New York.
www.randomhouse.com

THREE RIVERS PRESS and the Tugboat Design are registered trademarks of Random House, Inc.

Originally published by Prima Publishing, Roseville, California, in 2002.

Interior Design: Melanie Haage
Illustrator: Nathaniel Levine

Printed in the United States of America

Library of Congress Cataloging-in-Publication Data
Dobson, Linda.
    The ultimate book of homeschooling ideas: 500+ fun and creative learning activities for kids ages 3–12 / Linda Dobson.
        p.   cm.
    Includes index.
        1. Homeschooling—Handbooks, manuals, etc. I. Title: Ultimate book of homeschooling ideas. II. Title.
LC40 .D655 2002
371.04'2—dc21   2002028534
ISBN 0-7615-6360-1

10 9 8 7 6 5

First Edition

Contents

Introduction

To laugh often and much;
To win the respect of intelligent people
And the affection of children;
To earn the appreciation of honest critics
And endure the betrayal of friends;
To appreciate beauty,
To find the best in others;
To leave the world a little bit better,
Whether by a healthy child,
A garden patch,
Or a redeemed social condition;
To know even one life has breathed easier
Because you lived.
This is to have succeeded.

—Ralph Waldo Emerson

Welcome to a wonderful environment where children learn without necessarily being "taught," where questions fly without embarrassment, and where learning—mingled with all the other "stuff" of life—happens day and night, weekday and weekend, winter, spring, summer, and fall. Oh, and did I mention that learning can be a lot of fun here, too?

"Here" is the world of families learning at home together. It's a place currently populated by hundreds of thousands of parents who choose to embrace the responsibility of educating approximately two million of their own children themselves. It's a local community connected by park days, museum trips, and face-to-face weekly or monthly meetings. It's a state- or nation-centered population intent on preserving parental rights in education. Even more of these families form an international community connected by the Internet and e-mail. They are black, white, rich, poor, urban, rural, Christian, Jewish, Muslim, and just about everyone else.

In acknowledging a diversity of members, you'd probably guess that a wide variety of curriculum materials and books exist to serve it, and you'd be right. However, until now, one could not find a convenient, commonsense collection of ideas and materials, tips, and how-tos that bypass curricula and textbooks on a different course toward education, one that is family centered and remarkably easy, rewarding, and enjoyable for both parent and child.

Parent Tested, Kid Approved

The great learning ideas gathered between the covers of this book aren't just projects someone *thinks* kids will learn from and, if they're lucky, enjoy at the same time. Rather, they arrive in your home as recommendations from very special parents who are aware of their responsibility to make sure their children grow and thrive. Having usually partaken in a deeper study of education than the average person, and having been on the receiving end of sales pitches for every book and learning system on Earth, these parents tend to be extremely savvy education consumers.

When the homeschooling parents sent ideas for consideration in this book, they *knew* the ideas worked because they had created and/or implemented the ideas in their own homes with their own children. All of these activities and suggestions, intended exclusively to enrich children's educational experiences, are parent tested, kid approved.

The Book's Organization

The organization of this book is by subject. I yielded to this rather loosely defined system of organization to bring some semblance of order to the ideas. You'll note that because so many ideas don't fit neatly into one, two, or even three subject categories, I created chapter 11, "Across the Curriculum," in which to gather them.

Having decided to organize the book by subject, I rejected the notion of adding age levels to the ideas for a couple of reasons. First, any assignment of age level would be based on the opinion of only a handful of people who initially work on the book, just as, I might add, people far removed from your children arbitrarily determine age levels for textbook content, curriculum, and test matter. Instead, here we'll trust the parent-readers to know what skill is *appropriate* for their own children.

If you're unsure of your child's current skill level, it doesn't take long to get a ballpark figure. Pick an activity that you believe your child already knows. If the activity is too easy, find another one that takes things up a notch; if that one is difficult, find an easier one. It should only take a few adjustments before you find you're in the right place.

That said, don't deny your child the opportunity to partake in activities because she "already knows" those things. Review never hurt anyone, and children, just like adults, enjoy the feeling of accomplishment that accompanies successful completion of a task, especially if it's also fun! Take plenty of time together to indulge in such learning luxury.

Second, I like to think that, at times, children will themselves pick up a book to look for something to do. I hate the thought that they might find something that sounds interesting, only to find that it's assigned to an age level they have yet to reach, and then perhaps not attempt it at all in response. Too limiting!

Let Your Imagination Fly

Some of the successful ideas that parents share in this book were found by them in sources long forgotten. Many more were their own creations, thought up to meet their children's particular needs at a given time. You'll notice how many of the contributors outline an idea, then give several additional suggestions for adapting the activity to different or extended needs. It's everyone's hope that not only will you use their ideas, but also that the ideas will serve as seeds from which will blossom your own ideas. Maybe you'll use different materials, because that's what you have in your household. Perhaps you'll make the activity a bit easier or harder as your children's current needs dictate, or you'll adapt the idea to an entirely different subject. Let your imagination fly.

Some of the ideas were created by the children themselves, and don't forget to let your children do the same! As your children engage in an activity, listen if they make suggestions or recommendations for improvement—chances are very good that if you implement their ideas, their learning will be quicker, deeper, and more fun than ever. Children's creative muscles haven't usually atrophied to the same degree as our adult muscles have, so frequent opportunity to flex them will keep them strong and supple.

Supplement for Traditional Schooling

Peruse just a few of the learning ideas and you'll quickly see that your children don't have to be homeschoolers to benefit from them. Each activity's description is short and thorough enough for you to quickly determine if it's something that could help your children

- Learn and enjoy a new concept
- Get some practice in skills they're working on
- Receive extra help with a stumbling block

When the neighborhood children gather and cry, "We're bored!" pick up this book to find something for them to do, either as a group or side-by-side. When you need materials, they're almost always things you have around the house already.

The activities can also become the center of enjoyable time spent together after school, in the evenings, on weekends, during vacations, or in the summer months. No matter where you choose to use the activities, join in! Your children will appreciate it, and it's an important way to demonstrate that learning is a lifelong activity that they can still enjoy long after they leave school.

Keep Learning Fun

You've likely noticed how often the word *fun* crept into this introduction. Critics who are sold on the order, measurability, and supposed accountability of traditional schooling charge that an educational approach incorporating a good deal of fun is somehow overly protective and fails to prepare children for life's hard knocks, the tougher lessons from which no one is immune. Certainly they're right that *someday* there may be times when life and learning aren't going to be a picnic for our children. Seeing to it, though, that the hard knocks start sooner rather than later, that learning becomes a chore on someone else's timetable using someone else's methods, especially at the tender ages of three, or five, or even eight years old, is counterproductive.

The odds are good that someday our children will be involved in some sort of car accident. Does this mean we should purposefully engage them in an accident today so they're prepared for a future one? The odds are also good that someday our children will spend time in a hospital. Should we poison their dinners today so they get the hang of lying in a hospital bed?

Of course, we don't prepare children for *possible* perils by bringing on all of life's turmoil sooner than necessary. Rather, we smooth the way through education, giving them the tools they will need to handle whatever life throws their way. We teach them, through the words and actions of daily life, how to properly ride in a car, who it's safe to ride with, and, eventually, how to be good drivers themselves. We feed them nutritious meals, encourage good hygiene, and see to it that their lives include a healthy balance of work, exercise, and play. In other words, rather than make sure that they face the challenges at a young age, we make the effort necessary to *protect and prepare* them just in case bad things do happen one day.

So how does one ready young children for future learning experiences that may get rough? First, we protect the joy they naturally experience from learning something new, just as we protect the good health they enjoy as youngsters. Next, we prepare them with the knowledge and skills they'll need to "be a good driver" on any learning road they may travel. The best preparation for this is learning how to learn. Maintaining the joy of learning and knowing how to teach *themselves* whatever they need to know are necessary for future learning

I can't think of *any* good reasons learning can't or shouldn't be fun for both the young and the young at heart, and I've witnessed many good reasons why it should. Blessed to have spent years traveling around the country meeting homeschooling families wherever I go, I've seen the same smile and enthusiasm for learning emanating from little faces from Massachusetts to California and all stops in between. The reason, I'm convinced, is because of a lack of focus on "schooling" and all the baggage that accompanies it, and devoting the time freed from this focus to education instead. We'll look more closely at this much needed distinction in chapter 1, so don't miss it.

Let your first goal of using this book, then, be to have fun—let the learning be incidental! Your children *will* learn from every activity. It's what they do, and they're mighty good at it. Join them, for they have a lot to teach you if you're open to the possibilities.

I know you're eager to get into the meat of this book, the exciting learning activities that lie ahead. Please, however, read chapters 1 and 2 first, as they will be of immense help in understanding the value of the rest of the book. *Then* you can play!

1

Helping Your Child
Love Learning

Imagine growing up with the entire world's information instantaneously available, literally at your fingertips. Your children, racing toward adulthood just as the Information Age kicks into high gear, will know nothing different. If gaining access to information was what children used to be sent to school for, what are school attendance, knowledge, and education really about in this day and age?

One of the greatest tributes to homeschooling's success is not the children's well-touted abundance of academic achievements but rather the *way* in which children who have grown up at home instead of at school accomplish learning. This is not to say that the results of homeschooling are universal. Success is no more ensured by going about learning this way than it is by institutional—public or private—school attendance. Success is, however, much more likely with homeschooling, due in large part to fundamental differences in learning principles that guide the homeschooler's course.

To better understand the value of the material in this book, we must first dichotomize the thinking behind institutional and home approaches to learning. In so doing, we may deepen our appreciation for the opportunity our children have to learn in ways suited to their natural inclinations instead of in ways that help the school institution function *despite* the needs of those it professes to serve.

School Mind

Let's begin with what is, by far, the most popular way to think about education, at least for the past 160 years. We'll call it "school mind." This thinking originates with a simple basic premise: Schools are necessary for children to learn and be socialized. Because of this starting point, the school mind places its trust about learning and socialization in the schools (theoretically, learning institutions; hereafter I will use the terms *schools* and *institutions* interchangeably). Despite the natural and numerous variations among human beings— you know, the ones we rave about when we recognize them in adults—*all* young human beings get sent to the same institutions to learn the same things at the same time in the same way. This is the essence of a system, as in "school system," described by *The American Heritage Dictionary* as an entity that "stresses order and regularity affecting all parts of a relatively complex procedure."

Certainly, the workings of school have become ordered and regulated. But anyone who has spent even a cursory amount of time studying how human beings learn knows it's complex and rather messy. Where one child needs to see, another has to hear. Where one child grasps concepts quickly, another must sleep on them before they make sense. Where one child requires a quiet environment, another can't take the silence. Where one child uses more of the left brain, another favors the right. There's little, if any, "order and regularity" here among the folks that the "system" is supposed to serve.

The school system, then, exists to apply artificial order where none naturally resides. In the school mind, this makes sense. Remember, in this mind, the institution is the necessary ingredient. As such, much time, energy, and attention is spent keeping the system, which is striving for order and regularity, functioning. The more order and regularity accomplished, the smoother the sailing *for the system itself.*

Of course, the people whose livelihoods depend on survival of the system must implement practices that serve this end. These practices include regularity—in the ages at which children begin and end attendance, in the subjects presented for study, in the content of the books they read, in the daily schedule they keep. These practices include order—assignments, right answers, grades, standardized tests, diplomas signifying that the order was followed.

As pillars for order and regulation, school minds believe in the necessity of the following:

- *Compulsory attendance.* This demands, by force of law, that children spend large amounts of their time in the institution and away from the reality of daily life.

- *Curriculum.* A course of study laid out ahead of time for everyone, chosen by people who are strangers to the children, who lack personal involvement in the children's interests in the subject matter, and who are not affected by their success or failure.

- *A focus on the children's inability to meet existing standards.* Children need to be tested, then measured against other children to determine, among other things, if they need to be "fixed" to become part of the desired "regularity."

Here's what we end up with:

Compulsory attendance + Curriculum + Focus on lack of meeting existing standards = Schooling

Everyone who has been ordered and regulated via these methods has been "schooled." (This certainly explains how there are so many people walking around with school mind.) It also sheds light on how we, as a nation, can spend so much money and time and energy on keeping the system going, even while witnessing an astonishingly large percentage of children going through the process and coming out unable to read, write, think, or tell Jay Leno whether the Revolutionary War or the Civil War came first.

Although children may be legally forced to sit through more than a decade of order and regularity, not a single school administrator will guarantee any form of actual learning. Courts will not hear cases in which parents take school systems to task for failing to educate their children. With school as the essential ingredient, the only certainty is that children will be schooled. We can no longer afford, however, to believe that being schooled is synonymous with receiving an education.

Education Mind

Due to the modern experience of homeschooling, increasing numbers of adults *and* children possess what I call "education mind." The basic premise of education mind is that a school and its system are *not* elements necessary for children's education and socialization. Without a requirement to create and maintain a system to instill order and regularity, the starting point of thinking about learning and socialization naturally shifts to the child, who is to be served by any efforts in this direction. The need to apply order and regularity to an organically "messy" process disappears. Instead, increased time, energy, and attention (and money!) can be devoted directly to children, which increases the odds for their own smoother sailing.

The pillars to hold up order and regulation, mentioned earlier, are no longer necessary, because system support can be replaced by direct support of the children's needs:

- *Autonomous use of time.* Compulsory attendance laws control children's time for approximately half a year of regular forty-hour workweeks each school year. The freedom of individuals to use this large block of time in ways more appropriate to their own needs and desires creates much more opportunity for meaningful learning.

- *Purpose.* When children are curious about (interested in) something, they can see a purpose to learn about it. Interest creates intrinsic motivation to learn. This leads to a quicker grasp of information, concepts, or skills desired. Because interest leads children to apply the knowledge once acquired, they retain it.

- *Focus on what is being achieved.* Serving the needs of individual children negates comparisons with other children. Emphasis and attention shift to each child's forward progress. Someone who knows the child well, and loves and supports her, can accomplish this positive focus.

Where does this lead us?

Time + Purpose + Focus on what is being achieved = Education

Learning that begins in freedom, that is guided by curiosity, and that is conducted without a need for external rewards and punishments gives children an understanding that life *is* learning. As I wrote in *The Art of Education: Reclaiming Your Family, Community, and Self,* "In the singular act of living life to its fullest, in appreciating every moment as it unfolds, true education occurs. A child who grows knowing he already has inside happiness, love, success, and fulfillment is building a life and an education on a strong foundation. The inner gifts shine forth in play, work, busy time, quiet time, triumphs and failures. Each action becomes its own reward."

Certainly this formula is not the only way to create education in lieu of schooling (and, yes, an education is possible simultaneously with schooling), but it is one that has proven to work. It is also inexpensive and accessible to millions of families within their own homes.

School Mind Versus Education Mind

School Mind

**Compulsory Attendance (time in institution away from real world) +
Curriculum (study chosen by strangers and lack of interest) + Focus on
Lack of Meeting Existing Standards (tests, measuring against others +
"fix the child to fit in" mentality) = Schooling**

Education Mind

**Time (freedom and opportunity) + Purpose (intrinsic motivation and interest)
+ Focus on What Is Being Achieved (love and support) = Education**

Real Learning Is Messy

The school mind believes that one should go about educating children by "delivering answers." As part of the necessary regulation, a curriculum determines which answers are to be delivered at a specific time, using the children's ages as a guide. The answers arrive at the children's desks all clean and polished and organized in textbooks, presented in allegedly easy-to-digest bits and pieces. Order and regulation are as necessary for an "answer delivery service" as they are for a package delivery service. Testing acts as quality control to determine how many answers hit their marks.

I entered the workforce almost immediately after public high school graduation. After so many years in school, the real world seemed a strange place, for which I was ill prepared. On that first workday, I sat at my desk thinking, "I can't do this!" People were so busy flitting around the office doing their own thing that no one had time to spoon-feed me little bits of digestible knowledge. Instead, they handed me the whole enchilada and expected me to start chomping off huge bits—*now*. Yeah, it was messy.

More than half a dozen jobs later, and after the experience of teaching myself numerous skills to accomplish personal goals, I've faced a lot of messes. When no one delivers the answers, there's the disarray of trial and error while you dig around for them yourself. There's also all that additional information you bump into that creates even more questions. Often there's the confusion—and frustration—of failure, followed by a hard, close look at what went wrong so you don't waste your precious time making the same mistake again. There's the hope and enthusiasm that grow from the excitement of leaving the wrong path behind and starting down a new one. And then there's that indescribably delicious exhilaration of the "aha!" moment when you *know* you've found the missing piece. You own the knowledge gained. If ever necessary, it's available for you to *apply* in myriad ways in the future. *That's* education.

This description is one person's perspective on the way adults learn outside of schools. Indeed, many homeschooling parents report that as they take on responsibility for their children's education, they closely examine how they learn what is important in their lives. This scrutiny tends to add another mark in favor of homeschooling, because the school approach emerges as an artificial process, as unsatisfying as a glass of orange-flavored soda when you're thirsting for orange juice.

Why deny curious children the learning route we adults allow ourselves? Or rather, why put them through the artificial "order" when the "mess" of real learning offers so many valuable life experiences in the search for answers? This mess is just an open mind away. Indeed, your mind must be open if you want to discard school mind to make room for education mind.

School mind asks, "What should my child know at grade level X?" Education mind asks children what they are interested in and further observes active children to gather its own clues. School mind asks, "Do they need to know this for a test?" Education mind asks, "Do they need to know this to improve their lives in some way?" School mind asks, "What can I teach them?" Education mind asks, "What can they learn?" School mind asks, "What answers have they retained?" Education mind asks, "Have they learned how to learn?" With just a little practice, you'll be turning around similar questions yourself in no time.

How Children Learn

Whoever said "a little knowledge is a dangerous thing" may have been talking about education reformers when they get their hands on the emerging research about early childhood development. For several years, news flash after news flash has heralded new understanding of everything from neural connections to "windows of opportunity," and educators still scramble to bend the research to fit into the order and regularity of schooling.

Let's use as an example the report that resulted from a two-and-a-half-year review of hundreds of early childhood studies by the National Research Council, the research arm of the National Academy of Sciences, the National Academy of Engineering, and the Institute of Medicine. Jack Shonkoff, dean of Heller Graduate School, headed the panel and granted an interview to the *Washington Post* in March 2001, shortly after the report's release.

First, Mr. Shonkoff states that "one of the most important findings in the early childhood domain is the importance of nurturing, stable relationships as the key to promoting competence in young children." My education mind considered this confirmation of an oft-cited benefit of homeschooling.

Mr. Shonkoff's school mind, though, worries about why we "are paying so little attention to the issues of training and compensation for the professionals who provide the care and education of children before they start school."

He continues by stating that "research tells us that children's social and emotional development is critical to their learning." Education mind says, well, of course one needs to nurture all aspects of the child, and home is a safe, easy place to do so. "School mind" worries because Head Start teachers say their biggest challenge "is difficulty in managing emotional and behavioral problems."

In both cases, school mind looks at perfectly logical arguments for later, not earlier, school attendance, yet it continues to put the system first by focusing, in these cases, on how teachers (within the system) can achieve the benefits that would more naturally occur if the children remained at home. The school mind totally ignores the fact that children are rushed out of the home environment *despite* what the research says.

A Brief but Important Introduction to What Research Says

There's now enough research on early learning to fill a set of encyclopedias many times over. Therefore, I will hit some highlights relevant to using the activities in this book to your child's best advantage. Remember to let this exploration of research exercise your education mind.

Background on the Brain

Brains are made up of two kinds of cells: nerve cells (neurons), with branches called dendrites, and glial cells. Basically, the glial cells nourish the billions of neurons that busily create and maintain connections for thinking. This is accomplished when a neuron's dendrites pick up messages from other neurons and send them to the cell's body, from which the message travels further still to the axon, the neuron's out box. When leaving the out box, the message must "jump" across a gap (synapse) to be picked up by another neuron's dendrites. This feat happens billions of times each day as we participate in mental activity.

Enter new experiences for a child. These new experiences create new connections, changing the structure of dendrites and synapses to create new paths down which messages may travel. A child can learn new skills as the brain becomes more flexible now that alternative paths to the old destinations are developing. Ah, so experience is a key to learning? Let's find out.

Rats!

This has been one of my favorite research results since I discovered it over a decade ago in Dr. Jane Healy's *Endangered Minds: Why Children Don't Think and What We Can Do About It* (Touchstone, 1990). Dr. Healy reports on an experiment in which all rats received the same food and water, but some lived in "impoverished" cages while others enjoyed an "enriched" environment—larger cages, more friends, and lots of toys that kept them curious and active. Researchers found that although the impoverished rats weighed more, their brains were inferior in two aspects significant to learning. "First," explains Dr. Healy, "there are many more glial support cells in the enriched brains, and second, the neurons themselves have more dendrite spines and thus, presumably, more synapses." In addition, the enriched rats "appear to pick up more and different information during exploration as a result of their lively curiosity."

Although this research does not translate directly to humans, we can still stretch our imaginations and think of the impoverished environment as a bad school where life experience is limited and the enriched environment as a good school offering more opportunity for life experiences.

And then there are the rats that grew up "in the wild" outside the lab, exposed "to the real challenges of living in a free environment," explains Dr. Healy, "finding food, defending themselves, and moving about when and where they wish." Rather than being in school, these rats participated in activities that are part of real life in a rat community. These rats are, in comparison, the "homeschooled" rats.

Researchers have found that the "enriched" environment isn't as stimulating to the rats' brain as is the natural one, from which come rats that "tend to have larger and heavier cortexes than do those raised in cages." Cortexes, Dr. Healy explains in her book, are "the control panels for processing information at three levels: receiving sensory stimuli, organizing them into meaningful patterns so that we can make sense out of our world, and associating patterns to develop abstract types of learning and thinking."

This sure gives us something to chew on.

Parents with Education Mind Know

- Experience provides young children with the "files" of information they need for learning, thinking, reasoning, and making decisions in the future.

- Cramming things into children's heads under even the best artificial circumstances isn't as efficient as allowing time for natural processes to unfold.

- Given sufficient time, children quench natural curiosity that results in learning.

Relevance to this book's activities: Rather than waiting for the possibility that your child will receive sufficient, stimulating experience, you provide that experience with activities that can become part of your lifestyle.

Children Need Touch and Attention

Examining brain function, emotional learning in infants, and cultural differences, two Harvard Medical School researchers, Michael L. Commons and Patrice M. Miller, told us in 1998 that early separation of babies from parents creates stress that causes unnecessary, permanent harm. "It changes the nervous system so [children] are overly sensitive to future trauma," researcher Commons states.

Indeed, the research partners say that the way we are brought up colors our entire society. "We've stressed independence so much that it's having some very negative effects," explains Miller. Parents distance themselves in separate beds, often separate rooms, and don't respond quickly to crying for fear that their children will grow up dependent. Commons and Miller say this is a backward way of going about independence. "Physical contact and reassurance," they declare, "will make children more secure and better able to form adult relationships when they finally head out on their own."

When the Gusii people of Kenya, whose culture includes sleeping with their babies, watched videotapes of U.S. mothers with their infants, they grew upset that American moms took so long to respond to crying. The researchers called ours a violent nation marked by loose, nonphysical relationships. "I think there's a real resistance in this culture to caring for children," Commons concludes, "but punishment and abandonment have never been good ways to get warm, caring, independent people."

Parents with Education Mind Know

- People criticize them for being "overly protective."
- Their children often appear less stressed than their peers.
- The reassurance of their presence and attention builds a firm foundation of security from which their children venture out into the world.

- Others who meet their children after a period of home-schooling notice how warm, caring, and independent they have become.

Relevance to this book's activities: As a parent, your participation in activities is essential so that the necessary social and emotional growth occurs along with the academic enrichment.

Play It Again, Children

Thanks to magnetic resonance imaging (MRI), research shows that when humans learn a motor movement (such as playing the piano), a large portion of the brain's motor region is used. But according to a report in a 2000 issue of *Cognitive Brain Research,* the brain uses smaller and smaller regions of the motor cortex as the person gains experience, or begins to master the skill. In other words, repetition, alternatively called practice, makes neural networks more efficient to the point that regions of the cortex are free for still other uses.

Parents with Education Mind Know

- Children with the time available to do so will naturally gravitate toward practice, alternatively viewed as repetitive play with regard to children.

- Children have the perseverance to immerse themselves in repetition if free to do so.

- Play is a child's most important work.

Relevance to this book's activities: Your child may become so enamored with a particular activity and want to repeat it to the point where you think you'll go mad if you do it one more time! Do it one more time.

Age Integration

An analysis of fifty-seven studies from 1968 to 1990 revealed that 52 percent of multiage classrooms outscored single-grade ones, reported the *Chicago Sun Times* in May 2001. Multiage classrooms group together two or three grades, and the teacher stays with the children for more than a year. Some research indicates that such grouping reduces bullying, aggression, and discipline problems and increases self-esteem, cooperation, and social skills.

According to the article, advocates report that "multiage classrooms feel more like families." "Veterans nurture younger students, teach them classroom rules and routines, and help them with academic tasks that solidify their own understanding." Test scores in many schools rose, even as some parents complained that "it didn't look like learning was going on. It looked like kids were having a ball." (Now is that school mind or what? Can't have fun and learn at the same time!)

"I get help from the fifth-graders, but I can also help the third-graders," explains Mike, a fourth-grader in the middle of a third-to-fifth-grade classroom. "It's fun . . . it's almost like we're brother and sister."

Parents with Education Mind Know

- Younger children listen and pick up knowledge seemingly by osmosis when older children are learning in the vicinity.

- That warm, family feeling naturally supports social and emotional development so that it doesn't need to be artificially enhanced.

- Everyone likes to feel useful, helpful, and needed. This includes children.

Relevance to this book's activities: Enlist the whole family in activities whenever possible. Younger children take clues about growing up from older siblings. Interaction between children of mixed ages mirrors the real world, and children grow more inclined to accept and help each other.

How Are *You* Doing?

When children feel their social and emotional needs are met, they are more inclined to ask for help, says the *Journal of Educational Psychology.* In relation to schools, where were these important needs best met? According to University of Illinois researchers, the needs are met in classrooms "that emphasize self-improvement rather than relative ability" and where the opportunity to "take risks" is allowed. Where relative ability rules, children with self-imposed low academic expectations seek help less often. As a result, educators are encouraged to "let your students focus on how well they personally have improved rather than on comparing themselves to others in the room."

Parents with Education Mind Know

- A child's self-improvement is more important than high test scores that prove nothing except that the child is good at taking tests.

- Self-improvement is a clear indicator of individual progress readily and easily observable to the learner and to an attentive adult who knows the learner well.

- Focusing on one's own improvement helps a student realize his education is a gift to himself instead of a competition that only a small minority "wins."

- Effort as opposed to a grade (the journey as opposed to the destination) becomes valuable in its own right.

Relevance to this book's activities: Use the activities for fun time together, not to increase your child's test scores. Watch for improvement of academic skills for its own sake. Encourage your child to do the same.

Calling All Parents to Talk

Jane Healy's *Endangered Minds* includes a chapter on language. In it she reports on a conversation with Dr. Arnold Scheibel, coauthor of a preliminary study on postnatal development of the brain's motor speech area. After what was still a limited study of "normal" brains of children aged three months to six years, Dr. Scheibel "is personally convinced that interaction with adults, including language stimulation, is one of the growing brain's most important assets."

"Without being melodramatic," he further stated, "I think it would be very important to tell parents they are participating with the physical development of their youngsters' brains to the exact degree that they interact with them, communicate with them. Language interaction is actually building tissue in their brains—so it's also helping build youngsters' futures."

Parents with Education Mind Know

- Children need interaction with caring adults.
- Parents need to spend a decent amount of time with their children in order to have opportunities for interaction.
- The better you know your children, the deeper and more significant the communication. The deeper and more significant the communication, the better you know your children.

Relevance to this book's activities: Building stronger, lasting relationships by participating in these activities is even more important than the academic benefits realized.

Supporting Autonomy

Research on "student-centered classrooms" is most interesting to homeschoolers. It drips with irony. Even as critics, especially those from state teachers unions, continue to decry homeschooling's child-centeredness as ill preparation for their entry into the adult world of "having to do things you don't want to do," the *Journal of Educational Psychology* shared a 1999 study of teachers who use "autonomy supportive" teaching methods as opposed to "relatively controlling" methods.

Students of autonomy supportive teachers were found to be more likely to stay in school, perform better academically, and show more positive emotion, among other things. Here are some of the qualities that set these teachers apart from their more controlling counterparts. These teachers

- Listened more
- Supported the students' intrinsic motivation
- Verbalized fewer directives
- Asked more questions about what the students wanted to do
- Responded more to student-generated questions
- Didn't hold the instructional material in front of the class as often

Along the same lines, a Yale University study compared instruction involving analytical, creative, and practical methods of instruction to the rote, memory-based approach typically used in public school. Students exposed to the former methods had superior results in performance-based and memory-based multiple choice tests.

Parents with Education Mind Know

- Removal of complete external control on children's education allows space for all-important self-motivation.
- Students maintain their joy of learning when they feel they "own" the education they receive because they have had a large say in determining its course for themselves.

- Children in charge of their own education are more inclined to take risks, exhibit high amounts of creativity, and possess many practical skills.

- It is possible for parents to help their children learn without being a "relatively controlling" teacher.

Relevance to this book's activities: Allow your children to choose the activities most appealing to them. Pepper your conversation with open-ended questions that help your children create and analyze. Encourage suggestions for activity improvements or new activities, and follow through with them.

Don't Sit Around Holding Your Breath!

As you exercise your education mind, you're probably wondering why all this knowledge about how children learn hasn't been more visible in the present educational reform that is all the rage. Truth is, one of the prices of all that order and regularity is a huge bureaucracy running all the way from the school in your neighborhood to the U.S. Department of Education in Washington, D.C., with many other state and federal organizations' hands in the system. The system is incapable of rapid change, *even* in the rare cases in which service to the children is a primary goal.

You don't have to wait for others to provide rich educational experience for your child. You can take a giant leap ahead of educational reform by using your education mind to create your own curriculum, or bypass curriculum use all together.

2

Creating Your Own
Educational Reform

Because of the ever-increasing number of laws related to schooling, politics and educational reform go hand in hand. The first President Bush called it "America 2000." With a few tweaks and a slight name change, President Clinton gave us "Goals 2000." (You don't hear anything about those goals anymore!) Today, the second President Bush touts the "No Child Left Behind Act of 2001," which, by the way, represents $44.5 billion for the U.S. Department of Education in fiscal 2002 (one year, at the federal level!). The next president will ballyhoo a new brand of educational reform with an equally catchy name, setting forth yet another set of standards and his or her ideas about how the government will see to it that those standards are met or, better yet, exceeded. Federal education funds are the carrot ensuring compliance, as any school that "doesn't play" loses a sizeable chunk of cash.

Every time the program changes, new panels are commissioned to perform new studies and then issue new guidelines for necessary curriculum alterations and their implementation. Eventually, this all filters down to the local school administrators and teachers, who merely carry out the orders from on high, whatever those orders may be.

In some cases, these orders trickle down to the children in the form of tweaks to their course of study. If, for example, current research shows that American kids lag too far behind other industrialized nations' children in science, the U.S. kids find, at least in theory, a more vigorous science program. After the April 1999 Columbine tragedy, American children suddenly found themselves exposed to additional lessons in respecting diversity, new classes on how not to be a bully, and what to do when they see a bully in action. The kids with the best grades were treated to a few weeks of training as peer counselors to theoretically help head off troubles at the pass. Additional training in everything from the joy of vegetarianism to condom use, if not part of the curriculum proper, enters via special assemblies.

Of course, there are only so many hours in the day, even at school. With so much material to cover, and pressure to produce outstanding test scores as well, the number of hours spent on the school agenda must expand beyond the time during which the school doors are open. Enter lots of homework.

As a society that needs television commercials to remind us to have an occasional dinner together as a family, the homework agenda confiscates additional limited, yet still precious, family time. "Homework creep" must be epidemic. I've lost count of the number of parents who relate homework horror stories as their impetus to homeschool; but they're not the only ones who recognize the damage inflicted on familial relations when homework wars permeate the sanctuary of home.

In a February 2002 special to the *Washington Post,* psychotherapist Wendy Zevin, who carefully notes how much she appreciates her child's school and teachers, argues for more parental say in what happens in our homes. "We need a dialogue," says Zevin, "wherein parents can remind teachers that we have so much more to offer our kids in a family game of Monopoly (capitalist math, learning to be a good winner and a good loser) than in a fight over finishing 'just three more' problems that really don't amount to a hill of beans."

Zevin urges parents and educators to remember "not to waste what time we have with our children, and not to waste their time, either. That means," she explains, "that we have to look beyond intent, beyond effect on test scores, and take an accounting of unwanted side effects of homework. We must make certain that we are not squandering the rich resources of family relationships—or worse, damaging them."

Bypass (or Leap Ahead of) School Reform

There are two schools of thought on the state of American education. The first and most commonly held notion centers on the academic side of the topic. It considers illiteracy rates, falling test scores, failure to meet new standards, the trend of college remedial classes for incoming freshmen, and so on. By these criteria, American education is failing.

The second less publicized or discussed notion is that, despite all the rhetoric to the contrary, the school agenda is a raging success as it works against independent thinking and trains children to accept confinement, classification, movement en masse as a bell tolls, unquestioned authority of others, and an unexamined life as an obedient consumer and producer. (Please see *The Underground History of American Education: A Schoolteacher's Intimate Investigation into the Problem of Modern Schooling* by John Taylor Gatto (Oxford Village Press, 2000/2001) for a thorough treatise of this issue.) No matter which point of view you claim as your own, there is nothing here but a lose-lose situation for children.

You are reading this book for a reason. Perhaps you're a parent who has chosen to take your child out of school or not to send your child in the first place. If so, you are bypassing educational reform. Or maybe you're one of the growing number of parents tired of waiting for any possible benefits of reform to trickle down to your child's school. If so, you are leaping ahead of educational reform. In either case, congratulations. For your potential use, a list of wonderful, remarkably low cost resources to help you is shown in Table 2.1.

Do-It-Yourself Reform

In 1985, as I watched a laid-back little boy turn into a bundle of raw nerves as he attended kindergarten, the word "homeschooling" almost miraculously came to my attention. I spent subsequent weeks turning the idea over and over in my head, and I kept coming back to this phrase: "If you want something done right, do it yourself."

No matter what your guiding motivations are, if you're looking for change in your child's education, you can do it yourself. In fact, that's your *only* insurance that change will happen quickly enough to impact your child's experience positively. The beauty of the process is that it begins in the comfort of your own home with some of the people you most love.

Table 2.1   Educational Materials You Already Have Around the House

Material	Uses
Aluminum foil	You'll use it for everything.
Analog and digital clocks	Telling time
Baking supplies	Arithmetic basics; home economic skills
Balloons and cork	Art and science projects
Beans	Counting; planting; dissecting; making pictures
Books	Information on a variety of subjects
Buttons	Sorting; making mosaics
Calculator	Arithmetic

Material	Uses
Calendars	Basic time concepts
Computer programs	Edutainment
Contact Paper	Cheap lamination material
Crayons	Colorful art
Dice	Basic arithmetic skills; creating your own games
Food coloring	Learning about colors
Game spinners	Learning about probability
Graph paper and M&M's or other small colorful candies	Sorting; making graphs (weigh when finished, then graph results)
Index cards	Making your own note cards, flash cards, games
Internet connection	Accessing information
Library card	Key to a world of books
Math manipulatives (Lego bricks, milk jug lids, buttons, dry beans, M&M's as counters)	Arithmetic
Measuring cups and spoons	Studying fractions; multiplication, division, and more
Measuring tape (standard and metric)	Measuring
Note cards, paper, stamps, envelopes	Playing post office; writing
Paper	Writing; arts and crafts
Pencils	Writing
Puzzles	Great brain exercise
Real coins and bills	Understanding money; arithmetic skills
Recorded music	Appreciation; learning about styles; instruments; foreign countries
Ruler	Measuring
Salt dough ingredients	1,001 uses
Sidewalk chalk	Art; learning in the fresh air
Small plastic containers from yogurt, ricotta cheese, etc.	Starting seeds; making a phone with string; storing manipulatives; studying shapes; arts and crafts
Straws	Arts and crafts
Tape	Holding things together

Why You Don't Need *a Curriculum*

Remember, a curriculum is a course of study. It might help if you think of it as a highly planned tour through learning. If, in your exploration of do-it-yourself reform, you feel more comfortable using such a tour guide, then by all means use a tour guide! There are many sources of lists and general outlines of what someone somewhere has deemed that children should know and in what order they should learn these things. You can use the information to see where your child is and where your child will go.

But what if, in your learning journey, you begin with no particular place to go? What if, instead of being a professionally planned excursion complete with an itinerary some travel agency thought would be worthwhile, your family's trip becomes more like a jaunt on a beautiful spring afternoon, taken not to get anywhere in particular but only to enjoy being free to enjoy? Instead of getting on a bus with forty strangers, you might decide to walk, or ride a bike, horse, or four-wheeler, or drive around in circles stopping at inviting places along the way.

You may not see every classic site that those on the guided tour witness, but if they are among the places that interest you, you will visit some. You will also have under your belt experiences of value to you personally. For example, let's say you've tried fly fishing a time or two and enjoyed it, so for you, a visit to that funky little fly fishing museum is in order. While there you pick up ideas for new flies to make, talk with the proprietor about a few streams to try, and take home a couple of specialty books you've never seen elsewhere in order to learn even more at home. Had you traveled with that professional tour, you might not even know the museum exists because it wasn't on that itinerary.

You see, learning happens whether or not it is directed from without. Indeed, I would say that *more* learning (and remembering) occurs when you follow your interest to a meaningful destination than happens among those strangers who take the much more trav-

Using Curriculum Information as Guides

Developing Educational Standards:
edstandards.org/Standards.html

World Book Encyclopedia Scope and Sequence:
www2.worldbook.com/parents/course_study_index.asp

Kids Connection: www.kidsconn.com/first.html

eled route. This is why curriculum is not the necessity that the educational bureaucracy makes it out to be. In an article for the March 2002 *Life Learning* magazine, John Gatto said, "You can be *trained* from outside, but only educated from within; one is a habit of memory and reaction, the other *a matter of seizing the initiative*" (emphasis added).

You don't necessarily require a curriculum at home, because you're addressing education instead of training. I can't prove it at this point, because it hasn't yet been done, but I would bet that children who are guided by education mind, whose "learning time" was filled with the activities in this book, as well as the subsequent explorations these activities would engender because their time is their own, would wind up as educated people.

Just a Few Benefits of Do-It-Yourself Reform

The first and perhaps greatest benefit of do-it-yourself educational reform is the example of courage, will, and care you display to your child when you declare, "By golly, I'll do it myself." Perhaps, even subconsciously, this is what leads to the next benefit—good family relationships.

Whether you homeschool full time, part time, or simply use these activities because you think they'd be fun to share, the greater the quantity of time you spend in mutual involvement will almost undoubtedly increase the quality of your relationship with your child.

Perhaps it's because, as human beings, it's not natural that we even try to build our concept of self while we're subject to legally compulsory confinement in an institution. Mutual involvement allows time and opportunity for necessary family experience and, therefore, family identity. Home is also a safe place in which to experiment, one where a child may fail without humiliation, and try again. It's a location that lends itself to self-discovery through freedom to pursue personal interests, possibly with the help of talented (through experience) mentors. In "From Womb to World: Rethinking Self-Education" (*Life Learning* magazine, March 2002), author and interfaith community minister Katharine Houk explains, "It is in relationship that we grow. [My children] also enjoyed the richness of solitary play, something sorely lacking in the rushed and overstimulated world children find themselves in today."

Schools, Houk continues, "offer little opportunity for free play, deep dialogue with others, or solitude. Fostering growth of meaning-making and meaning-sharing is a fundamental responsibility of family and wider community."

The industrial revolution–inspired approach to schooling includes the adoption of many mass production methods, among them the breaking up of a sizeable process, such as making a car, into numerous functions in which individual workers "specialized." Joe worked at the automobile factory, but he didn't build an entire car; he put the tires on the right side of many cars, over and over and over again.

Similarly, schools artificially separate learning into "subjects" in which teachers theoretically specialize. However, you need only choose any one of the activities in this book (despite the fact that they are organized according to subjects because of the prevalence of school mind) to see that drawing lines between subjects in real-life activities is ludicrous. How does one learn about social studies without reading? Can one study science without incorporating at least some mathematics? How about history without geographic awareness?

"Intelligence enhancement involves creating as many neural linkages as possible," says neurologist Richard Restak in *Mozart's Brain and the Fighter Pilot: Unleashing Your Brain's Potential* (Harmony Publishers, 2002). "But in order to do this, we have to extricate ourselves from the confining and limiting idea that knowledge can be broken down into separate 'disciplines' that bear little relation to one another." (Notice how you're already building on what you learned in chapter 1.)

It's only natural—and much more effective *and* efficient—to allow integration its genuine place in the act of learning. This gift to your children is impossible in a school setting, yet extremely possible, and likely, when you choose your own educational reform.

As long as you're making a concerted effort to change education for the better for your child, it only makes sense to mold it in a way that best fits you and your family. Despite compulsory attendance laws, parents still have the right to secure for their children an education consistent with their family's values, beliefs, and principles. Custom-made education allows these to be easily integrated into life lessons.

Because school administrators are beholden to both taxpayers and the "keepers of the purse," they do their best to be all things to all people, and they do it with political correctness to boot. After the process of sorting and sifting, we're left with education's white bread equivalent: something that will fill little heads but that is void of almost all useful nourishment.

Home educators have historically described the thrill of watching a child discover then dive into a topic that so tickles his imagination that it creates in him an unquenchable thirst for knowledge. While satisfying that thirst, peripheral education, or knowledge of other topics related to the chosen topic, occurs. The specifics of the peripheral education can never be foreseen, but so what? Is it the end of the world if in pursuit of knowledge about the airplanes he loves, your third-grader bumps up against the scientific principle of the Doppler effect? Sure, the typical curriculum says he isn't supposed to learn about this until fifth grade, but isn't he much more likely to care about it and therefore understand the principle *now*?

John M. Jenkins and James W. Keefe, authors of a lengthy article for the February 2002 issue of the *Kappan Professional Journal,* called what we're talking about "personalized learning," and they wrote as if the two schools they discovered in Canada and the United States that approach education in this way are revolutionary. "The future," they wrote, "will demand flexible and thoughtful people unafraid to meet the unknown head-on." This type of person is just what the freedom and autonomy available in home education creates. "Self directed learning may not touch all students equally at first," claim Jenkins and Keefe, "but in time it makes them work harder and prepares them for life." Here are the personalized instruction components they credit with accomplishing this (keep in mind the elements of home education you've already discovered as you ponder them):

- *A dual teacher role of coach and adviser.* Homeschooling parents frequently recognize that they spend more time as advisers than as teachers, which is why they pooh-pooh the idea that anyone needs teacher training to be an effective home educator.

- *The diagnosis of relevant student learning characteristics.* More simply stated, this means figuring out your child's favored learning style, which is easy to do with the aid of several good books to guide you, such as *In Their Own Way: Discovering and Encouraging Your Child's Personal Learning Style* by Thomas Armstrong (Tarcher, 1987) and *Discover Your Child's*

Learning Style by Mariaemma Willis and Victoria Kindle Hodson (Prima, 1999).

- *A collegial school culture.* The schools in the study used multi-age groups of students. It doesn't get much more like home than home is.

- *An interactive learning environment.* Living and experiencing "real life" in the community is as interactive as it gets.

- *Flexible scheduling and pacing.* When you're in charge, the pace and schedule are what you *choose* them to be.

- *Authentic assessment.* Jenkins and Keefe are talking about school, and they explain that students "redo any unsatisfactory work until all errors are corrected." This naturally happens at home, without the necessity of tests.

The U.S. school in the study, a new charter school in Massachusetts, serves children in grades seven through twelve. Several of those students shared their observations with a reporter from the *Providence Journal:* "Teachers explain why you got the grade you got," said one. "They give you feedback." Another interviewee added, "There's a lot of revision here. You don't just do an assignment and turn it in." "The school lets you operate at your own pace," said another. "You get a 'gateway' halfway through the year if you show you know the material."

Real education requires some sort of investment on the part of the learners, be it intellectual or emotional. Educational customization leads the learners to understand that they own the knowledge acquired and are indeed the ones responsible for *taking,* not passively receiving, whatever they get. "It is our view," concluded Jenkins and Keefe, "that the kind of vital personalization at [these schools]—not state testing or rigid standardization—must become the cornerstone of school renewal if educators and the communities they serve hope to change, in any significant way, the basic grammar of schooling."

You can actually put this research to intelligent use. As long as school mind places so much more value on content than on process, grand-scale educational reform attempts will remain as useless as wishing you were getting younger. The underlying foundation of much of the new research on learning acknowledges the role of process, both by verifying numerous learning styles and by recognizing that context lends meaning to true education.

Creating your own educational reform means you can actually put all of the emerging research to intelligent use. The studies discussed in this book are merely the tip of a huge research iceberg, so keep your eyes and ears open for news stories, and comb the Internet for up-to-date developments.

For your personal use, we'll (dramatically) condense the results of a two-year study conducted by the National Research Council at the request of the Office of Educational Research and Improvement of the U.S. Department of Education. (They, too, used the rat research.) "The primary goal of the project," explain Bransford, Brown, and Cocking, editors of the book that resulted from the study (*How People Learn: Brain, Mind, Experience, and School,* National Academy Press, 1999), "is to convey to teachers, school officials, parents, and policymakers the most immediately useful findings from the . . . research on learning in subject areas such as science, mathematics, and history." (Did the folks at your child's school let you know this was written for your use?)

Applicable to your family's use of the activities herein are the researchers' key findings "about how early cognitive abilities relate to learning." They are observations that parents learning alongside their children recognize every day.

- Young children actively engage in making sense of their world.
  Translation: Little ones are predisposed to learn.

- Young children have abilities to reason with the knowledge they understand.

  Translation: Children are ignorant but not stupid.

- Children are problem solvers and, through curiosity, generate questions and problems; they also seek novel challenges.

  Translation: Children are persistent as learners because success and understanding are motivating in their own right. (When did we forget this?)

- Children develop knowledge of their own learning capacities (metacognition) very early.

  Translation: Children are capable of planning and monitoring their own success and correcting their own errors.

- Children's natural capabilities require assistance for learning.

  Translation: Caring adults can promote children's curiosity and persistence by supporting their learning attempts and keeping the complexity and difficulty of information appropriate for success.

Another important aspect of education is to use what is learned in new and unique ways. The researchers call it "adaptive, flexible learning." What do the studies reveal?

- A lot of "time on task" doesn't ensure learning if it's reading and rereading a text.

  Translation: Busywork doesn't mean learning is happening.

- Learning with understanding is more likely to promote transfer than simply memorizing information from a text or a lecture.

  No translation available yet: Because schools still almost exclusively test only students' memories, the researchers still haven't had a lot of experience with the advantages of learning with understanding.

- Knowledge taught in a single context is less subject to transfer than knowledge acquired through a variety of contexts.

  Translation: As previously stated, the process of learning needs to be considered along with content. Children are more likely to hang on to the relevant features of concepts when material is presented in multiple contexts (just as it is in natural contexts). As a bonus, multiple context presentation also increases understanding of how and when to put knowledge to use (conditions of applicability).

- Learning and transfer should not be evaluated by "one-shot" tests of transfer.

  Translation: The typical tests are useless! How well children transfer knowledge, an integral step in learning, can't possibly be perceived until they have an opportunity to learn something new, at which point transfer is evident when they grasp that new information more rapidly. Assessing such evidence of learning is difficult to impossible in a classroom, but easy with your own children.

- All learning involves transfer from previous experience.

  Translation: There is no guarantee that children will necessarily bring their previous knowledge to a new learning task. To increase the odds that they *will* do so, researchers recommend that teachers actively identify the "learning" strengths that the children possess, and build on them. With the customized learning of home education, this is easy and natural to achieve.

As the editors of *How People Learn* conclude their book, they address "learning and connections to community," a subject near and dear to homeschoolers' hearts. Here's the good news. The editors recognize that:

> [T]he success of the family as a learning environment, especially in the early years, has provided inspiration and guidance for some of the changes recommended in schools. *The rapid development of children from birth to ages four or five is generally supported by family interactions in which children learn by observing and interacting with others in shared endeavors. Conversations and other interactions that occur around events of interest with trusted and skilled adults and child companions are especially powerful environments for learning. Many of the recommendations for changes in schools can be seen as extensions of the learning activities that occur within families.* (emphasis added)

It almost sounds like they're thinking with education minds, doesn't it? Now the bad news. The remarks above were prefaced with a caveat:

> None of the following points about the importance of out-of-school learning institutions . . . should be taken to de-emphasize the central role of schools and the kinds of information that can be most efficiently and effectively taught there.

Despite the fact that everything they've uncovered points directly to individualized, learner-inspired education, these folks cannot and will not let go of "the central role of schools." In this tunnel-vision (single) context, the research will remain worthless. This information can best be put to intelligent use by *you* in *your own home*. Use it with "the central role of your child's education" always guiding you.

Table 2.2 All the Curriculum Materials You Need for Less Than $100

Resource	Use	Approximate Cost	Bargains at
	FOR ALL AGES:		
Library card	Key to a world of learning	Free	Your local library
Lego bricks	Math, spatial, fine motor, imagination	$10–$40 or more	Yard sales
Maps: world, U.S., other	Geography, history, social studies	$3–$10	Secondhand *National Geographic* magazines
Small aquarium with top (fish, plants, tadpoles, or dry for amphibians, worms, butterflies, and other insects)	Science	$15	Yard sale
Desk pad calendar	Planning, learning about time	$3	Office supply store
Newspaper end roll	Artwork, time line, banners, other projects	$3	Small local newspaper
Clear plastic measuring cups	Science, volume, fractions, multiplication	$2	"Dollar Days" at variety store
Cardboard appliance box	Playhouse/puppet theater, other imaginative play	Free	Appliance retailer
Nature identification books	Identifying local flora and fauna	$8 each	a
Homeschool support group membership	Support, activities, friendships	$10–$25/year	Find info on the Internet
Cassette player/recorder	Language arts, producing commercials, shows, preserving memories	$40	Yard sale
Dress-up clothes, hats, wigs	Drama, imaginative play	$10	Yard sale, thrift stores

Current globe	Geography, social studies	$15	b
Family Math for Grades K–8	Hands-on math activities for the whole family	$19.95	a
Cheap science equipment (funnels, measuring cups and spoons, spatulas, cups, bowls, etc.)	Science experiments	$10	"Dollar Days" sales at variety stores
Books	Home library	$0.25 and up	a
Dough/salt dough	Making 3-D letters and numbers, crafting	pennies	Homemade (recipes available on the Internet)
Geoboards scraps and nails	Math concepts: geometry, area	$3	Homemade from wood
Percussion instruments around the house (find book at library)	Music, science, math	$15	Homemade from things
			Total $70–$235

For 3- to 7-year-olds add:

Resource	Use	Approximate Cost	Bargains at
Picture dictionary	Spelling	$12	a
Bug net	Catching insects, amphibians, fish for observation	$3	Homemade from scrap of sheer curtain

a. Homeschooler's discount card at bookseller, secondhand at used bookstore, used curriculum sale, yard sale, or online.
b. Used curriculum sale, yard sale, online.

(continues)

Resource	Use	Approximate Cost	Bargains at
Magnifying glass	Inspecting almost anything	$2	"Dollar Days" sale at variety store
Kid's toy/learning clock	Telling time	$15	Homemade from poster board or paper plate and metal brad
Plastic-coated U.S. and world map placemats	Geography, spelling, social studies	$1 each	Variety store
Primary school balance scale	Estimation, weighing	$17	b
Family Math for Young Children: Comparing	Hands-on introduction to math concepts	$19.95	a
			Total $15–$70

For 8- to 12-year-olds add:

Resource	Use	Approximate Cost	Bargains at
Youth dictionary	Language arts: spelling, vocabulary	$8	a
Microscope	Science: exploration of tiny objects	$200, or $89.99 (My First Lab Microscope) at Amazon.com	b
Binoculars	Bird and animal watching	$15	b
Family Math, The Middle School Years: Algebraic Reasoning and Number Sense for Grades 5–8	Math concepts	$20.95	a

Resource	Use	Approximate Cost	Bargains at
Mancala game	Strategy, counting	$15	Homemade from egg carton and beans or [b]
Disposable camera	Art: composition, light, preserving memories	$7	Multipacks from buying club
Musical instruments	Music, pleasure	Recorder $7, Melodica $35	Used from music store or b
Time line	History, time, social studies	$12	Homemade from adding machine tape
Self-adhesive glow-in-the-dark stars plus star chart or book	Astronomy, mythology	$5	Homemade star maps of black construction paper with pinholes
			Total $140–$325

Bonus add-ons for all ages:

Resource	Use	Approximate Cost	Bargains at
Pattern blocks	Math concepts: geometry, multiplication, division	$16	Homemade from pattern downloaded from the Internet
Cuisenaire rods (72 rods)	Math concepts: multiplication, division, area, volume, algebraic thinking	$50 wood; $10 plastic	b
Annual family pass to historic site, zoo, museum	Culture, history, science	$35–$80	Reciprocal memberships allow for visits to other sites
			Total $45–$150

a. Homeschooler's discount card at bookseller, secondhand at used bookstore, used curriculum sale, yard sale, or online.

b. Used curriculum sale, yard sale, online.

3

We Have
Your Numbers

Okay, I guess I've been doing it long enough to call it a habit. As a writer specializing in homeschooling, I'm always gathering information and ideas from those I consider the pros—experienced homeschooling parents. The habit is that each time a collection grows, I begin noticing what seemingly disparate pieces have in common, even though I know (or maybe *because* I know) the collection is gathered from a widely diverse population.

I'd hazard a guess that a sizeable number of homeschooling families skipped a long study of others' research and went straight to their own learning laboratories for some observation and experimenting. With information from those education scientists who were kind enough to report to me, I was able to amass the great learning ideas of homeschooling parents, and I was thus given another chance to exercise my search for commonalties. I think we're onto something here, folks. No matter what philosophy underlay the families' homeschooling experience, amazing similarities popped up in the way the youngest children become inspired to explore pre-arithmetic skills. The most frequently mentioned motivators, in no particular order of importance, are food, money, games, and the great outdoors.

Yes, you could probably present a good argument that these four elements remain top inspirations for children straight through college, and for the entire lives of a good many adults, for that matter. But then you'd also be making a strong point for the more natural approach to learning available through homeschooling. These elements are, indeed, important real-life materials, much like those that encouraged "homeschooled" rats to learn as they explored their outdoor environment.

Many classroom settings preclude the use of these natural "arithmetic literacy inducers," but, luckily for you, that's not the case at home. Here's just a brief list of the ideas you'll find in this chapter to help you put these inducers to great use:

Food
- Sorting
- Counting
- Graphing
- Patterns
- Subtraction-by-eating (even more fun when more is "added" to replace the "subtracted")
- Standard measurement and fractions through baking and cooking

Money
- Values
- Making change
- Interest
- Tithing
- Carrying and borrowing
- Decimals
- Percentage

Games

- War with a twist and other card games
- Concentration
- Star Trek subtraction
- Yahtzee dice game
- Life board game
- Monopoly board game
- Dominoes
- Legos toys
- Tangrams
- Make-believe shopping

Outdoors

- Multiplication through a popular basketball game
- Hoppable number lines
- Parking lot multiplication
- Bird-feeding fractions
- Number hopscotch
- Open house measurement

Number Phobia

Although there has not been a formal study, anecdotal evidence suggests that a prevalent concern of beginning homeschoolers is their own number phobia, a phobia echoed throughout our society. I believe this could very well stem from the way schools go about "teaching" arithmetic. The perception is that among academic subjects, this one requires a linear approach, in which concepts must be understood in a particular order for the learner to acquire competence. Most frequently, this is accomplished through the "drill it into their

Conversational Math

Our children initially learned to do math problems conversationally; that is, they didn't have to read them or approach them with pencil and paper until much later. All we did was include mathematical word problems into our everyday speech. We knew it was important to keep it casual and related to what was going on in our lives at the time, be it baking (doubling amounts, halving, paring on the scales, and adding on amounts, etc.), climbing stairs (counting how many, up and down, how many in multiple flights), talking about shapes of buildings, packaging, patterns in the sand at the beach, on leaves and trees.

Using mathematical terminology and solving problems quickly became a way of life. I introduced more and more art projects, knowing that they were building real math skills in a concrete way. The children were involved in the planning and building stages of our house and garden, and we all used math every day. They assimilated mathematical concepts and skills without realizing it.

I didn't introduce "paper" math until I knew they could work things out in their heads. If anything was introduced on paper before they fully understood the concept, I found they were confused and didn't retain the concept or knowledge. Around ages seven or eight, they could do simple addition and subtraction on paper; at nine, ten, and eleven, they could tackle multiplication and division. Fractions were left until last, and decimals until they had done so much spending, measuring, and constructing that they already knew all about them and could do the sums easily.

—*Beverley Paine, Yankalilla, South Australia*

heads" approach. No doubt this often cements necessary facts inside little brains forever, but it doesn't typically foster fascination, appreciation, or a desire to explore beyond whatever is deemed required.

Exploring the world of numbers is exactly what you encourage your child to do with the ideas that follow. If you're one of the millions of math phobics, lose the idea that your child will suddenly become Einstein through these activities; instead just take a relaxing number exploration right along with your offspring. You'll be surprised at how much fun it can be. More importantly, you may help a member of the next generation grow up without math phobia. In the process, I guarantee that you'll discover things either you never knew or you totally forgot.

Kid-Friendly Arithmetic Exploration Turn-Ons

When my youngest was about five years old, he and his older sister spent a few days with Grandma while I went out of town. Although I dropped off with them a good stack of reading material and a few educational games to play, I told Mom not to worry about what, if anything, was accomplished; it was more important that they enjoy their time together. But her school mind just couldn't accept this notion.

I called one evening to see how things were going, and my youngest got on the phone. "Grandma gave me a whole page full of subtraction problems, but I like addition better so I changed all the minuses to pluses and then I did them, but Grandma got mad at me." Grandma was *not* used to the educational autonomy felt by homeschooled kids, even those who are five years old.

That page of problems was a definite arithmetic turnoff. So what have homeschoolers found to get reluctant kids to play with numbers? Here are a few starting places you might like to consider.

Graphs. Graphs come in all shapes and sizes and can be as colorful and complex as the creator wants. In addition, any collection of information may be graphed. (See "Graphing Activities," later in this chapter, for some starting ideas, then use your imagination.) Graphs open opportunities to discuss fractions (pie graphs are especially useful for this), percentages, greater than and less than, comparing, sorting, statistics, and so forth.

Extreme Numbers. Although lots of kids get a kick out of wildly large numbers (what's a googol?), introducing them to the other end of the scale can be equally interesting. Extreme numbers abound—plain

Read Math

Most of our math is very hands-on and comes from real-life situations, but for more advanced math concepts, we read books by or about math and mathematicians. There are books for every age and level—just visit your library's math section. Some of our favorites are:

Beyond Numeracy: Ruminations of a Numbers Man by John Allen Paulos (Vintage Books, 1992)

G Is for Googol: A Math Alphabet Book by David M. Schwartz (Tricycle Press, 1998)

Math Curse by Jon Scieszka (Viking Children's Books, 1995)

My Brain Is Open: The Mathematical Journeys of Paul Erdos by Bruce Schecter (Touchstone Books, 2000)

Number Mysteries by Cyril and Dympna Hayes (Durking Hayes, 1987)

Realm of Algebra by Isaac Asimov (Fawcett Crest Premier, 1961)

Realm of Numbers by Isaac Asimov (Houghton Mifflin, 1959)

Socrates and the Three Little Pigs by Tuyosi Mori (Philomel Books, 1986)

—*Holly Furgason, Houston, Texas*

old counting, weight, and length are good ones to begin with. How about a graph of some of the world's fish, including the longest and shortest? What are the heaviest and lightest animals? How does a milligram compare with a kilogram? What are all those zeros for, and do I have to write them all out?

Arts and Crafts. What hands-on learner will be able to resist creating her very own geoboard or set of tangrams? How about an exploration of geometric shapes with nothing more than some string and a couple of boxes of straws? Pattern blocks are great inspiration for various projects, and to really get your artists going, turn them on to the work of M. C. Escher.

Remember, math is all around you. Real life presents opportunities to use math in the grocery store, in the car as the odometer spins, as you figure out how many forks you need on the table when company comes. You may even find paying bills is at least a little more fun when you have help. And who knows? After seeing the electric bill a few times, it might even inspire your youngsters to turn off the lights when they're done in the room!

For Those New to Numbers

I Love You
Therese Peterson, Milwaukee, Wisconsin

With this activity, not only do little ones learn to count, but it also helps to keep boredom at bay during long walks or car rides. Mom (or the instigator) says, "I love you," and hopefully the inevitable "I love you, too" is returned. The immediate comeback is "I love you three!" baiting the child to say, "I love you four!" This turns into a game that can be played by all in the immediate area. Change the game for older kids by counting by twos, fives, tens. When my sons were ten years old or so, the game would dissolve into laughter when one would shout, "I love you a bazillion jillion!"

Coin I.D. Game
Shay Seaborne, Woodbridge, Virginia

When I make a purchase and have some coins as change, I let my children earn them by demonstrating their knowledge about the coins. At first they just had to state the correct name of each coin. As their mastery improved, they had to name the value and the name of the president depicted. Once they mastered that, they could earn coins by adding the amount of the change. When they became good at that, the game was over!

Edible Manipulatives

Pamela Jorrick, Korbel, California

Preschoolers love counting raisins, nuts, or grapes for fun. Tell them to subtract as they eat, then add more to the pile. Chocolate chips seem to hold my kids' attention the best—they don't want to lose track of any of them. Divide a sandwich or pie into equal parts and introduce fractions.

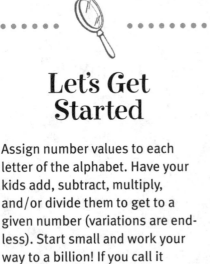

Let's Get Started

Assign number values to each letter of the alphabet. Have your kids add, subtract, multiply, and/or divide them to get to a given number (variations are endless). Start small and work your way to a billion! If you call it "breaking the code," kids will find it even more fun.

Practice Is Child's Play

Kris Bordessa, Diamond Springs, California

Have a family game night! Yahtzee, Life, Monopoly, and many other board games require frequent (and painless) math calculations. The time also fosters a sense of togetherness that just doesn't happen during your average TV viewing night.

Stress-Free New Concepts

Alexis D. Gutzman, Bethel, Connecticut

My oldest daughter is something of a Nervous Nelly. She loves to do things she has mastered, but she is reluctant to tackle new concepts. I notice that whenever I talk about something new related to academics while she brushes her teeth, she completely gets it, without any, "Oh, no, this is something new" resistance. The next day, I can say, "This is just like what we talked about last night," and things go swimmingly.

Count the Dots

Cindy Allas, Fairfield, California

I use simple dot-to-dots to reinforce counting. I make them with coloring books that teach counting. I trace the numbers in the book, but instead of using a solid line, I make dots every so often along the outline. I also use this for even or odd number counting.

Sorting Beans and Pasta

Jane Powell, Bowie, Maryland

Buy fifteen-bean soup mix, and give your child a portion of the beans and several containers. Ask your child to sort the beans according to size, shape, color, or design (speckled or not). Once he has sorted one way, ask him to sort another.

Sorting is also fun with various shapes of uncooked pasta. You can buy tri-colored pasta. Or you can create your own colored pasta: put a few shapes in a plastic bag, add a few drops of food coloring, shake the bag thoroughly, and allow the pasta to dry overnight.

Animal Crackers on My Table

Fiona Bayrock, Chilliwack, British Columbia, Canada

Dump a box of animal crackers onto the table, and challenge your kids to sort the crackers in some way. Your children will be sure to find characteristics: four legs/two legs, jungle/farm/zoo, carnivores/herbivores, continent where they come from, habitat.

The conversation can evolve to include endangered species, circuses and zoos, animal adaptations, food chains, or even arithmetic questions, such as "If an elephant eats one hundred pounds per day, how much does he eat in a month?"

Paper Towel Number Line

Rosemarie Larose-Renner, Port Orange, Florida

Use a roll of paper towels and write numbers in order on each successive paper towel. Unroll the towels onto the floor. Because individual towels are just the right size for young children's feet, your kids can really understand how the number line works by walking it.

Versatile Dominoes

Tonna Dodd, Eddyville, Kentucky

You can use dominoes for addition sentences, fractions, matching, grouping, and counting. We have the color double 9's, and even my two-year-old gets in on the fun. Of course, you can also stand them up in a row and watch them tumble—there's got to be a science lesson in there somewhere.

Line 'Em Up Straight

Ruth Dunnavan, Moultonborough, New Hampshire

When my children had trouble lining up numbers in arithmetic problems, I found that having them write their lessons in a spiral notebook—with the spiral at the top—helps. The lines on the paper become guides for aligning the problems correctly, and the notebook keeps the lessons together.

Alien Patterns

Hope Ware, Peoria, Illinois

As I tried to figure out how to incorporate math into our day, my son, James, asked if I'd play Legos with him. He was playing Robot, and explained that my job would be to make aliens and try to get them on board his newly constructed ferry boat, which was guarded by the robot. Obviously, the robot wanted to let "friendly" passengers on board the ferry, but not hostile aliens. I said, "Sure." Who could resist such an elaborate scheme by a nearly five-year-old boy?

After I made several figures from the Legos, I said, "James, your robot will have to identify the aliens in this group of passengers by using some clues." The clues went something like this: "The alien has a pattern that could be described mathematically as *ABAB*." "The alien is made of seven blocks." "The alien has three yellow blocks and four green blocks." Voilà! He didn't even suspect we were working on math concepts!

Addition/Subtraction

More Aliens Invade!

Hope Ware, Peoria, Illinois

When my son, James, wanted me to play Star Trek one day, I quickly formulated a secret plan in my mind. In a yogurt shipping box, with twelve round indented areas in the bottom where the yogurt cups sat, I placed twelve construction paper circles using four different colors. I wrote numbers on the circles, then pasted them randomly on the bottom of the box. (For a smaller version you can use an egg carton.)

No sooner had we begun Star Trek than aliens abducted the captain. I pulled out the "secret math box" and told James that the

A Few Words About Math and Symbols

Math is all around you and your children every day. Let your imagination fly and use all of the opportunities everyday life presents to talk and learn about concepts and application. Here are a few places to start. Can you think of more?

Fingers and toes, pattern blocks, 2 × 2, 4 × 4, narrow gauge, ruler, tape measure, scale, model, profit (loss), earn, spend, save, interest, checkbook, recipe, batting average, Captain, May I?, soccer, baseball, basketball, love, fault, birdie, strike, spare, first and ten, penalty box, map, compass, Pokemon, Candyland, Monopoly, Go, chess, Sorry!, dominoes, dice, poker chips, bridge, Crazy Eights, Go Fish, graphs, charts, origami, mileage, knit 1 purl 2, weave, weigh, motor, engine, pulley, ratio, odds, chances, statistics, average, more or less, even, odd, yards, scale, circumference, volume, area, score, speed limit, braking distance, fourth dimension, sixth sense, Indy 500, build, plan, rate, estimate, predict, revise, garden, yardage, height, depth, angle, trade, straight, curve, spiral, high tide, low ball, tempo, quarter note, half pound, temperature, weather forecast, bargain, budget, price, half off, plus tax, sequence, 7 percent solution, 100 percent markup, latitude, longitude, light years, escape velocity, precession of the equinoxes (oh, Best Beloved), range, set, stitch, sort, size, tally, calculator, plot, dozen, gain, lose, exactly, approximately, income, borrow, allowance, loan, design, diagram, knots, beads, gear ration, minutes, degrees, timer, computer, fathoms, grid, meters, half pipe, quarter turn, double time,

aliens demanded that he solve math questions using the colors and numbers on the bottom of their math box before they would release the captain.

I gave him simple questions that he could answer using the box, such as, "If you have two aliens watching the captain and one goes to lunch, how many are left? Show me the circle with that number on it." "Add the numbers on the three green circles. This is how many of the captain's crew are coming to rescue him."

I gave my youngest child twelve wooden beads that matched the colors of the construction paper circles. After he matched up the correct bead colors to each circle color, the captain was released! You full bore, safe speed, abacus, credit, debit, limit, infinity, first class, third rate, equal share, short shrift, waxing, waning, phase, rhythm, balance, cycle, magnitude, perspective, value, apogee, perigee, frequency, rotation, revolution, dollars, cents, pennies, wooden nickels, full deck, full house, double helix, time zone, millennium, program, binary, generation, epoch, era, nanosecond, code, puzzle, calendar, fiscal year, progression, midpoint, watts, lumens, horsepower, ohms, Great Circle Route, '52 Pickup, '55 Chevy, Hundredth Monkey, altitude, make change, Lego, shopping, tangrams, Battleships, Fibonacci series, checkers, speed, height, width, length, volume, sphere, output, displacement, schedule, time limit, collection, add up, count down, age, four score, last full measure, census, (Are we there yet?), gigabytes, googol, powers of 10, increase, decrease, supply and demand, links, contour lines, Great Divide, Bingo! Group, air pressure, stock market, daily log, rent, bills, discretionary income, arc, geometric proportions, geologic time, navigation, Dewey Decimal System #510, stone circle, dosage, grams/ounces, meters/feet, 16 mm, 22 caliber, shutter speed, f-stop, twenty-pound test, dot-to-dot, orienteering, yield, squared, low bid, etc., etc., etc. See also:

- The Math Forum @ Drexel: www.mathforum.com/dr.math
- NRICH Mathematics Enrichment Club: www.nrich.maths.org.uk
- Consumer Reports.org 4 Kids: www.zillions.org

—Courtesy of Unschoolers Unlimited, www.borntoexplore.org/unschool

don't necessarily need a yogurt packing box to play this game, but it made it easy for the two-year-old to put matching beads in the indented areas because they didn't roll.

Extra Dice

Andrea Hargreaves, San Antonio, Texas

When playing any game with dice, I add more than what the game actually requires. We've played with up to four dice so far because it's a fun way to get a little extra practice with addition facts.

War

Cindy Allas, Fairfield, California

Play the old card game, War, but with a twist. Each person plays two cards instead of one. Let your child add up the cards to see whose sum is larger and who wins the cards.

Domino Drop

Laura Cleary, Vista, California

My daughter drops two dominoes on the floor, then adds or subtracts, whichever subject we're working on. It beats worksheets.

Like Golf, the Lowest Score Wins

Jane Salemi, Camino, California, courtesy of *Right at Home* newsletter

Lay out number cards from 1 to 9. Have your child roll two dice, then eliminate the total rolled in any combination. For example, if your child rolls 3 and 4, he can eliminate the number cards 3 and 4, or 1 and 6, or 5 and 2, or just 7.

Pennies and Dimes, Ones and Tens

Kim Weaver, Victoria, British Columbia, Canada

Our daughter was having difficulty understanding the carry over idea when adding larger numbers. Drawing diagrams didn't help the concept click, so I turned to the tried and true money idea, using pennies to show that when adding two numbers, such as 27 + 28, you add the 1s column numbers first. You can't, however, have fifteen 1s in your answer or else it would look like four (10s) and fifteen (1s) = 415. Because she can add in her head, she knew this answer wasn't right. I explained the carry over by *trading* ten pennies for one dime, and she then understood that the dime had to be with the other dimes, so the answer was actually five (10s) and five (1s) equals 55. She easily made the skill/understanding transfer to numbers without money manipulatives and quickly added hundreds, thousands, and even tens of thousands using her new carry over skill.

Carry Over Charades

Andrea Hargreaves, San Antonio, Texas

This is a "pre" exercise to use when you're ready to teach carrying in addition. You need a set of Cuisinaire rods or similar base 10 blocks (we use Math-U-See blocks), a game, and possibly a deck of cards. Take any game you have in which you earn points for each turn. You could also use a deck of cards to assign points earned for each turn in any game. For example, you can play charades, but draw a card from the deck before each turn so you know how many points you'll earn on that turn. Use the blocks to keep score, making sure that no one accumulates more than nine units at a time. When ten or more units are acquired, the units must be traded in for a 10-bar.

Example using a game of Charades:

Player 1 draws a 7 from the deck. Player 1 acts out her charade. If another player guesses, Player 1 earns 7 points, which she takes from the set of base 10 blocks. (We would use a 7-bar, but it would also work with 7 units.)

Player 2 draws a 9 from the deck, acts out his charade, and gets nine points, which he takes from the set of base 10 blocks.

On her second turn, Player 1 draws an 8 from the deck, acts out her charade, and gets her eight points from the set of blocks. Now she must do a trade-in, because, in this game, anything 10 or above must be traded in for a 10-bar. So she lines up her original 7 and her newly acquired 8 and trades them in for a 10-bar and a 5-bar.

We continue this process until someone reaches 100, or after a predetermined amount of time has passed. We also use a 100-block as a scoreboard so it's easy to see when someone has acquired 10 units and needs to trade the units for a 10-bar.

- Connecting Cuisenaire Rods: 800-445-5985, www.etacuisenaire.com
- Math-U-See: 888-854-MATH, www.mathusee.com

Shop 'Til You Drop

Tara Hall, Colliersville, Tennessee

Our son Martin sets up shop and prices toys between $1 and $10. We make pretend Martin Money, and his younger sisters and I are given $10 to spend. It's up to him as cashier to calculate how much money his sisters have left and what toys they can still afford. We use old book bags as store bags, the girls enjoy it, and our son loves teaching them how much money they have left and what they can buy—great simple addition and subtraction practice.

Shopping Part Two

Shay Seaborne, Woodbridge, Virginia

To help my children learn more about money, the exchange of money, and making change, the girls and I set up a "store" on our dining table. Together we price items purchased from the dollar store, such as cute erasers, pencils, marbles, and small note pads. Most items cost a nickel or a penny, but some cost a dime or a quarter. I give each of the children a dollar bill and let them shop at my store. With help, the girls determine how much they can buy, add up the cost of their purchases, and count out the change.

Dinosaurs Come and Go

Cristina Ramos-Payne, White Plains, New York

My five-year-old loves dinosaurs, so our game begins when I lay a number flash card face up. He must then cover each number with the same number of dinosaurs, then add them up. I usually recite the equation as he does it for reinforcement (two dinos plus two dinos equals . . .). He improved the game on his own by setting the toys on a chair and knocking dinos off for subtraction (four dinos take away three dinos—ROAR!). It's a great alternative to expensive math manipulatives.

Twisted Concentration

Cindy Allas, Fairfield, California

We play Concentration, but instead of matching pairs, we match two numbers that add up to 10.

Fair Weather Number Line

Maria Hammer, Marshall, Illinois, courtesy of *Right at Home* newsletter

I draw a number line with chalk on the sidewalk, going as high as need be to focus on the number groups we're currently studying. My son starts on zero. I say, "Plus two!" "Minus one!" "Plus seven!" He goes to the proper spot and shouts the answer. Get him going fast enough and I have a giggling blond lump on the sidewalk.

Use this for multiplication and division for older kids; just create your number line in multiples of 4, 5, 12, whatever. Give them a problem and have them jump to the answer.

Personal Best with Flash Cards

Julie Swegle, Colorado Springs, Colorado

If you have more than one child at a time memorizing arithmetic facts, you can always turn the use of flash cards into a race. If competition isn't your style, try timing each child and keeping a My Best Time chart for each one. On poster board, draw a goal time and a place to record the child's time every day. When the goal is reached, throw a little family party complete with decorations, such as hanging flash cards and a rectangular cake decorated with the most difficult math fact that was memorized.

Multiplication/Division

Dicey Body Parts

Jen Blake, Rapid City, South Dakota

Create a worksheet with a blank spot for a number determined by the roll of a die or dice, then an operation sign, then another spot for a rolled number. Finally, list a body part, so it would look like this:

___ × ___ = ___ **Heads** or ___ + ___ = ___ **Arms**

When my daughter is finished filling in the sheet, she gets to draw her creation based on the answers she came up with. For example, a creature with six heads and three arms. She asks for this game over and over.

Marching to the Beat of a Different Drummer

Linda Dobson, Saranac Lake, New York

With your child, march around the room and count with each step. If you're practicing the two times tables, clap on each multiple of 2; if the three times tables, clap on each multiple of 3. Have fun high-stepping, and march more quickly as your child gets better and better.

Traveling Times Tables
Holly Furgason, Houston, Texas

While in the car, we count together by each number ten times until we reach that number's multiple of 10. So, for the 2 times table, we count by 2s until we reach 20; for the 3 times table, we count by 3s until we reach 30; and so on.

H-O-R-S-E
Jeanne Faulconer, Stanardsville, Virginia

Remember the basketball game H-O-R-S-E? Here's a variation for which I wrote numbers on the patio, using the "hard" multiplication factors 7, 8, and 9. Each of us took basketball shots from each of those spots, saying the math facts for that number, in order. For instance, when I stood on the 7, I shot, saying, "Seven times seven equals forty-nine." If my shot went in, I got another shot, saying, "Seven times eight equals fifty-six." When I missed (either the basketball shot *or* the multiplication fact), it was the next person's turn. When my turn came back around, I would start where I left off. The first person to get all of his shots in from all locations—and to say all the facts correctly—was the winner. This was great for my energetic, hands-on, kinesthetic learners.

Visual Square Number Patterns
Lillian Jones, Sebastopol, California

Get a bag of miniature marshmallows and a box of toothpicks. Arrange a square pattern of toothpicks five across and five down, making twenty-five squares in the grid. Fasten the toothpicks together by sticking the ends into marshmallows so that they form a grid.

On top of that grid, build a similar grid with only four toothpicks across, then attach it with vertical toothpicks into the marshmallows on the bottom. Keep working up, with one less number in each level, until you've completed an attractive and interesting structure. At some point, count the squares on the bottom, the next level, and so on, and note that these are numbers that are made by multiplying a number by itself, square numbers (for instance, 3 is the square root of 9).

Try lining up a three-toothpick by four-toothpick grid—is that a square number? It's fun to see the multiplication facts displayed so graphically and to watch children make their own discoveries, noticing the interesting patterns that come about.

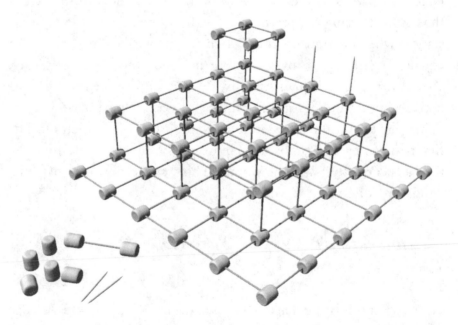

Parking Lot Multiplication

Leslie Redweik, North Judson, Indiana

Use those moments waiting in a parking lot. How many cars are five cars by two rows deep? For our six- and eight-year-old boys, this really helped the concept stick.

Cooking Up Some Math

Julie Swegle, Colorado Springs, Colorado

Cooking is our favorite math activity. Teaching a child to use measuring cups and spoons, to multiply and divide each recipe as needed, and even setting the table with the right number of forks, spoons, and knives are wonderful activities.

Let's Get Started

Check the car odometer when you leave home and again when you return. How far did you travel? If appropriate, have your child perform calculations mentally or keep track of gas mileage.

On the Mighty Jungle Gym

Rosemarie LaRose-Renner, Port Orange, Florida

Head for the jungle gym to practice multiplication. Your child can only climb to the next level when she gets a multiplication answer right.

More War

Jeanne Faulconer, Stanardsville, Virginia

We play the card game War in the usual way, but the person with the higher card must recite the multiplication fact and answers before he wins the hand. For instance, if I have a seven and my son has an eight, he says, "Eight times seven is fifty-six," and then he gets to pick up the cards.

Dinosaur Eggs

Cindy Watson, Levittown, Pennsylvania

My son was having trouble understanding the concepts of sets and multiplication, but he loves dinosaurs! We drew a large map with fields, rocks, caves, woods, and a pond. I gave him some cut-up dry grass to make nest sites for different dinosaurs. Then we took various colored circles (holes left over from a paper punch) and put "eggs" in the nests. We used this as the basis for mathematical equations. "T-Rex has three nests with two eggs in each, so three times two equals six." He loved it and got the concept in one day. My five-year-old twins did a similar project by counting the nests. My three-year-old just glued.

Practice, Practice, Practice

Jeanne Faulconer, Stanardsville, Virginia

To learn times tables, we put blank times tables charts up on the refrigerator and let the guys fill them in as they felt moved to do so. We did this over and over for much of one school year, and they seemed to enjoy the no drill/no pressure aspect.

We also used the dry erase white boards and place mats you can buy at discount stores to practice multiplication facts.

Who Gets the Card?

Rosemarie LaRose-Renner, Port Orange, Florida

My children loved the game where they won the flash card if they got the answer right. Mom keeps the card if they get it wrong.

"Distance" Learning
Fiona Bayrock, Chilliwack, British Columbia, Canada

When the kids are learning multiplication or division facts, hang up posters for them to refer to at any time while doing pencil work. The trick is to hang it as far away as possible from where they're working and instruct them that they must leave their pencils and paper behind if they want to check a poster. Repeating a fact over and over out loud or to themselves to keep it in their heads all the way back from down the hall, around the corner, into another room, and behind the door (where the poster is located) reinforces it in memory. They're also very motivated to commit the facts to memory as soon as possible so they don't have to make the l-o-n-g trek each time they need a fact.

Multiplication Table Patterns Exploration
Lillian Jones, Sebastopol, California

Make a large 14-square by 14-square chart with a blank upper left square. Write the numbers 0 through 12 across the top edge, and 0 through 12 along the left edge under the blank square. Run the line of zeros down the first column under the 0 and along the top column across from the 0. Fill in the rest of the multiplied numbers, then start to explore. After a while, start to extend the columns even further beyond the edge of the chart. It's really fun for kids to discover the repeated patterns, some of which are not obvious until you extend the columns of numbers.

Photocopy the chart so you can play around with colored pencils or crayons. The kids can, for instance, color in all the multiples of 3. Instead of memorizing the multiplication facts, they learn them from becoming friendly with them, and there are lots of years ahead during which they naturally learn the facts with use.

	0	1	2	3	4	5	6	7	8	9	10	11	12
0	0	0	0	0	0	0	0	0	0	0	0	0	0
1	0	1	2	3	4	5	6	7	8	9	10	11	12
2	0	2	4	6	8	10	12	14	16	18	20	22	24
3	0	3	6	9	12	15	18	21	24	27	30	33	36
4	0	4	8	12	16	20	24	28	32	36	40	44	48
5	0	5	10	15	20	25	30	35	40	45	50	55	60
6	0	6	12	18	24	30	36	42	48	54	60	66	72
7	0	7	14	21	28	35	42	49	56	63	70	77	84
8	0	8	16	24	32	40	48	56	64	72	80	88	96
9	0	9	18	27	36	45	54	63	72	81	90	99	108
10	0	10	20	30	40	50	60	70	80	90	100	110	120
11	0	11	22	33	44	55	66	77	88	99	110	121	132
12	0	12	24	36	48	60	72	84	96	108	120	132	144

Your kids might also enjoy decorating the charts. You can even laminate favorite charts for future reference on which they can look up facts. Help them draw pictures showing multiplication principles, like a green vine with four berries near each of twelve leaves, so by looking at the drawing they can count "four, eight, twelve, sixteen, twenty," and so on along the vine. You might also use objects—such as seeds, beans, or pasta shapes—glued on to heavy paper in number patterns.

Make up games together: Who can be the first to find the number that is $2 \times 2 \times 6$ and so forth? Obviously, the possibilities of these charts are endless.

Fractions/Decimals/Percentages

The Gobble Guts Pizza Fraction Game

Beverley Paine, Yankalilla, South Australia

Making this game was challenging and a lesson in math in itself. First we made a fractions "pizza" from cardboard. Using a pair of compasses, we drew equal size circles on stiff cardboard and cut them out. We then dissected them into all the fractions up to twelfths. This was tricky and took a few hours, with much learning and experimentation. Accuracy is important.

We labeled each fraction of each pizza, then colored all the pieces. The whole was green, the halves orange, the thirds pink, and so on. I made a cardboard holder, like a cylinder with a base, to store all the pieces. We disregarded the sevenths and elevenths for the game but used them for other fraction activities.

Making the board is easy. On a stiff piece of cardboard, I drew twelve circles in a 4×3 grid, using a small bowl as a template. The circles are connected with two-way horizontal and vertical arrows, indicating that you can move in any direction from each circle. Each circle was labeled as follows, and a small circle within illustrates the fraction shown.

- Make $1/2$
- Eat $1/4$
- Start
- Eat $1/8$
- Make $1/3$
- Make $1/10$
- Make $1/12$

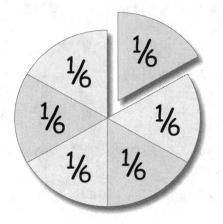

- Eat $1/6$
- Eat $1/3$
- Finish
- Eat $1/5$
- Make $1/9$

We made "men" from beads glued together, but use anything you have. Players begin on Start, and move the number shown on the throw of one die. If the player lands on "Make $1/3$," he must take the $1/3$ fraction from the pizza "bank." On the player's next turn, he can move in any direction the number of spaces rolled on the dice, but he must be able to do what the circle he lands on says. For example, he can "Eat $1/6$" by exchanging his $1/3$ for two $1/6$s and returning one $1/6$ to the bank. Alternatively he can "Eat $1/12$" by exchanging his $1/3$ for four $1/12$s and then return one $1/12$ to the bank. Another option would be to "Make $1/10$" by collecting a tenth from the bank. This is where the game can get tricky.

The object is to make a complete (or more than one complete) pizza and try to land on Finish. This is much harder than it first ap-

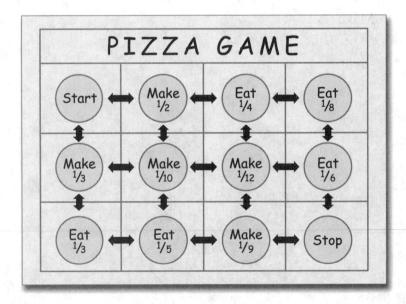

pears, and cooperative play is almost essential for someone to win. If you'd like to make the game easier, leave out the fifths and tenths, which can frustrate younger players. Better yet, play as partners with the youngest and really help them out; otherwise you may just confuse fractions in their minds. The game teaches equivalent fractions in a hands-on, concrete manner.

Measuring Is for the Birds

Hope Ware, Peoria, Illinois

I fill a small bowl with birdseed and send my young boys outside with several measuring cups and spoons. They practice spooning the seed into the measuring cups to improve small group motor skills. Then they see how many (fractional) cups it takes to fill a (fractional) cup, and how many (fractional) cups it takes to fill one cup, and so on. Using birdseed means I don't have to worry about leaving the birds something that will hurt their digestive systems, like rice! When learning time is over, just leave the birdseed to give the birds a treat. You can watch from the window with your bird book and identify who comes to enjoy the feast—including the squirrels, of course!

Fall Fractions

Amy DeRusha, Somersworth, New Hampshire

While raking the yard one day, I saw that I had completed about one-third of the work. Realizing that I was using fractions, I called my seven-year-old out to the yard, and we began discussing fractions. It was clear she was grasping the concept within forty-five minutes. Within a month, after raking our yard and several neighbors' yards several times, she understood well. As bonuses, my five-year-old started to grasp fractions, and the yard looked great.

Baking Knowledge Transfers to Problems on Paper

Jennifer Miller, Puyallup, Washington

I taught my children to add and subtract fractions through baking. I put all the ingredients on the counter and provide only one measuring cup and one measuring spoon. I might use a one-third measuring cup one time and a one-fourth measuring cup another time. My children then must figure out how to measure one and (some fractional amount) cups using only the cup they are given. When they got really good at that, we started doubling and tripling recipes. Out of curiosity, I tested my son once to see if his baking experience transferred to working problems on paper. I'm proud to report that he aced the test!

Fraction Circles Game

Maria Hammer, Marshall, Illinois

I purchased an inexpensive set of colored foam fraction circles from Wal-Mart, but you can easily make them from durable materials. I explained that one-eighth means "it takes eight of these to make one whole circle," and so on. I wrote the fractions on the circles to make it easier. I then wrote some fractions on slips of paper and folded them up really tiny (hone those fine motor skills!) and asked my son to pick one out of a bowl. If he picked $3/6$, he had to pick up three $1/6$ pieces and show them to me. Then I asked him to find other pieces—or combinations of pieces—that were the same size as $3/6$. By placing them on top of each other, he soon discovered that $3/6$ equals $4/8$ equals $2/4$ equals $1/2$.

Easy Decimal Practice

Athena Dalrymple, Columbia, Maryland

I gave my child a catalog and asked her to use the item number to tell what the price would be if that number was the price. She had to add a decimal point two places from the right. For example, if the item number was 944369, she would say, "Nine thousand, four hundred, forty-three dollars and sixty-nine cents." The point was to give the amount in dollars and cents. If we didn't have a catalog, we just gave out random digits, which worked as well. For example, if I gave her the numbers 1, 5, 6, 9, 8, 2, she would say, "One thousand, five hundred, sixty-nine dollars and eight-two cents."

The Incredible, Versatile Egg Carton

Lillian Jones, Sebastopol, California

Kids can make endless hands-on discoveries with egg cartons. Save your empty ones or get extra large ones that hold twenty-five eggs in rows of five by five. Fastened together, four of these bigger cartons create a perfect square of one hundred little egg holes.

Use plastic eggs from discount stores to play around with visual representations of fractions, percentages, and decimals. It's fun to see what $1/100$ looks like, or to discover that $25/100$ and $1/4$ are the same thing.

If you write numerals from 1 to 100 on the plastic eggs, kids can insert them in numerical order. They can even "skip count" to learn multiplication and/or addition facts. You can write all the numbers for a multiplication table on the other end of the eggs (the fatter end) in a different color (to keep track of which is what).

Kids can use other things, such as beans, large pasta shells, and pom-poms, for other exploration. (Put two beans in two holes, in three, in four, then count them to learn to count by twos. The learning is more fruitful if left to fun and exploration rather than turning it all into lessons. It's fun to point out things you see, but the children learn more if those observations are part of mutual sharing of discoveries.)

Let's Get Started

Practice estimating while in stores. Have your kids estimate the total cost of everything you are buying and see how close they get.

Negative Numbers

Another Twist on War

Dona Braswell, Gaithersburg, Maryland

In this twist on the card game War, the red cards are negatives, and the black cards are positives. So a seven of hearts would be worth less than a four of clubs. If there is a tie (that is, if both players have a seven of clubs, for example), each player puts three cards face down and the fourth card determines who wins that hand. For yet more practice, each player can put the three cards face up, then add or subtract the negative/positive numbers to determine who has the highest number.

Measurement

Open House Measuring

Athena Dalrymple, Columbia, Maryland

While visiting open houses of homes for sale, give your child a measuring tape and allow her to take measurements and tell you the total square footage for each room (or as many as you have time for). Later give the child the floor plan of the house and allow her to find the total square footage for each level and the entire home. Don't forget to try this at home, too!

Olympic Rings

Fiona Bayrock, Chilliwack, British Columbia, Canada

Have your children make the Olympic Games rings symbol out of construction paper using a compass. Tell them what the diameters of the inner and outer circles should be, and have them figure out how to set the compass to the correct radius. Afterward, they can cut it out and color it in.

Money

Interest Builds Interest

Diana Tashjian, Fremont, California

When our now eight-year-old son showed no interest in doing arithmetic on paper, we gave him an allowance to spend as he wanted. He could receive one week's allowance in advance but he had to pay 1 percent interest. Likewise, we also paid him interest on that portion of allowance he didn't spend. He kept track of it all, and now he has his own savings account and ATM card!

Do You Want to Be a Muffin Man?

Cindy Maricle, Bend, Oregon

Make homemade giant cookies or muffins or cinnamon rolls to sell once a week at Dad's office or at a nearby industrial park (no restaurants), selling your wares at coffee break time. Be consistent and on schedule if the demand is there. Prices can range from $0.50 to $2.00 each, depending on what it is, how big it is, and the demand. Make sure there is plenty of profit and lots of quality. Grocery store bakery cookies cost a lot and don't taste very good, and most families don't spend time baking, so there's a market for homemade goodies at a premium price. Be sure to first obtain permission from Dad's boss, company head, or the industrial park.

Independence
Pamela Jorrick, Korbel, California

Letting children have some independence and say in how their money is spent seems to make the concept real. My own mother started letting me be in charge of my clothing budget at about twelve years of age. She designated the amount to spend and dropped me off for a day of shopping with my friends (where I would put on hold the items I wanted). She would then purchase up to the agreed amount when she picked me up. I realized in no time that I could have one pair of pricey jeans or find five cool outfits on the sales racks. I learned how to make the most of my dollars at a young age and had a better wardrobe than some friends who spent twice as much. I will never forget how to live well on a budget.

Coin Value Game
Laura Cleary, Vista, California

For this activity, you need only a pile of a few of each type of coin and a die. Have your child pick a monetary amount as the game's goal (any amount, but start low, maybe twenty cents). Take turns rolling the die. The number rolled is the amount of money the person rolling can take from the pile. When you get enough money to trade for a higher value coin, you *have* to do it. For example, if you roll a four, you pick up four pennies. On your next turn you might roll a three, so you pick up three pennies. Because you have seven pennies, you must trade in five pennies for a nickel. Whoever reaches the goal first wins.

Food Fight
Robin Norell, Orlando, Florida

(If wasting food bothers you, please skip this one!)

When asked what she'd like if she could do anything she wanted, my second-grade daughter replied, "Have a food fight!" To turn it into a learning experience, both she and our son were given $5 to spend on food and materials, and they needed to be creative. For example, Jell-o *sounded* great, but it just bounced right off. Creamed corn worked well, but the smell made everyone nauseous. The following year, the kids invited their friends. They all had the same budget restrictions and responsibility for cleanup.

So what works best? Take a cheap liter or quart of soda, shake it up, then spray it. This works great when you first open the container, and you just pour it over people's heads. A box of instant mashed potatoes was cheap, and with extra water in the mix (and no butter) it was nice and soupy. Applesauce and pudding are good for grabbing handfuls and throwing. Overall, it's an interesting math/budget lesson as the children quickly learn how far $5 can (or can't) go in a grocery store. Soon they work hard to stretch their money as far as it will go. This is also a tactile experience, a lesson in responsibility (cleaning up!), and just all-around fun.

Time

Impatience Is a Teacher
Kris Bordessa, Diamond Springs, California

I use my six-year-old son's inability to wait for *anything* to ease him into telling time. When anticipating an event, I set the time it will happen on a small clock with moveable hands. He then compares that time with the "real" time as he waits. By figuring out how long he has to wait, he is already telling time to the hour. A bonus is that this has eliminated many of the "when will it be time?" questions! You can find manipulative clocks in educational materials stores or catalogs, or you can make your own with a paper plate and construction paper hands held on with a brass fastener.

Graphing

Edible Bar Graphs
Fiona Bayrock, Chilliwack, British Columbia, Canada

Have your child make a bar graph using Smarties or M&M's. Dump a package on the table and tell your child to organize the candies into rows of each color. She should arrange them so the first Smartie of each row starts at the same level, so together the rows look like a bar graph and you can easily compare quantities. Then, using a piece of graph paper and colored pencils that correspond to the Smartie colors, your child can make a bar graph, coloring one square for each Smartie and ending up with a bar for each color. Talk about least, most, twice as much, half as much, and so on. Hypothesize why there is a discrepancy in distribution. Maybe write a letter to the company to find out—oh, but that would make this fall into the language arts category! Amazing how one thing leads to another.

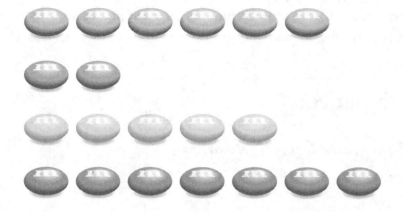

You're How *Old?*
Shay Seaborne, Woodbridge, Virginia

Show children how they can use Cuisenaire rods to make a graph that compares ages of people in the family. My children were amazed at how long the Grandaddy's line was!

Random Legos
Fiona Bayrock, Chilliwack, British Columbia, Canada

Have your child grab a couple handfuls of Legos, then take each kind of block and build a tower with a single block on each level. It's easy to see the distribution.

Velcro-Aided Graphs
Laura Cleary, Vista, California

Velcro dots work great for making games or graphs. Once we created an animal race, researching animals and how fast they move. Then we drew a race track and put Velcro dots on it, with matching dots on pictures of animals. The kids could move the animals as in a race, but ultimately needed to place the animals according to their actual speeds.

Miscellaneous

Make Your Own Tangrams
Linda Dobson, Saranac Lake, New York

I can't even wager a guess as to how many hours my children spent playing with tangrams, an ancient and simple Chinese puzzle. A set consists of seven pieces: five triangles, one rhomboid, and one square. You are given a solid silhouette of a picture, perhaps an animal, boat, or geometric shape, and it's your challenge to re-create the picture, always using all seven pieces.

You can purchase a set (with which you typically get silhouettes to re-create), or you can use any material you want to make your

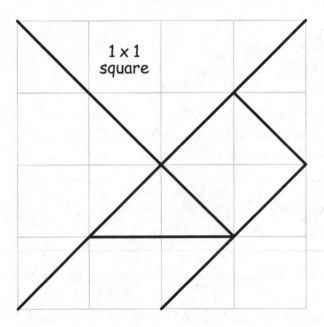

1 x 1
square

very own. Paper or cardboard are quick and easy; wood or metal more durable.

Begin with a 4-inch square of material on which you draw a 1-inch grid (sixteen squares). Next draw on the grid the patterns noted on the illustration. Carefully cut your material along these lines. Your child can arrange the pieces back into a square, or experiment to see what "pictures" she can make. She can combine the pieces to create even more geometric shapes for you to discuss. Check the library for tangram books or the Internet for silhouettes to duplicate.

On the box of the tangram set I bought for my children, it states, "You give it your concentration and patience, and it gives you the joy of discovery." It really does.

Covering the Gamut While Eating

Athena Dalrymple, Columbia, Maryland

When dining out, have your child guess how much the bill will be, including the tax. You can give individual item amounts or let your child guess those, too. Then give the amount on the bill and have your child calculate a 15 percent tip, then a 20 percent tip, and suggest which it should be, given the service rendered. Let your child use a calculator until able to calculate mentally. Finally, have your child give the total amount of the meal (add the amount on the bill and the amount of the tip).

String and Straw Geodesics

Helen Hegener, Tonasket, Washington

I started making string and straw geodesic forms as a child, and my kids always enjoyed creating various shapes and structures with the same materials. With a box or two of drinking straws (the thinnest ones work best), some strong string (carpet thread works great), and

More Math Reading

The following books all have a variety of fun puzzles, facts, activities, and games for learning about math:

- *Help Your Child Learn Number Skills* by Frances Mosley and Susan Meredith (Usborne Parents' Guides, EDC Publishing, 1991) This colorful little paperback is one of the best buys around and is packed with creative activities you can do with inexpensive things around the house.

- *The I Hate Mathematics! Book* by Marilyn Burns (Little, Brown & Company, 1976)

- *The Joy of Mathematics: Discovering Mathematics All Around You* by Theoni Pappas (Wide World Publishing/Tetra, 1989)

- *Math for Kids and Other People, Too!* By Theoni Pappas (Wide World Publishing/Tetra, 1997)

- *Math for Smarty Pants* by Marilyn Burns (Scott Foresman, 1982)

- *More Joy of Mathematics* by Theoni Pappas (Wide World Publishing/Tetra, 1991)

- *The Wonderful World of Mathematics* by Lancelot Hogben (Doubleday and Company, 1968) This lovely big picture book has interesting stories of how mathematics developed around the world from earliest times. It also shows

a blunt needle (available at your local crafts or fabric store), build cubes, pyramids, geodesic domes, balls, and other wonderfully complex creations.

The instructions are simple: Thread about 6 feet onto the needle, and thread three straws onto it, or four straws for a cube. Run the needle back through the first straw again, and thread on two more and go back through the base straw. You should end up with a simple techniques that people once used to calculate for everyday needs. To get a feel for how and why people developed the study of mathematics, your family can easily duplicate these historical techniques as fun activities.

In addition to those just listed, the following books have wonderfully imaginative ideas, but they are specifically written for Waldorf School classroom teachers. The best approach is to read through them to find fun and creative things you and your kids can explore together. The books are available from the Rudolph Steiner College Bookstore, 916-961-8721, www.steinercollege.org/bookstore.html:

- *Math Lessons for Elementary Grades* by Dorothy Harrer (Mercury Press, 1971)
- *Teaching Mathematics* by Roy Wilkinson (Rudolph Steiner College Press, 1990)

These last two books are written for homeschool and classroom teachers and contain games and activities that use pattern blocks and other simple materials for younger children to use. A goal is to have students learn to think as mathematicians think. A Web site provides some sample activities from the books: Pattern Press, P.O. Box 2737, Fallbrook, CA 92088-2737, members.aol.com/patternpr/patterns.html

- *Patterns in Arithmetic* by Suki Glenn
- *Understanding Fractions* by Suki Glenn

A helpful online resource is the HomeSchool Association of California Web site: Go Figure! The Fascinating World of Mathematics (www.hsc.org/intedo3.html).

—*Lillian Jones, Sebastopol, California*

diamond shape with a crossbar through the middle. Run the string through one of the side straws, string on one more straw, and take the thread through the straw at the other point of the diamond. Presto! You should have your first pyramid! By continuing to add straws—sometimes two at a time, sometimes only one—you should be able to build domes, balls, multipointed star shapes, and many other wonderful structures.

See photos and more instructions on this principle at BuckyBalls Triangulated, www.earth360.com/sci-c60.html.

Just Foolin' Around

Sandra Dodd, Albuquerque, New Mexico

We have geoboards, drawing compasses, graph paper, rulers, pattern blocks, and pattern puzzles that we use as toys. They're not just for kids. We do things together, just goofing around, and sometimes a serious question and pursuit comes along for a minute or twelve, and the concepts grow. Once my daughter, Holly, showed me how she finds the middle of a square on the computer art program Kid Pix, and I showed her how, similarly, to bisect a line on paper with a compass. We were each impressed with the other's knowledge.

More Foolin' Around

Linda Dobson, Saranac Lake, New York

This game makes long car trips seem to go faster while helping your children expand their understanding of numbers by playing with them.

Ask your child to think of a number in a certain range (such as between one and one hundred). You need to guess the number by asking questions of the child that give you clues. For example, you might begin by asking, "Is it an even number?" Your child either answers or you get a chance to discuss even and odd numbers.

Next, you could ask, "Is the number greater than fifty?" (Note the use of the terms used in mathematical language.) If the child says no, you can hone in by asking, "Is it more than ten but less than thirty?"

With older children, add questions that review more concepts, such as division and multiplication. Don't forget to let your child take a turn asking questions.

Mystifying Möbius Strips

Linda Dobson, Saranac Lake, New York

When you turn a strip of paper into a continuous one-sided surface, you have a Möbius strip, a source of much investigation and experimentation and a great introduction to topology (a branch of geometry that concentrates on how surfaces can be pulled, stretched, twisted, bent, or otherwise manipulated to change form).

To make your strip, you'll need a piece of paper about 14 to 15 inches long and 2 inches wide (adding machine tape works perfectly). Also get some tape, scissors, a pencil, and a couple of crayons.

Lay your paper flat on the table, and mark an *X* and an *O* in alternate corners on the side facing up. (The letters will be at a diagonal to each other.) Now twist the paper until the two *X*'s are facing and the two *O*'s are facing. Hold that position and tape together the ends of the paper so you make a sort of circle. With your pencil, draw a line lengthwise down the middle of the strip. What happens with the line? Is it coming or going, does it come back where it started? For more fun, try to color one side of the strip green and the other side purple. (You can't because a Möbius strip only has one side.) Cut the Möbius strip in half with the scissors—do you now have two Möbius strips?

Overlap

Conversation Starters

- Which occupations use a lot of math? How?

- Machines are performing many calculations for us today. What are the benefits and drawbacks?

- Using a real-life math problem, talk about (and write down) how many different ways there are to find the answer.

- What do you suppose is the (longest, shortest, heaviest, lightest) (animal, plant, planet, fish, person) in the world? How will we find out?

- Clip and save those coupons you won't use in the stores. Spread out a handful of them on the table and converse about everything from best buys to prices to savings percentages to . . .

4

Communicate!

The Joy of Language

Recently, a mom on a homeschooling e-mail list shared a story:

> Jennifer, the little girl next door, said to the woman's homeschooled daughter, "Of course you're reading more than I am, Samantha. *I don't have time to read. I have to go to school.*"

Oh, the irony. A young child experiencing daily "schooling" can so clearly see that school attendance doesn't allow her the time needed to truly *read*, certainly not the amount of time her homeschooled friend finds for reading.

More irony: When, in 2000, homeschooled contestants swept the top three places in the Scripps Howard National Spelling Bee, many spokespeople for the public educational establishment voiced the same complaint to the media about the homeschoolers' performances. "Well, of course the homeschoolers are going to do better," they lamented, "they have more time to prepare!" Doesn't preparing for a national spelling bee mean learning how to spell? And that's *bad*?

Homeschooled children possess more time to read and to learn how to spell. Next thing you know, you'll hear complaints that homeschooled kids also have more time to practice handwriting, stretch their vocabularies, "play" phonics, and free their imaginations in poetry and stories of their own making.

Well, yes, in general they do have more time. And if you're open to listening to someone other than the critics, homeschoolers will share a secret with you: Little ones learn and use language easily, at least easily relative to the complicated production educators and politicians have made out of the process.

With days free from compulsory school attendance, children have time to observe and participate in "language," meaningful communication that is a part of real life. As a homeschooling parent, you get the chance to observe for "teachable moments" and spice things up, presenting opportunities to make it all that much more fun.

Reading

Although all aspects of communication are important, in the past several decades, reading has ripped away center stage from its sisters, writing and speaking. The attention has been dubbed "The Reading Wars"—heated controversy over two teaching theories, each with soldiers vocally carrying its battle flag.

The first side swears by the direct instruction of phonics, or the predictable relationship between letters—and letter combinations—and their sounds. While everyone knows words whose spelling defies this correspondence, the actuality is that more than 85 percent of English words are phonic and more than 90 percent follow regular spelling rules (it's only 10 percent that are out to get you!).

The second side believes children best learn to read through a method commonly called whole language, but also alternatively referred to as look-say, paired reading, shared reading, sentence method, emergent literacy, balance literacy approach, and animated literacy, among others. Because it's also frequently described as "literature based," as the theory (simplistically) contends that children learn how to read by being read to, many people mistakenly believe that the teaching of phonics ignores literature, which is not the case.

After hearing all of this, one might believe that the two methods are mutually exclusive. Not so, say National Institutes of Health researchers who spent twenty years studying how we learn to read. They discovered that different sections of the brain handle different aspects of reading. One part helps us identify letters, another recognizes the sounds of the letters, the third section reaches for meaning. Based on these discoveries, the researchers recommend a three-part formula for getting children onto the reading road:

1. Help children learn the sounds that make up the language, such as "puh" as the sound of *P*. This is known as phonemic awareness.

2. Help them understand letter-sound relationships. This is the phonics aspect.

3. Expose them to meaning by helping them enjoy literature by being read to and by reading independently as skill allows. This is the core of whole language.

Yes, the most effective way to master reading skills takes a little from both sides of the argument and combines them. The nice thing about this formula is that it's natural, easy, and powerful when applied in the home setting. The reading activities you'll find in this chapter will serve your children well as they use this commonsense approach. A love of reading, an ever-expanding vocabulary, often encouraged by enjoying and discussing good literature together, and attention to spelling and grammar via reading create a terrific foundation upon which your children can build their education.

Helpful Language Arts Resources

Books

- *The Princeton Review Writing Smart, Jr.: The Art and Craft of Writing (Grades 6–8)* by C. L. Brantley and Cynthia Johnson (Random House, 1995)
- Writing Adventures Book 1 Workbook and Journal (Create Press; 760-730-9550; www.createpress.com)

Sources

- Chinaberry Book Service: 2780 Via Orange Way, Suite B, Spring Valley, California 91978, 800-776-2242, www.chinaberry.com
- Greathall Productions, Inc. (stories on cassette or CD): P.O. Box 5061, Charlottesville, Virginia 22905, 800-477-6234, www.greathall.com
- Sonlight Curriculum, Ltd.: 8185 S. Grant Way, Littleton, Colorado 80127, www.sonlight.com

Reading Programs

- Ball-Stick-Bird (learn to read): P.O. Box 13, Colebrook, Connecticut 06021, 860-738-8871, www.ballstickbird.com
- Headsprout Reading (online delivery beginning to read): www.headsprout.com
- Reading Kids Olympics: www.readingolympics.org

Web Sites

- American Library Association Resources for Parents, Teens, and Kids: www.ala.org/parents/index.html
- Carol Hurst's Children's Literature Site: www.carolhurst.com
- Children's Literature and Art: www.mgfx.com/kidlit/
- Literature Resources Online: www.literatureplace.com
- Write Guide: www.writeguide.com

Writing

There are two aspects of writing—the physical act itself and getting one's ideas down on paper. While there is much less attention paid to handwriting these days, thanks to the proliferation of computer keyboards, it's still nice to be able to read what your child writes. Because many kids hate writing just for its own sake, you'll find activities that give your children a *reason* to hone their penmanship. Also included are activities to motivate your children to create works of written art, as well as fun ways to achieve them.

Listening and Speaking

True communication occurs when the parties involved know how to listen to comprehend, then to express their thoughts and ideas logically and clearly. This aspect of language often receives short shrift in schools, as it doesn't result in a concrete final product that is easily scored. At the other end of this continuum, you don't need to force your child to become the king of debating either (and you might be sorry if you do).

Homeschooling parents report that adults meeting their children for the first time are often pleasantly surprised by how openly and articulately the kids relate to them. I believe this is a result of the relatively large amount of time home-educating families spend together in discussion, honing those listening and speaking skills in many ways. As families, they talk about current events and pressing social issues, challenge each other's thinking (playing devil's advocate is a lot of fun!), and, of course, maintaining a healthy dose of curiosity as they question everything. Enjoy paying attention to these very important aspects of language.

Beginners: Getting Ready for Reading

Pocket Alphabet

Tara Hall, Colliersville, Tennessee

For my two- and three-year-olds, I took pockets from old shirts and pants and sewed twenty-six of them onto a colorful beach towel. With a marker, I wrote one letter on each pocket, then surprised the girls with items placed in the pockets: a toy apple in "A," a bear in "B," a car in "C," and so on. I only do this once a week so that the novelty doesn't wear off too quickly. They spend an hour going through the pockets, looking at the letters on front, and playing with the toys.

They've already figured out that the xylophone is always in the "X" pocket and the yo-yo in the "Y". It's fun to see them fill the pockets themselves during the week to surprise me—and most of the time they get it right.

Kinesthetic Alphabet

Cindy Watson, Levittown, Pennsylvania

One of my twins is struggling with learning letters, so every night when he takes his shower, I use cheap shaving cream to spray a new letter on the shower wall. He has to tell me what letter it is and something that starts with that letter before he can play with the shaving cream and make his own picture. I do more cleaning of soap scum, but he's really learned his letters this way.

Also, after we've studied a new letter, the twins find something in the house that begins with the letter, then I take a picture of them with it. This activity involves running around the house after sitting and applying what they've learned about a letter. They love getting their pictures taken, and these become part of their very own alphabet books that we read over and over again.

Fun with Letter Cards

Shay Seaborne, Woodbridge, Virginia

Cut thirteen 3-by-5-inch cards in half vertically, and write one letter of the alphabet on each. Let your child spell words, organize by consonant versus vowel, or organize alphabetically. I still vividly recall my daughter's beaming face when she lined up her cards in alphabetical order after making the connection between the cards and the alphabet song.

Plywood Alphabet Chart
LeCee Galmiche Johnson, New York, New York

Cut a piece of plywood (about $18) into strips 10 inches by 2 feet, enough to hold four letters. Sand the plywood. Using a stencil or freehand, draw letters, about four to a section, onto the plywood strips. Paste small bow tie and shell pasta onto the letters. Have your child, with help if appropriate, decorate the border with pasta as well, if you like.

Paint the boards with glitter paint, use shellac to make them glossy, or use a matte paint. Be sure to get your child's input so each letter can be as individual as he is. Use shiny confetti, beads, rhinestones, or glitter to decorate the boards. Paint the letters gold so they stand out. After all the work is done, paint shellac on the boards to set the creation. The fumes are overbearing, so it's best to do this outdoors.

The result is a vibrant, fun alphabet (or numbers, if you like) chart. The shells give sensory feedback when the children trace the letters with a finger.

We hang our letter on the wall. Each letter is attached to the chart with two-sided, reusable tape squares from an art supply store. We take down the letters that we're working on and then put them back on display when we're finished with them.

"Starts With . . ."
Carron Steele, Traverse City, Michigan

I don't teach the ABCs to beginning readers. Instead, I play the "Starts With" game. Because my four-year-old daughter loves this game, she'll start by asking, "What does *rabbit* start with?" I tell her, "rrr" (sounding the letter), and then say the letter. She goes on to a new word. This teaches a meaning behind the alphabet instead of just a bunch of letters in a song. As she has gotten better, she plays the game in stores and other places, with the next step being *me* asking her what words start with. She now spells simple words orally, such as *sat, Dad, Mom, dog*, and so on.

Tactile Letters
Chrissy Walser, Murrells Inlet, South Carolina

Cut out letters from sandpaper. As your child identifies the letters, give him a crayon that has been peeled and a piece of white paper. He can place the paper over the cut-out and then use the crayon to make a rubbing of the letter. This works well with numbers, too, of course.

Letter Hide and Seek
Jane Powell, Bowie, Maryland

Purchase or make a set of letters out of cardboard, index cards, construction paper, or just about any other material you may have on hand, and select just a few of the letters. Hide the letters in various locations in a room, and ask your children to find them. Once they find a letter, have them tell you what it is, what sound it makes, or both. This also works well for number recognition.

The World Is Full of Letters
Linda Sunderland, Calgary, Alberta, Canada

Give your youngsters disposable cameras and have them take pictures of letters in the community. Don't use signs or meaningful symbols; instead use things like cracks in the sidewalk that look like a "B" or a curled-up hose that looks like a "Q."

Then develop the photos in 5-by-7-inch format. Paste each picture on 8 ½-by-11 construction paper and have your children, make "frames" by writing the letter represented by the picture all around the outside.

This activity was inspired by *Alphabet City* by Stephen Johnson (Puffin, 1999).

Life-Sized Alphabet Game

Meg Grooms, Orlando, Florida

Use sidewalk chalk to draw twenty-six large squares on the sidewalk or on your driveway. Write one letter in each square. Call out a letter and have your child jump into that square. You can add squares for blend sounds, as well. Or you can write numbers in the squares and use the game for number recognition.

To play indoors, write one letter on each of twenty-six pieces of paper and spread them around the room.

Made-Up Magnet Words

Pamela Jorrick, Korbel, California

My three-year-old daughter loves to arrange magnetic letters into new words that I "read." I phonetically sound out words like "Fjuswapi" and point to each letter as I say the sound. She laughs at what she spelled, then moves a few letters around, adds or removes a few, and asks me to read the new word. Even though the words aren't real, she's learning the sounds of the letters. I see her sounding them out herself sometimes, too.

Hop to It
Joanna Simpson, Dallas, Oregon

Using a cooler temperature hot glue gun, connect two clear shower curtains with long vertical and horizontal lines of glue, and finish by gluing the entire perimeter. You will have formed many squares. Carefully cut an opening in the top of each square, on one side only, creating many pockets. In each pocket, place the letters, numbers, or words your children are working on, lay the curtain on the ground, and play hopscotch, having the kids say whatever they land on.

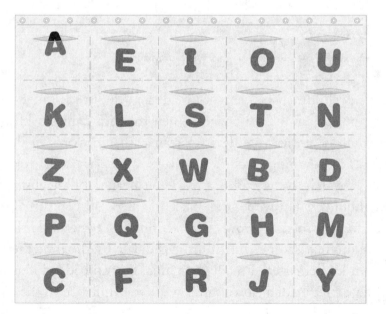

Hanging Letter Blends, Digraphs, and Diphthongs

Kim Weaver, Victoria, British Columbia, Canada

To help learn letter blends, digraphs, and diphthongs, create shapes of objects (about the size of two fists) out of construction paper. Each object that you create should contain the letter blend to be learned, such as a rain cloud. Next, write the word containing the blend on the large shape (*rain* on the rain cloud, usually in lowercase letters) with the letter blend underlined. Then make smaller, related shapes (in the above example, you can use raindrop shapes) and cut them out. Write other words containing the same blend (one per small shape, such as "aim," "train," "bait," etc.). Suspend the smaller shapes from the large one with yarn and hang them on the wall. The visual reminder of the sounds, as well as the process of creating them, can help your child internalize the blends more easily.

To Do Lists

Ruth Dunnavan, Moultonborough, New Hampshire

When my children were young, I made a to-do list each night, using large type and simple language. When the kids came to breakfast, they could begin learning how to read with the words in the day's agenda. I wrote things such as "vacuum," "go to the store to buy ice cream," "watch *Barney* at 8 A.M." The beauty of the list is that throughout the day, we'd check back and cross off completed items. My children associated words with actions and focused on the same meaningful text several times during the day. By the time they were ready for kindergarten, I made individual lists and added items such as "draw a picture of a clown" and "write the alphabet on the back of this paper."

Up on the Ceiling, It's the Alphabet!
Tara Hall, Colliersville, Tennessee

Use an extension pole and shortened roller to paint the alphabet on the ceiling. Then make mobiles: Attach to each letter a picture of something that begins with that letter. You can use pictures that your child drew, or you can go through old magazines and newspapers with your children and have them point out, and then cut out, pictures that start with different letters.

Letter of the Day
Pamela Jorrick, Korbel, California

Some days we choose a letter on which to focus. I make a few dotted examples of the capital and lowercase for my daughter to trace, and then she'll copy a few on her own. We talk about the sound the letter makes, and then we brainstorm words that begin with it. She draws or cuts out pictures of a few of the words as I browse our bookshelves to find a few stories to go with the theme.

Every Picture Tells a Story
Hope Ware, Peoria, Illinois

Cut out pictures from a magazine that are related in some way—or not. Cover the pictures in clear contact paper so they last longer. Hand them to your children and say, "Make up a story using these pictures." After they make up the story, have them act it out using the pictures. As they narrate, write the story on paper. Crayola makes *huge* "story" paper with lines at the bottom and a blank space at the top. Have your children illustrate the story at the top of the

No Pressure

Children learn to read when you and they enjoy it. They also learn by seeing others read for pleasure and curiosity and by playing with books, letters, words, maps, puzzles, board games, and comic books. Some children learn to read at four years of age, some at twelve. By the time they are sixteen, no one can tell the difference.

—Luz Shosie, Guilford, Connecticut

page. You can also make sentence strips for the story. To do this, simply make a word-for-word duplicate of the story and cut it apart into sentences. Later your children can match the words on the sentence strips to the words in *their* story.

Phonics for Children with Speech or Hearing Problems
Danni Williams, Richardson, Texas

Color Phonics is based on the theory that there is a connection between being able to say sounds and being able to read, and that children who have had or do have speech and hearing problems will have trouble learning to read.

Color Phonics is a computer program that starts with a cutaway of a face, showing an air puff while it tells and shows how to make a sound. Each vowel sound is given a different color so the child knows what it sounds like. If a consonant has a special sound or one that is not normal (such as the *f* in "of"), it's slanted in the writing. The letter for a silent sound is very skinny. The program offers lots of pronunciation practice.

At approximately $40, Color Phonics is *very* inexpensive compared with most of the other programs we examined, and it's available online.

- Color Phonics: www.inspireidea.com

Getting Ready for Writing

Add Pictures and Codes to the Mix

Athena Dalrymple, Columbia, Maryland

To help inspire a new writer to share his thoughts, show him how to add rebuses (depictions of words or syllables by pictures that suggest the sounds they represent) in his writing. Young ones find secret codes a lot of fun, too.

Practice on the Dotted Letter

Jane Powell, Bowie, Maryland

As children begin to write, they are often overwhelmed by the amount and complication of letters, coupled with the difficulties of holding a writing instrument properly. Make writing fun by creating dot-to-dots for your children. With a large-tipped marker, draw large letters using only dots. Let your children connect the dots to form letters. Extend the lesson with identification of letters and sounds.

Match 'Em Up with the Real Thing

Joanna Simpson, Dallas, Oregon

Put a single word (such as "duck") on an index card, then either get a small toy (a rubber duck) or draw a picture of whatever the word is.

Handwriting Help

Building upper body, arm, and hand and finger strength helps improve handwriting. With children it helps if it's play instead of work. Here are some fun ways to achieve the goal.

- Hang a climbing rope from a tree. Put knots in the rope every foot or so for beginning climbers.
- Have your children lie on their stomachs on the floor propped up with elbows to do schoolwork, watch TV, or listen to stories.
- Use an easel or tape paper to a wall to draw or paint on. This not only strengthens muscles, but it also puts the writing/drawing utensil in a natural pencil-grip.
- Have your children string Fruit Loops on a string. This helps when learning colors and patterns, too.
- When eating, have your children spear grapes and other fruit pieces with a toothpick.
- When making lunch, have your children spread peanut butter on crackers.
- Have your children play with an Etch-a-Sketch, Cat's Cradle, or other games using hands and wrists.

Have your child match the word to the toy or picture. As her skills progress, she can put the words into vowel groups or word family groups.

Yes, We'd Like Fries with That

Angela Preimesberger, Sumter, South Carolina

What kid doesn't like going out for some fast food? While at the restaurant, our children make letters out of the French fries. It's a lot of fun and the kids "just eat it up."

So That's What My Story Looks Like

Sue Patterson, Wichita Falls, Texas

Sometimes "writing" is much more than penmanship. It's really difficult to develop a story when you aren't sure of the difference between a "B" and a "D," but that doesn't mean that an action-packed story isn't waiting to be told.

Dictation solves the problem. Have your child dictate her story (this will also help you improve your typing skills!). Try using different fonts at different ages—use simple block lettering font when she's young, "graduating" to a more cursive look as she gets a little older. When my children were trying to learn to read cursive writing, this really helped because they already knew the story.

During the dictation, you can toss in some comments, but only after your child knows that you are not going to tweak her ideas. For example, "Tell me more about Jake. What does he look like? What is his attitude?" Sometimes your input may be welcome. But other times it could be an intrusion on her creative process. It is always perfectly acceptable for your child to say, "Not yet, Mom, I'm on a roll!"

"I Can" and "I Feel" Books

Beverley Paine, Yankalilla, South Australia

We make "I Can" books by cutting A4 blank exercise books in half. Each page in these A4 landscape-oriented books begins with "I can _____." When young, my son, Thomas, would just draw a picture, and I'd scribe. Sometimes he'd "write" for himself, filling the space with scribble or strings of figures that were close approximations of letters and numbers.

As he grew and his skills developed, he began to finish the sentence himself. Sometimes a story evolved from the "I can" statement, and I would record it for him, as the writing often spilled over onto the next page. I encouraged fiction as well as actual abilities.

The "I Feel" book can be explored forever, but it does need a creative parent to come up with never-ending possibilities once the usual emotions are covered. Start with pictures on love, hate, anger, and so on, and then move on to frustration, pity, and more. We began with pictures of how Thomas looked when he felt a certain emotion, or we would use pictures of things that made him feel a certain emotion. Use anything in which feelings are explored, such as poetry, song lyrics, films, or television.

Looking through these books years later is fun because they trace his development—physically, socially, intellectually, and emotionally.

Reading Skills

Building Motivation
Barb Beideman, Pittsburgh, Pennsylvania

We've started a monthly book club for our five-year-old and seven of his friends. Unlike adult book clubs, the book club for kids allows the children to bring their own favorite books and to talk about why they like them. (These are books that have been read to them.) Most of the kids are just starting to read, so this activity builds motivation. They're also welcome to bring projects that they've created.

Rhyming Word Memory Game
Maria Hammer, Marshall, Illinois

This is a great phonics exercise for beginning readers. Cut an index card in half and write a rhyming word on each half, such as "hop/pop" or "bought/thought" for advanced readers. Mix up several rhyming pairs and turn them upside down. The one who discovers the most pairs—and reads them correctly—wins.

Look How Much You Know!

Kim Weaver, Victoria, British Columbia, Canada

Each day, take a section of the newspaper and circle or highlight words that your child already knows how to read or can sound out. Have your child read the words, then cut them out and glue them onto another piece of paper. In a few days, your child will have her own "newspaper" made of words from the actual newspaper. This shows her that she can read words from many sources and encourages her to look around the world for other sources of print to unlock. After just a few days, our daughter realized she could read a lot more than she thought she could.

Let's Get Started

Have your child read three books by his favorite author.

Ring My Bell

Hope Ware, Peoria, Illinois

We sit on the floor facing each other. I say a word and my son James has to respond with a rhyming word. His younger brother, John, rings a small metal bell if the word rhymes, and James gets a point. Then James gives me a word, and I have to think of a rhyming word. If it rhymes, John again rings the bell, and I get a point. John, in case you haven't guessed, just likes ringing the bell! We play until we reach a certain number of points or get tired of rhyming.

Dealing with Dyslexic Difficulties

Ten years ago, it was difficult to find hints for teaching a differently abled child. Many people said I was crazy to try, but my dyslexic son and I pressed forward and got past the basic phonics, which were out of fashion at the time. Still, reading wasn't fun for him at all.

I stocked up on all of the Children's Illustrated Classics we could find, since as an English major I couldn't bear the thought that my child wouldn't know these wonderful stories. During the following year, he steadily read them all and his confidence grew. I knew he was ready for something else, but what?

We found the answer in the library's large print books. They had all the helpful aspects he was used to — large print generously laid out, but not "watered down" for children. He began with *The Diary of Anne Frank* and loved it. He'd found the key to enjoying reading. My son is a senior in high school now and continues to find books he likes. He just finished reading the Tolkien trilogy and likes Voltaire — go figure! The jump from children's books with large print to "normal" books from the large print section did the trick.

—*Jean Forbes, Alexandria, Virginia*

The Beanie Baby Reading Method

Su Crutchfield, North Beach, Maryland

When my son, JT, wanted to learn how to read at age six or seven, he balked at anything that smacked of phonics, and he grew frustrated and angry with himself if he made a mistake. He came up with a way to practice reading without the stress.

He would gather a group of Beanie Babies to sit on the sofa with us, and we took turns reading. JT played himself as well as a couple of Beanies, and I played myself and sometimes a Beanie, too. Each of the Beanies had its own personality, and some had better reading skills than others. It seemed so real at times that I talked to the Beanies as if they were my other children!

We'd all take turns reading, and since all the Beanies read less well than JT, he didn't feel any pressure. Some of the Beanies made horrible mistakes, or threw tantrums, or obnoxiously corrected each other (all via JT). It sounds pretty weird, but it really worked, and it was all JT's idea, which always works better for him. He reads quite well now, spending hours every day reading just for the joy of it—*without* Beanies.

Out Loud, Taking Turns, and Comprehension Check

Cindy Allas, Fairfield, California

My children and I read together orally because my son told me that he grasps more when he hears the information. We take turns reading. My daughter loves to read, but I noticed that she doesn't always remember or comprehend. To help her, I have her tell me about what she has just read (often chapter by chapter), or I find questions about the story on the Internet that we can discuss. I don't make her write the answers because she would hate that and thus kill her joy of reading.

Piece the Words Together Game

Jennifer Miller, Puyallup, Washington

Write the words "beginnings" and "endings" on index cards. Examples of word beginnings are *bl*, *st*, or *m*, and word endings are *ow*, *op*, and *end*. Place the cards face down in two piles, one of beginnings and one of endings. Players take turns turning over two cards. If the two cards make a word, the player keeps the match and goes again. If they don't make a word, it's the next player's turn. When all cards are gone, the player with the most cards wins.

Word Bingo
Theresa Doolan, Riva, Maryland

This game is great for phonics reinforcement of short vowel families, blends, digraphs, homonyms, and so on. Cut a piece of poster board into cards about 10-by-10-inches square. Divide each card into columns and rows, just like Bingo cards. Fill in the squares with words you are learning or reviewing. Remember to make each card different so you know the child is really reading and not just memorizing the location of a word.

For markers, use Goldfish crackers, Teddy Grahams, chocolate chips, M&M's, or other small edible items. Call out a word, have your child locate it and cover it with a "marker." The game goes on until either a row is filled or, more often, the card is filled and the

Dog	Cat	Pig	Duck	Cow
Hen	Bug	Rug	Rag	Log
Rig	Hat	Bat	Pow	Wow
Luck	Hog	★	Puck	Sow
Now	Nag	How	Zag	Low
Mow	Zig	Log	Big	Pen
Nog	Dig	Muck	Bog	Zen

child delights in eating all the markers. (A lesson in delayed gratification provided free of charge.)

This Old Magazine
Jane Powell, Bowie, Maryland

Have your child cut out pictures from old magazines: a house, tree, kitchen table, chair, characters, cars, food—nothing is off limits. Attach the pictures to individual sheets of paper. Lay about a dozen pictures face down. Ask your child to choose four (or however many you want), then invite him to create a story with those four pictures (orally or written, depending on his skill level).

What's the Word?
Linda Dobson, Saranac Lake, New York

Have your children choose a word from the dictionary, the bigger the word the better. (While you're in the dictionary, note what part of speech the word is and read and discuss the definition.) Give each person a piece of paper, and have her write the word on the top of her sheet of paper. Set a time limit for writing as many words as possible using only the letters in the big word. Use a point system depending on how many letters are in the created words (three letters = one point, four letters = two points, etc.). This can be a competition, or children can enjoy beating their previous best score.

Adjective Hunt
Maria Hammer, Marshall, Illinois

This was a favorite warm weather activity for my six-year-old. I made a list in advance of things found around and inside our apartment complex. Jake read the first word on the list and ran to it. (Choose things far apart, and include physical education.) He then touched, smelled, threw, or tasted the object to provide an adjective that described it. No colors were allowed; that's too easy. Even if your child has to make up a word, write it down; the most hilarious results are the best remembered.

Wiggle Words

Dianne Rigdon, Bakersfield, California

To keep my five-year-old son's attention, we turned phonics recognition into a moving game. For example, if I said a word that started with a short *a* sound, he had to wiggle as much as possible; if it didn't, he sat still. This was great fun, but only good for about five minutes at a time or every word would have earned a squirm!

When this got old, we turned it into a "Mother, May I?" type of game. He would move forward if the word matched the criterion given and stay still if it didn't. This could be used in a variety of situations.

Take-Out Books

Andrea Hargreaves, San Antonio, Texas

We take our "read aloud" books with us wherever we go, especially to doctors' offices and other places where we're likely to wait in lines. This practice keeps us from being bored and helps us get our reading done.

Fun with Proofreading

Athena Dalrymple, Columbia, Maryland

When attending a concert, wedding, or other event with a program, everyone begins reading the program at the same time. The first one to spot a typographical error (typo) wins. Another alternative is to have the winner be the person who spots the most typos. You can also do this with books, restaurant menus, or other materials that you can all read at the same time.

Try this activity at home. Let your child read your writing, such as journal notes or business letters. Have him correct your spelling or grammatical errors, as well as suggest more precise words. If you model happiness about getting the corrections and suggestions, so might the child when you correct his errors or make recommendations.

Go Read TV, Please

Jean Forbes, Alexandria, Virginia

Our new television came equipped with closed captioning. One day, when my younger son was really bugging me and I was desperately trying to finish an algebra concept with his big brother, I turned on the closed captioning, turned off the sound, and told my son he could watch television for a while.

What a surprise! The child who wouldn't read to me giggled as he easily read the captions.

Make-Your-Own Books 101

Jennifer Miller, Puyallup, Washington

My children and I made some of their early readers. I stapled several pieces of paper together and wrote a simple story using words that we were working on. ("The fat cat sat on a mat.") The children either drew pictures or took photographs to illustrate the books. They loved reading their very own little books.

Advanced Make-Your-Own Books
Ned Vare, Guilford, Connecticut

Years before I discovered homeschooling, while I was a private school teacher for three years, all of my students from grades two to six wrote, illustrated, and bound an original book. The projects began with a short story, perhaps more than one, from which the children chose a favorite. (I took dictation for those who couldn't get their stories down on their own.)

With the story on paper, rewriting and the addition of passages began when we divided the stories into several parts, with each part the basis for a chapter. This provides an "outline" of sorts to follow. Young children might write a one- or two-page chapter with a full-page illustration. Older kids could use story boards and incorporate passages describing places, people, weather conditions, animals, culture, and so on.

Each chapter can be a separate project, combining additional writing, printing, and illustrations with captions. You can include front and back matter, such as title page, dedication, author biography, and index. Binding can be as simple as staples or as elaborate as you can afford.

This experience so changed my attitude about books that I became an author of two. Authors have said that writing a book is one way of attaining immortality. Not a bad result of a rainy day project. Kids and parents, go for it.

If Not a Published Book . . .
Judith Waite Allee, from *Educational Travel on a Shoestring*

Watch for opportunities for your child to submit stories, poetry, drawings, or photographs for publication. Check your library for *The Young Writer's Guide to Getting Published* by Kathy Henderson

(Writer's Digest, 2001) and other resources, including children's magazines that often provide submission information in each issue.

- *Educational Travel on a Shoestring* by Judith Waite Allee and Melissa L. Morgan (Shaw Books, 2002)

Literature and Poetry

M.A.S.H. and Donne

Juleigh Howard-Hobson, Sacramento, California

John Donne's poem "A Valediction Against Mourning" can be set to the *M.A.S.H.* theme tune and very rapidly memorized. It fits perfectly.

Poetry Rocks

Beverley Paine, Yankalilla, South Australia

Gather thirty smooth, oval river stones and clean them. With black paint or black felt tip pen, write single words on each: *he, she, you, river, glistening, fire*; you get the gist. Include some full stops, exclamation marks, and question marks.

Paint each stone with clear lacquer. If you'd like, you could paint the rock first with whatever color you like. Put the rocks in a clean cardboard milk container that has been suitably decorated. You now have poetry rocks that can be arranged into sentences to make up poetry.

Let's Get Started

Make up a first line of a poem. Have everyone write a few more lines, or have each family member add a line, then move on to the next person until everyone has had at least one turn.

Poem of the Week

Fiona Bayrock, Chilliwack, British Columbia, Canada

Buy a blank laminated poster—one that looks like a giant piece of notepaper is great. Each week place one member of the family (Mom and Dad included) in charge of the "Poem of the Week." That person selects or composes a poem and writes it in dry erase marker on the poster. The poem hangs on the refrigerator until the next week, when someone else has a turn.

Bring home a fresh supply of poetry books from the library each week and watch noses get stuck in them. Soon the whole family will be immersed in poetry as each person searches for just the right poem. "Hey, listen to this!" will become common. Watch for opportunities to discuss tone, tempo, and meaning when someone inadvertently omits or adds punctuation, spacing, or capitalization. Look for patterns—boy, will you find patterns! Think emotion, perspective, style, and synonyms. Use your imagination. This will snowball.

Three Questions

Judith Waite Allee, from *Educational Travel on a Shoestring*

Find five or more favorite bible verses. Write them on paper for each child. Then say, "I'm thinking of a bible verse. You can ask me three (or ten, depending on the children's skill) questions." Your children will look at all the verses many times, trying to figure out the verse. They will also think about the meaning of the verses, looking for clues and cementing the verses in their memories.

- *Educational Travel on a Shoestring* by Judith Waite Allee and Melissa L. Morgan (Shaw Books, 2002)

Clustering

Linda Dobson, Saranac Lake, New York

"Clustering" is an idea from a book for adult writers from which even young poets can benefit.

Start with a word for a broad concept, such as "winter." Write the word in the middle of a piece of paper or on a chalkboard and draw a circle around it. For a few minutes, the child writes (or dictates) whatever words pop into her mind related to the central word ("cold," "hot cocoa," "slippers," "fire," etc.). She then connects each word to the central word by spokes. If one of the words leads to another, it is "attached" to the subordinate word with its own spoke. The most important point—no editing by parent or child!

When the few minutes are up, the child is left with lots of related words that she can consider for inclusion in a poem that can rhyme—or not. Most of the work is already done, and you have an opportunity to talk about metaphors, similes, and, my favorite, alliteration. ("Sliding into slippers, sipping hot cocoa by the fire.")

Adapted from Natalie Goldberg, *Writing Down the Bones: Freeing the Writer Within* (Shambhala Publications, 1986).

More Ways to Create a "Must Read" Book List

- Use book club mailers for library book suggestions.
- Go to a children's book club Web site and select the appropriate age.
- Go to Barnes & Noble's or Amazon.com's Web site and select appropriate age ranges.

—Jane Powell, Bowie, Maryland

Book Lists

Jeanne Faulconer, Stanardsville, Virginia

I print out book lists from the Internet and other sources to help jog my memory of the good books I want my sons to read. Many colleges have suggested reading lists online, as do the American Library Association and individual libraries. I keep a list in my planner, too, jotting down suggestions I get from other homeschooling parents and librarians.

Book and Movie Comparisons

Terese Peterson, Milwaukee, Wisconsin

We really enjoy reading books that have become more familiar as movies, such as *Mary Poppins, Peter Pan,* and *The Wizard of Oz.* We have great discussions about how different the movies are from the books. We also compare the original movie to any remakes, such as *The Miracle Worker.* This movie helped my daughter to understand that the people are actors, since Patty Duke is Helen Keller in the first movie and Annie Sullivan in the second.

We also have great discussions about the differences between *Peter Pan* with Mary Martin, *Peter Pan* with Cathy Rigby, *Hook,* and the animated Disney version of *Peter Pan.*

Stories and Art, a Natural Partnership
Jeanne Faulconer, Stanardsville, Virginia

I read lots of fairy tales and folklore to my children when they were in their early and elementary years. While I read, they would draw a scene from the story in their sketchbooks. After a few months, they possessed lovely books full of their own interpretations of classic children's stories.

Writing Skills

Present a Writing Buffet
Beverley Paine, Yankalilla, South Australia

Variety can be the spice of writing. We keep many writing instruments around—lead pencils of varying grades and thickness, different types of colored pencils, biros, ink pens (cartridge and nib), chalk, felt tip pens (fine and thick), charcoal. In addition to all of the regular art materials, we also include things like lemon juice and candles for "secret writing."

Vary the color and texture of paper, too. Our children enjoyed making paper, and cards and envelopes appeared all over the place, resulting in many letters mailed. Don't stop at paper and cards to write on—try chalkboards, brick walls, pavements, round surfaces, and so on.

Are Your Ideas in Order?

Laura Cleary, Vista, California

We were talking about the order of beginning, middle, and end, and learning about how you need your ideas in order when you write so that your reader can understand. We took pictures of my daughter making some simple recipes, like noodles and sauce or peanut butter and jelly sandwiches. When the photos were developed, she put them in order, wrote directions to go along with the pictures, and made a little cookbook. You could do this with craft projects, fix-it projects, and others.

These Are a Few of My Favorite Things

Cindy Prechtel, North Fort Myers, Florida

My grades one and four children love making notebooks on specific subjects. For instance, my older son recently worked on a shark notebook. For a few weeks, he added pictures and diagrams almost daily. I asked him to write a few sentences about a specific kind of shark. Then we used those sentences to write a paragraph. We practiced using adjectives by writing descriptive words about sharks and then decorating that page of the notebook. He continues to add to the notebooks, so they'll be works in progress for many years, I'm sure!

My younger son has an ocean life notebook with a section on sea turtles. I write basic words or captions that he dictates to me, sometimes with a yellow highlighter so he can trace my writing. I help the notebook projects along by checking out tons of library books and placing them all over the house.

Extra, Extra, Read All About It

Athena Dalrymple, Columbia, Maryland

Rather than keeping a diary, your child could create a daily newspaper. Using a computer, it's easy to make it look authentic. The child might write a script as if she were telling about her day to a friend or even a robot.

Create Your Own Community

Beverley Paine, Yankalilla, South Australia

Role-playing games are a great way to introduce writing into our children's lives. One great game went on for more than a week in our home. My children constructed a shop in our living area that slowly evolved into a whole community of shops.

I helped out with props and costumes and made suggestions, like designing and printing play money, forms for the bank and post office, menu cards for the restaurant, travel brochures for the travel agents, a magazine of hair styles for the hairdressers, and a newspaper. The amount of writing that happened that week still astounds me!

Mad Libs

Jeanne Faulconer, Stanardsville, Virginia

You can buy Mad Libs word game booklets at most stores, including discount stores. We take turns asking each other to supply each story's missing noun, verb, "name of a person in the room," adjectives, and so on. The words are written down in the appropriate blanks, then read back in the story in the order they were given. The kids love the hilarious results. Not only is this a good way to learn the parts of speech and the importance of context in making words work correctly, but it also encourages the physical act of handwriting for children who are reluctant to write things down. Children also learn how fun it is to play with words.

We've just started an advanced version of this game. We write our own stories, leaving blanks in certain places for others to supply the missing words to be read back at the end. This provides even more practice on handwriting and helps kids develop an "ear" for language. Related to this, we sometimes take out a paragraph from a book or magazine and "mad lib" it. It's terrific to see the kids scouring through all the reading material looking for what might turn out to be the funniest.

Penmanship

Rice Write
Jane Powell, Bowie, Maryland

Pour uncooked rice in the bottom of a pan. Using a finger or spoon, have your child write letters in the rice, just as you would in sand, and "erase" them by gently shaking the pan. Experiment with sand, Jell-o mix, and other similar materials.

Handwriting Treasure Box

Dianne Rigdon, Bakersfield, California

My nine-year-old son is still reticent about handwriting, yet we pursue a classical-style education. To cut down on "pressure," we've combined his copy work with his memory work. Now he copies catechism answers and bible verses as he memorizes them. We print his memory verses on business cards, and as he memorizes them, we place them in his treasure box—a small wooden box on which he painted, "For where your heart is, there your treasure is also."

Fill Out This Form, Please

Jeanne Faulconer, Stanardsville, Virginia

To help my boys get interested in handwriting, I have them fill out forms. They've been reluctant to practice handwriting, but they are only too happy to send off for a rebate or prize offered by a cereal company. Fitting the letters on the lines or in the little boxes is great for practicing those fine motor skills, and it demonstrates the value of being able to communicate clearly in writing. Then the rebate or prize arrives—a great "natural" reward.

Thank You Very Much

Sue Patterson, Wichita Falls, Texas

Gone are the days when I have to "dot out" letter shapes so my budding writers can dash off a quick note. Thanks to StartWrite, a handwriting software from Idea Maker Inc., it does it for me. You or your child can choose from several interesting fonts. We've even "cheated" by typing out a thank-you letter (child dictated, of course), put the letter on a very light setting, and let the child trace over it with a fine-line marker. Grandma will be *so* impressed.

- StartWrite: www.startwrite.com or 888-974-8322

Young Pen Pals, Start with Postcards

Beverley Paine, Yankalilla, South Australia

Let's Get Started

Help your child find e-mail pals for writing practice.

Homeschooled kids are famous for accruing long lists of pen pals. For beginner writers, use postcards, which have limited space so are quick and easy to write. The small space on the postcard is less intimidating for new writers, and the whole exercise takes just a few minutes. My children transitioned easily to sending letters, drawings, homemade magazines, and puzzles to their pen pals.

Add interest by making your own postcards out of old cards with interesting pictures or old photographs.

Letter Writing Thursday

Merelee Syron, New Egypt, New Jersey

On Thursday, each child must write a letter to someone. It can be a relative, author, famous person, or corporation. We have received postcards from the president, our favorite author (Gail Gibbons), coupons for products they like, a free model kit due to a complaint about something they disliked, and lots of information about topics we were studying. The handwriting, spelling, and grammar has improved like no workbook could ever accomplish, and the children can't wait to see what rewards the mailbox has for their efforts.

Spelling

Spell Check Spelling

Shay Seaborne, Woodbridge, Virginia

My eleven-year-old used to be a horrible speller until she started e-mailing messages to her friends. When one friend's e-mails contained invented spelling that was almost impossible to read, my daughter decided to improve hers because she realized decent spelling is crucial to written communication. She learned how to use the spell checker on our e-mail program, and using it improved her spelling, because she had to choose the correct word from the pop-up menu.

My daughter still asks how to spell words, especially if she's not using the computer, but most often, she's the one answering her eight-year-old sister's requests for spellings. Out of her own interest and choice of method, she now spells to her satisfaction, which is a pretty high standard.

Night Time's the Right Time

Bobbi Jo Baumgardner, Cloverdale, California, courtesy of *Right at Home* newsletter

Since it often takes my daughter a while to get to sleep, I hang a list of spelling words by her bed. She reads over the list at least a few times each night.

Vocabulary Building Leads to Spelling Proficiency

Jean Reed, Bridgewater, Maine, from *The Home School Source Book*

We began many days sharing vocabulary words. We didn't talk about the spelling of these words, but learning the spelling just seemed to happen. Sometimes we'd give the kids three or four words to look up and define for us. Usually we'd include at least one silly word to make sure enjoyment and appreciation of language remained high. Sometimes we asked the children to choose words to introduce to us. They liked the idea of knowing something we didn't know and educating us. We noted in the latter case that they frequently chose more obscure or difficult words than we expected or would have chosen.

• *The Home School Source Book* (Brook Farm Books, 2000)

Spell It in Radio Code

Scott Stevens, Paris, Tennessee

We were listening to a book on tape, *The Wanderer*. It's about a young girl and her family who are sailing across the Atlantic Ocean. The kids on the boat learn about the radio code alphabet: Alpha is for *A*, Bravo is for *B*, Charlie is for *C*, and so on. Since reading this book, my kids have been going around for weeks spelling everything in radio code. It makes spelling fun, and it really gets the brain firing as you think about spelling the words in a different way. The entire code is as follows:

A	Alpha	B	Bravo
C	Charlie	D	Delta
E	Echo	F	Foxtrot
G	Gulf	H	Hotel
I	India	J	Juliet
K	Kilo	L	Lima
M	Mike	N	November
O	Oscar	P	Papa
Q	Quebec	R	Romeo
S	Sierra	T	Tango
U	Uniform	V	Victor
W	Whiskey	X	X-ray
Y	Yankee	Z	Zulu

Spelling Challenge

Athena Dalrymple, Columbia, Maryland

As you read aloud to your child, ask him to try to spell a word you think might be a challenge. Do so in a nonconfrontational manner, of course. This is activity is for fun; it's not a spelling test.

Outdoor Spelling

Jennifer Miller, Puyallup, Washington

If you like giving your children spelling tests, try having the children write the words on the sidewalk with sidewalk chalk. It's amazing how enthusiastic they are about spelling outside.

Let the Spelling Shine In

Carron Steele, Traverse City, Michigan

My older daughter has always hated spelling, so with different colored dry erase markers, I have her spell her words on the window in our family room! If she spells it correctly, it gets erased, but misspelled words get corrected and stay on the window all day. She then sees the word all day, gets creative, and decorates the window with the markers to make the word look "cool." I'm now using the idea with my four-year-old, who is learning to write letters.

Always-a-Winner Hangman

Therese Peterson, Milwaukee, Wisconsin

In our version of Hangman, the good speller picks a word and tells the learning speller what it is. The learner then attempts to fill in the blank for each letter of the word. Many letters can be sounded out, but then the guessing comes into play. We never have a loser in our game, as we give the poor hanged man fingers, toes, eyes, and so on until the word is completed. My daughter, who had trouble spelling, begs to play this game and is memorizing many of the words she's heard before.

Alphabetizing

Get Around Perfectionism

Ritzya Mitchell, Herndon, Virginia

My perfectionist son, who alphabetizes his spelling words, didn't like how messy his paper looked if he forgot a word and needed to squeeze it in. He was learning the means and reasons of alphabetizing, but the mechanics of getting it all down on paper were frustrating.

To solve the problem, he began writing each spelling word on an index card. If he didn't know the definition, he looked it up and wrote it on the card. Using a file box, he then placed each card in alphabetical order with alphabet divider tabs. If he missed one, he could just lift it out and move it, or easily rearrange the order of the cards. He never messed up alphabetizing again. For a little more fun, he chose a spelling word starting with each letter of the alphabet and used the words in a story.

Vocabulary

Mini Vocabulary Flash Cards

Ruth Dunnavan, Moultonborough, New Hampshire

When you read along in a textbook and come to a new word, you are doing several things at once. For example, you come across the word "ellipse" in a chapter on planets. You have to read the word, hear the sound of the word, know how to say it, know that it is related to orbits and planets in a solar system, and be aware that it is not the word "eclipse" or a similar word.

I developed mini flash cards to prepare my children for learning vocabulary. Preparing the cards is a little time consuming. I use the glossary, chapter reviews, or name lists from the text to find words to type into a spreadsheet with about four items across and wide spacing between lines. Then I print two copies of the spreadsheets onto card stock (available beside the copy paper at stationery stores). Finally, I cut the words into 2-by-$\frac{1}{2}$-inch mini flash cards and clip one corner on each card so I can keep track of which side is up. I sort them according to their text chapter, tie them with rubber bands, and store them in fishing tackle boxes. Having the vocabulary lists on the computer is a bonus because I can use them to make puzzles on the Discovery Channel Web site and insert them in the Mavis Beacon typing program.

Several days before we start a textbook chapter, we use the mini flash cards for games. The obvious game is Concentration, but there are many others. Sometimes I pick a flash card, say the word, my son says it, and then I throw it for him to catch. Other times I spill out the flash cards and my son pairs them up while saying the word. Still other times we play against a timer for two minutes as my son spreads out a group of cards, half up and half down. He is "up" and I am "down." I have to say the word on an "up" card and flip it "down." He does the opposite as we each try to turn over the other's cards while saying the word on the card before two minutes is up.

After we study the text, we use the flash cards for review games.

- Discover Channel Puzzlemaker: www.puzzlemaker.school.discover.com

- Mavis Beacon Teaches Typing: www.mavisbeacon.com

Dictionary Game
Hope Ware, Peoria, Illinois

Find in the dictionary some really interesting words. Pronounce one of the words aloud. Each person in the family (or divide into teams) has a minute to come up with the best guess of the word's meaning. Then the guessed meanings are read aloud, and the best or funniest one is selected to win the round. To finish it off, the *real* definition is read.

Use It, Don't Lose It
Lorrie DeCoursey-Thomas, Sylmar, California

We pick about five words per week that have come up in conversation that the kids don't know. After we've discussed and looked up the meanings, they write them on an index card. Throughout the week, they try to use each of the words in sentences during normal conversation at least three times. When they do, they mark it on their index cards. Our ten-year-old son carries his card in his pocket.

Speaking

Start with a Good Poem
Julie Swegle, Colorado Springs, Colorado

A good starting place for public speaking is the memorization of poetry. Help your child to memorize a poem and recite it with feeling and dramatic flair. When she is ready to recite in public, invite grandparents or friends for a bit of fun. If you can't get a live audience, videotape or audiotape the performance to share it. The following are a few great books to start with:

- *A Child's Garden of Verses* by Robert Louis Stevenson (Simon & Schuster, 1999)
- *Favorite Poems Old and New* by Helen Ferris, Editor (Doubleday, 1957)

Quick Reminders of Unnecessary Words

Ruth Dunnavan, Moultonborough, New Hampshire

Using "like" and "ya' know" as frequent interruptions in speech is very annoying. My husband and I find that simply repeating the unnecessary words immediately after they are said helps the children remember not to use them.

Make-Your-Own Books on Tape

Laura Cleary, Vista, California

My daughters love to record themselves reading books onto a tape as gifts for younger cousins. Sometimes we send the books along, and the girls will even make a sound when the page is to be turned; it often gets very fancy. I think this idea might encourage a reluctant reader or speaker, because she has to choose books with a listener in mind and practice reading until she reads and speaks the words smoothly.

Public Access TV, Anyone?

Linda Spaulding, Pattersonville, New York

Almost every community has a public access channel that shows videos of useful information to the community. My daughter and I were members of a recorded panel on homeschooling. We gathered together a few other panel members, divided up general topics, and went on the air. Our moderator was a homeschooler as well.

Comedy Night
Athena Dalrymple, Columbia, Maryland

Set up a Comedy Night for your homeschool group. Each child will have the opportunity to do a five-minute comedy routine. "Open Mike Nights" are fun, too. Children can play instruments and tell a bit about the pieces they play, do magic tricks, or put on a short play—the sky's the limit.

Comedy—It's the Delivery That Counts
Therese Peterson, Milwaukee, Wisconsin

My five-year-old granddaughter has trouble with pronunciation. Even though she's perfectly willing to chatter away, no one listens much because they can't understand her. My daughter and I found some simple jokes to teach her. We coached her to deliver them so she can entertain waitresses (we eat out a lot) and other people she meets.

The trick is to find jokes that she understands and knows why they're funny. This makes it easier for her to remember how the words are put together, making her delivery smoother and easier to understand. The delighted reactions she receives from the people who hear her jokes are a great reward and encouragement for her to keep improving her speaking skills.

Listening

Verbal Scavenger Hunt

Jennifer Miller, Puyallup, Washington

Instead of giving the kids a written list of things to find in a scavenger hunt, give them a verbal list. Start with just three or four items and go from there. See how many items they can remember from your list.

Say "I Don't Know"

Athena Dalrymple, Columbia, Maryland

As you read aloud, ask your child to point out words he doesn't know. Let him look them up, either on the spot or once the reading is over. Some might give points to a child for volunteering that he didn't know the words, but I would discourage that, as the idea is for the child to want to enjoy learning new words. A "reward" could put the focus elsewhere.

Scooting Around

Jeanne Falconer, Stanardsville, Virginia

My three boys are extremely active, and there is a large age difference between the two older and the youngest. Even though my youngest is interested in stories, it's often hard for him to sit still for read-aloud times. I discovered that I could read aloud as they all scootered around me in circles. We read a ton of Greek myths in rapt silence, save the wheels turning and the feet pushing and an occasional change in direction.

Foreign Language

Total Physical Response

Holly Furgason, Houston, Texas

Total Physical Response (TPR) is an easy method for learning foreign language vocabulary. Put the vocabulary into a command, give the child the command, and then help him act it out.

This works well for all parts of speech. If your child is learning the verb "to swim," tell her to "swim" by pretending to swim across the room. For nouns, you add a simple verb, such as touch, point, or walk to; "touch your nose," "point to the window," or "walk to the table."

Prepositions are the most fun. Use "stand" or "sit," then switch the prepositions around; "stand on the chair," "sit under the chair," "stand next to the chair," "walk over the chair."

You can create commands for teaching any vocabulary, and the sillier they are, the more easily the child remembers them. Be sure to always do the command with him so he always understands what you're saying.

Power Glide into Spanish

Linda Spaulding, Pattersonville, New York

When we thought about learning a new language, I first researched what language we should study, based on the size of the population of its speakers throughout the world. Then I adjusted the decision for level of difficulty; we decided to wait a bit on Chinese and study Spanish instead.

I researched several different programs and decided on Power Glide, because, although geared for adults, it revolves around a detective story and uses puzzles, games, diglot weaves (begins story in the known language, then gradually weaves in more of the target language), and stories to teach. Although it wasn't cheap (around $100 several years ago), it took us an entire year to go through the book and tape combination.

Conversation Starters

- Read a passage of a book out loud. Is the author stating fact or opinion? How can we learn to distinguish the difference?

- Have a family member say a word that has at least several synonyms and antonyms. Discuss the subtle differences in their meanings and the possible contexts in which you would use each one.

- Has the computer—and all the communication methods associated with it—helped or hindered the proper use of the English language?

- Who is your favorite author? Why?

- If you could, how might you rewrite the ending of your favorite movie? How much and what of the original story would have to change to get to a new ending?

5

Kitchen Chemistry and Backyard Bugs

Never in a million years did I believe that learning about science could be fun—until I began homeschooling, that is. The plethora of hands-on activities now available, most of which are easy to accomplish in your kitchen or backyard, are so much more interesting than just reading and memorizing science facts. We checked out science-based magazines from the library and left them around the house. The kids would pick up the magazines at their leisure and read an article or three that stimulated hours of discussion. Watching television news reports of scientific developments, or even *National Geographic News* or *Discovery News,* often sent us scurrying for additional information.

Compared with the way I learned science in school, our homeschooling approach more closely resembled that of real-world scientists. We were free to add accurate and timely knowledge in our search for understanding, think critically about what we were learning, and employ creativity to solve the problems we ran into.

Science, In Depth

Ethan, our middle son, spent his sixth, seventh, and eighth years obsessed with marine biology, oceanography, and all scientific aspects of water. We read immense numbers of books about the oceans, marine life (large and small), ships (ancient, modern, and famous), submarines, bathyscaphes, and the exploits of Jacques Cousteau, as well as a massive tome called *The Encyclopedia of Fish,* which Ethan (and only Ethan) adored. We visited aquariums; we raised fish, snails, and hermit crabs; we collected and classified shells. We watched ocean-related videos—everything from National Geographic specials to *Moby Dick*—and we played endless rounds of ocean-related games.

We experimented with techniques for mapping the ocean floor and turned out quite a nice contour map using a ruler and a dishpan ocean, filled with continental shelves and underwater mountains made of (horrendous amounts of) modeling clay. Ethan built a model submarine and a working periscope; he studied pond-water specimens under the microscope, and we tried to persuade him to dissect a fish, but he balked. He and his brothers took a marine biology class at a local science center, where they experimented with water pressure, temperature gradients, and salt concentrations, learned about tides, were allowed to handle sea cucumbers and sea urchins, and got up-close looks at piranhas and electric eels.

In the summer, we went snorkeling.

—Rebecca Rupp, The Complete Home Learning Source Book
(Three Rivers Press, 1998)

Scientific Method

The scientific method, vital as a basis to the study of science, is easily learned at home. Practice increases those important critical-thinking and problem-solving skills as a process of inquiry unfolds. In a nutshell, scientists

- Take into consideration everything they already know about the subject of an experiment (collects and organizes data)

- Ask questions, the answers to which help them formulate a hypothesis ("an assertion subject to verification or proof," according to the *American Heritage Dictionary*)

- Set about to prove—or possibly disprove—their hypothesis through objective, controlled (changing only one variable at a time) experimentation

- Keep track of experiment results (what they have observed)

- Analyze results

- Repeat the process, if necessary

Of course, you should begin this process at the level of your child's understanding and let it grow more complex as ability warrants. The Scientific Method 101 activity later in this chapter provides a simple starting point. You can go through the process yourself, thinking out loud, to show the steps in action. It's worth the effort, as a terrific benefit of this practice is that, once learned, these important skills are transferable to additional scientific study as well as to future learning opportunities beyond the subject of science.

The World Is Full of Science Opportunities

This chapter covers the science topics children usually study in elementary grades, but it also includes a little taste of additional branches of science to whet your children's appetite for further exploration. Kids tend to love oceanography and marine science, botany, and zoology. Try some earth science via paleontology or meteorology. There's also chemistry, physics, and biology for beginners, too.

Science in General

Scientific Method 101
Maria Hammer, Marshall, Illinois

My six-year-old and I purchased three bags of M&M's: one each of plain, peanut, and crispy. After I explained the scientific method to my son, I told him we were going to conduct an experiment of our own. I asked him several questions before and then after we opened the bags. I wrote down in one color his answers to the questions asked before we opened the bags (this was his estimate). After we opened the bags, I asked the questions again, he researched the answers, and I wrote down the answers in another color so he could easily note the differences between his estimate and the final results.

- Which bag has the most M&M's?
- Which candies are biggest?
- Which are smallest?
- How many kinds have something besides chocolate in the middle?
- Which bag costs the most?
- How many coins make 32 cents (the cost of a small bag of M&M's)?
- Which bag gives you the most M&M's for your money?

After the experiment was over, we would eat a couple M&M's and saved the rest for later.

Science for Four
Lillian Jones, Sebastopol, California

One of the best things we ever did was put together a weekly science club for four kids, ages eight to eleven. The object of the club was to create a social get-together that focused on something the children would find stimulating. When all the kids arrived, they played together, then they did the science activities, then they played some more.

I originally planned to make it like a little class with a demonstration, but I soon realized it was better to have each of them bring an experiment or activity each week, with all the supplies for it. This gave them something to think about and something to search for in science experiment books. Never did two kids bring the same experiment, even though we made no effort to coordinate what they brought. Preparation involved lots of skimming and reading, and they learned a lot on their own in the process. The parents just watched, enjoying but not directing. The group was such a success it continued for about two years.

Lecture, Anyone?

Linda Spaulding, Pattersonville, New York

Local libraries sometimes provide free science topic lectures. Often, if you become a Friend of the Library for a nominal fee, you'll receive announcements of forthcoming events. Attend the lectures on topics that your child is interested in, as there is usually some time afterward to ask questions of the speaker. Our library's lectures are taped for a local public access television station, so asking a question also results in a television appearance.

Science in the News

Cindy Watson, Levittown, Pennsylvania

Challenge your kids to find as many newspaper articles on science as they can within one week. Anything is permissible as long as they can list what branch of science each article represents. One girl in my

Adam's Brook

At times Mom and Dad had tears in their eyes and failure in their harsh voices because in kindergarten, Adam was deemed in need of the infamous *special education* that, of course, would make him learn.

In the fall of 2000, with great family opposition, six-year-old Adam showed his family his style of learning and exactly where that learning was to take place—in the brook across the street from his home. A quiet, peaceful, gentle place with fall colors, Mom and Adam pulled on their boots, packed their books, and sat by the brook to read, to add using the scattered sticks and rocks, and to clear the brook of litter. Soon, Adam brought the entire family to help, that is, when he wasn't measuring the sides of the brook to see if Mom could jump that high to get out, or writing silly letter games in the sand, or inspecting every rock to be sure they weren't 1 million-year-old fossils.

We turned our backs on a packaged public school system that obviously didn't suit Adam. In its stead, Adam found the right place, and each day we thank God for Adam's school, for Adam's brook.

—Patrese Bielinski, New Britain, Connecticut

homeschool general science class found a baseball advertisement and labeled it "physics—friction." Another had a birth announcement and labeled it "genetics." One student found 135 articles in one week! All the kids loved it, and it got them thinking outside the box.

Instant Internet Info

Jeanne Faulconer, Standardsville, Virginia

We enjoy the ability to look up something "instantly" on the Internet. When Kevin and Patrick began catching crayfish and examining them, it was such an immediate reward to go to the computer, do a bit of research, and then print out several articles that gave solid information about their current interest. The boys quickly learned to determine a crayfish's gender by combining what they observed firsthand with the information they found online.

The Human Body

The Five Senses Made Easy

Maria Hammer, Marshall, Illinois

> ## Let Curiosity Lead
>
> Humans are born scientists. Encourage curiosity and help children go where it leads—mud, pets, rocks, bugs, stars, trains, bicycles, fishing, swimming, computers.
>
> —*Luz Shosie, Guilford, Connecticut*

This activity is great for preschoolers. You'll need

- Scissors
- Old magazines with lots of pictures of people and animals
- Glue stick
- 5 pieces of construction paper

Write the names of the senses at the top of the five pieces of construction paper. After talking about the five senses with your child, encourage him to look through old magazines to find and cut out the body parts that illustrate those senses. If your child isn't reading yet, help him to paste the first picture of each sense on its corresponding piece of paper. Encourage him to be silly and cut out parts of animals or cartoon characters, or he can even draw his own illustrations. Mount the five senses on poster board for display.

Hearts and Valentines

Rebecca Rupp, adapted from *The Complete Home Learning Source Book*

My sons, ages five, seven, and eight, started making paper Valentines—which immediately led to questions about the size, shape, and workings of the human heart. We first showed how big the heart is (easy: make a fist) and demonstrated how hard it works (impossible: squeeze a tennis ball seventy times a minute). Then the kids took turns listening to each other's hearts with a stethoscope, learned how to measure a pulse, and took their own pulses both before and after exercise. We read about the heart in *Hear Your Heart* and *Blood and Guts*, and the boys colored diagrams of the heart, learning about atria, ventricles, valves, arteries, veins, capillaries, heart murmurs, and heart attacks.

We then played a homemade game of Circulation, in which various pieces of living room furniture became the heart, lungs, or the cells of the body. We connected these with red yarn (arteries) and blue yarn (veins). The boys played the parts of very excited red blood cells. First they were pumped (pushed by their mother) from the heart along an artery to the lungs, where they collected a paper oxygen token; then they returned along a vein to the heart, to be pumped out the aorta to the cells of the body, where they deposited their oxygen tokens; and finally back along a vein to the heart to start the process all over again.

After that, tired out, we settled down for lunch, during which we read a history of Valentine's Day.

- *Blood and Guts: A Working Guide to Your Own Insides* by Linda Allison (Little, Brown, 1976)

- *Hear Your Heart* by Paul Showers (HarperTrophy, 2001 re-issue)

- *The Complete Home Learning Source Book* by Rebecca Rupp (Three Rivers Press, 1998)

Hang a Body

Fiona Bayrock, Chilliwack, British Columbia, Canada

Trace your child's body on a large piece of paper and cut it out (your local newspaper should have remnant newsprint rolls free for the asking). As you and your child learn about each organ, have your child draw a life-size outline of the organ, color it, cut it out, and glue it to the paper body in the proper place. Hang the body in a prominent location—your child's bedroom door works well, and a whole row of bodies along a hallway is quite a sight.

The Body-Mars Connection
Cindy Watson, Levittown, Pennsylvania

First I had my children design a city that would allow humans to live on Mars. It was to be a self-contained environment, and their plans needed to include defense against hostile atmosphere, ways to obtain water and oxygen, and a strategy for disposing of waste.

After they had a well thought-out plan and a good drawing, we labeled the city with the different body systems. Waste recycling became kidneys; the protective bubble, skin; and the road system, a circulatory system.

Tasting Game
Ann Lahrson Fisher, Carson, Washington

Explore the sense of taste. Have your child sit on a kitchen chair and blindfold him. Place tiny amounts of various foods and condiments on his tongue and see if he can identify each. Use very tiny amounts at first. If he can't guess, give him a slightly bigger taste. Alternate different kinds of tastes, and have water handy to sip between samples.

Liquids to try:

- Ketchup
- Soy sauce
- Milk
- Tea
- Mustard
- Water
- Coffee
- Juice

- Soda
- Lemon juice or vinegar
  (dilute for young children)

- Pancake syrup
- Honey

Powders to try:

- Salt
- Flour
- A bit of ready-to-eat cereal
  that you have crushed into
  a powder

- Sugar
- Oatmeal

My kids loved this activity. Advance the game by having them hold their noses while tasting to see if they can still identify the items without smelling them.

Environment

Turn a Pool into a Pond

Rosemarie LaRose-Renner, Port Orange, Florida

We knew that next season we would replace the liner in our above-ground pool, so in the fall we turned the backyard pool into a back-yard pond. At the end of summer, we stopped adding chlorine and chemicals. When fall arrived, we visited a local lake, where we gathered plants, fish, snails and more, and just dropped them in. For plants, we took old stockings and filled them with sand and rocks to plant the ones that needed soil. We let the other plants just float.

With the pool transformed into a mini ecosystem, birds and bugs congregated in the yard, and everyone in the neighborhood loved it. When warm weather returned and we had to empty the pond, we built a smaller, permanent pond so the critters we had grown to love would have a home.

Guided Nature Walks

Linda Spaulding, Pattersonville, New York

We walk in the spring and fall with the Environmental Coalition of Schenectady (ECOS). Do some research, and you will probably be able to find a similar group in your area. ECOS offers six spring and six fall walks at various locations in the region. They mostly draw retired folks, as the walks take place on Tuesday mornings, but our group loves having the kids around. The leaders and most of the other participants know a great deal about the various flora and fauna of the area. Because we break into groups of about five to ten with a leader, the children have lots of people around to answer their many questions and point out interesting sites along the way. *Note:* With younger children, make sure ahead of time that the walk doesn't involve high cliffs or other dangerous spots. Our leaders scout the trails the day before, and there is usually a brief written description about the terrain for each walk in the literature they mail out at the beginning of the season.

Watching Water Cycles

Cindy Allas, Fairfield, California

When we studied birds, frogs, and wetlands, we took hikes to a large pond. First we went in the spring to see the tadpoles. A few months later, we revisited and found full-grown frogs. When we returned a few months later, the pond had completely dried up and there were no frogs left. We'll go back one more time after the rains replenish the pond and see the cycle continue. Then we talked about the water cycle and how this very large pond had slowly evaporated and how in a just a few months it was once again full of water and life.

We always take along our binoculars and do some bird watching as well as try to identify animal tracks. We've seen deer and once found a freshly killed frog that we carefully dissected with a stick on the spot.

Leisurely Walking in Nature's Wonderland

Pamela Jorrick, Korbel, California

Because of homeschooling, we're usually free to go to the beach and parks when the rest of the world is at school or work. The less-crowded environments allow for relaxed exploration and learning. Regular walks in the same area throughout the year allow a close-up view of each season's changes. Walks always elicit plenty of questions, such as "What is sand?" "Why are there waves?" "Why do dogs roll in gross things?" So many opportunities to learn.

Edible Plant Walk

Debbie Eaton, Rock Tavern, New York

While not everyone has "Wildman" Steve Brill to lead their children on edible plant walks, everyone can check out his book, *Identifying and Harvesting Edible and Medicinal Plants in the Wild (and Not So Wild) Places*. By using the information in the book, your family will be able to enjoy the act of actually picking a plant and eating it. Edible plant walks can give a child a sense of connection to nature that she might not otherwise experience.

- *Identifying and Harvesting Edible and Medicinal Plants in Wild (and Not So Wild) Places* by "Wildman" Steve Brill (Hearst Books, 1994)

The Versatile Treasure Hunt

Kris Bordessa, Diamond Springs, California

Treasure and scavenger hunts are a favorite at our house. The hunts take on many different forms. Have your kids "follow the clues," using pictures for nonreaders, written directions ("go to the large oak tree"), or riddles ("I make music, but I'm not a radio") to create more of a challenge.

Searching for certain items on a list works both indoors and out. Nature items create an opportunity to walk and explore as a family. Looking for descriptive items, such as "something fuzzy," encourages an understanding of adjectives. On occasion, I can even use this method to my advantage and get a little help cleaning up, as in, "Find something that belongs in the laundry basket and put it there."

Don't Forget the Nature Notebooks

Pamela Jorrick, Korbel, California

Just provide your children with colored pencils and blank sketchbooks in which to draw pictures of plants they observe during nature walks. In areas that are not environmentally sensitive, you can collect specimens that you dry and press at home and place in the notebook later. Use a field guide to help identify the plants, and record the name, date, and location in the notebook.

Zoology

Or How About a Zoo Journal?

Jennifer Miller, Puyallup, Washington

Create a zoo journal by punching several pieces of paper with two holes at the top and tying them together with yarn. Head for the zoo and let the kids draw the animals they see. Older children can write a bit about the animals, too.

Lovin' Lessons

Pamela Jorrick, Korbel, California

Feeding, grooming, and caring for animals are great learning opportunities. I wouldn't recommend experimenting with water and light, but by getting to know animals, you discover their individual needs and personalities. We love watching our dog, cats, ducks, and goats, especially when the species interact through play. Breeding season for the ducks elicited some questions from my daughter, and last spring we were lucky enough to see a baby lamb born while caring for our neighbor's sheep—it's all part of life.

Look What the Cat Dragged In

Fiona Bayrock, Chilliwack, British Columbia, Canada

If a bird breaks its neck flying into your window and the cat presents you with her latest "find," or if you come across road kill that isn't too badly squashed or rotten, take advantage. Be careful to protect yourself from disease by keeping dead animals out of the house and only handling them with rubber gloves, but have a good look. Identify the species, check out the camouflage and adaptations (bird feet and beaks, for example).

We've carried home a flat snake with a stick, identified a rare shrew (from the length of its tail, who knew?), and seen up close birds that we had previously only heard. If you're really adventurous, bury the

Let's Get Started

Catch snakes, frogs, or bugs and observe them up close before releasing them.

corpse in the backyard when you're finished with it and let it decompose for several months before digging up the skeleton for a whole new anatomy lesson.

Paleontology

Dino Wall

Tara Hall, Colliersville, Tennessee

We use butcher paper stretched across a wall and separate it into the three periods of the Mesozoic Era: Triassic, Jurassic, and Cretaceous. Then we subdivide each period into meat eaters and plant eaters. Each day my son picks a dinosaur and chooses as many books as he wants so he can to "research" that dinosaur. I trace a photo of the dinosaur—bumps and all. He colors it, cuts it out, and pastes it on our butcher paper time line before we label it with the name and origin of its fossils.

MESOZOIC ERA					
Triassic		Jurassic		Cretaceous	
Meat Eaters	Plant Eaters	Meat Eaters	Plant Eaters	Meat Eaters	Plant Eaters

Then we're off to our world map, where he places a dinosaur sticker on the location of that fossil. In addition, we keep a spiral-bound set of index cards on which we record the name, period, origin, whether it was a meat or plant eater, and a brief description from our readings. At the end of the week, Dad and I quiz him by only providing descriptions, then offering additional clues if he needs them. He is thrilled to jump from period to period and catch us when we try to trick him.

Dinosaur names are also wonderful for spelling and sounding out words. We usually spend no more than twenty minutes reading from books that cover a particular species. Next he wants to create a land mammal wall, then move on to sea creatures.

Dino Dig

Elizabeth Johnson, Philadelphia, Pennsylvania

After studying dinosaurs for a week, I hid several dino eggs (cardboard) around the basement with the name of a dinosaur on each. I gave the children three buckets labeled "Carnivore," "Herbivore," and "Omnivore." They also took flashlights, a small shovel, and whisk broom, tools that the pros might use. They had to consult with each other to decide which egg should go into which bucket. When they emerged from our dig site, we looked up each dinosaur to see if their classifications were correct and to see what the dinos would look like when they hatched.

Chocolate Excavation

Cindy Allas, Fairfield, California

Practice excavation with chocolate chip cookies. Each child gets two cookies and toothpicks. They use the toothpicks to pry out the chocolate chips as carefully as possible. One cookie gets excavated without water, and on the other they may use water to see which way is easier.

We're Going on a Fossil Hunt
Merelee Syron, New Egypt, New Jersey

We made a simple fossil-hunting device out of a wooden frame and large screen. Then we wrote to the geology department at our nearest university and received maps and information on where fossils can be found nearby and from what time period. We often head out in our rain boots into a fossil-laden stream and bring home the fossils we need help in identifying. This is an ongoing project about creatures that once lived in our neighborhood.

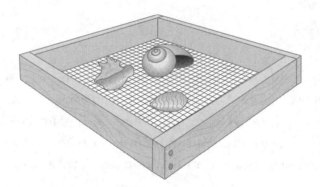

Chemistry

Wacky Cake Chemistry
Kim Weaver, Victoria, British Columbia, Canada

Baking a Wacky Cake demonstrates what happens when an alkali and an acid are mixed, causing a chemical reaction. Vinegar and baking soda are leavening agents in this recipe—they create gas bubbles that cause the cake to rise. During this science experiment, we discuss other types of leaveners (such as yeast), practice our fractions (how many 1/4 cups does it take to make 2 cups of flour?), and frequently end up making a volcano out of Play-Doh and using the same chemicals as in the cake to create the eruption (fill volcano with baking soda, add vinegar, then watch the fun). Then we eat cake!

Wacky Cake Recipe
1 1/2 cups flour
1/4 cup cocoa
1 cup white sugar
1 tsp. baking soda
1/2 tsp. salt
1/3 cup salad oil
1 tsp. vanilla
1 tsp. vinegar
1 cup water

Preheat oven to 350 degrees Fahrenheit. Mix dry ingredients into an ungreased 8-by-8-inch pan. Make three holes in the mixture. In one hole, pour the vinegar; in the next hole, pour the oil; and in the last, pour the vanilla. Pour water over the whole works and mix just until combined. Bake for thirty minutes. Cool and eat!

Laundry Room Laboratory
Diane Keith, Redwood City, California

When my sons were about seven and nine years old, I enticed them into the laundry room with the promise that they could use chemicals to conduct experiments! The very first thing I did was show them the effects of bleach on clothes. Before we experimented with the bleach, I took the precaution of explaining safe handling techniques. Then I took several colorful but raggedy shirts and invited the boys to sprinkle them with chlorine bleach. Just like magic, the bleach made color disappear, and the boys oohed and aahed in astonishment. The bleach experiments continued for several days as we soaked different kinds of fabrics from jeans to lace in the bleach for varying periods of time and noted the effect.

Our bleach testing led to other explorations. I had them experiment with starch to see how stiff they could make a shirt. We had a field day using various spot and stain removers (in many different forms) to determine which ones worked best. The boys really enjoyed creating tough stains on old socks for those experiments! Detergents and fabric softeners provided many hours of laundry room lab research, as they carefully measured powders and liquids into our washing machine. They had "loads of fun" (if you'll pardon the pun) using the various cycles on the washing machine and dryer to see which ones took the longest or dried the fastest. Occasionally we didn't use the fabric softener so that when it was dark that night, they could see the static sparks produced while pulling apart two socks. They examined the lint after every load, and began to think of ways to recycle it—as new stuffing for worn teddy bears, and even to create a lint ball that they could bat safely around the house.

Eventually, I showed them the fabric labels sewn into most clothes and had them read the manufacturer's instructions for how to launder a given item. I explained how excessive heat can cause some colors in fabric to fade, so we tested hot and cold water wash and rinse cycles, along with delicate and permanent press dryer settings. They noticed that some fabric tags said "Dry Clean Only," and that led to a field trip to our local dry cleaner. They recently discovered the new dry cleaning solvents that can be used in a dryer at home and have been experimenting with wool sweaters.

In our laundry room lab, my sons have learned a great deal about various household chemicals and can identify many different types of fabrics. They have even learned a little geography, because they noticed the country where clothes were made as they looked for the manufacturer's washing instructions. That led to quite a conversation about politics, economics, and ethics in business. But the best part of all is that I have sons who know how to do their own laundry.

Speaking of laundry, my kids experimented with borax on some wash loads. A friend told them that they could use borax to make a neat non-Newtonian solid that behaves like a liquid called Gick. They mixed up a batch in the laundry room sink, and it provided hours of educational fun. Here's the recipe:

Gick Recipe

- Paint bucket or plastic tub
- Paint stick or large, sturdy plastic spoon
- 2 cups Elmer's Liquid Glue
- 2 cups water
- 2 tsp. borax dissolved in 2/3 cup warm water
- Food coloring

Directions: In a clean, plastic paint bucket, mix together 2 cups glue and 2 cups water. Stir in food coloring with the paint stick. Pour in the dissolved borax-water mixture. Stir until a big, gooey lump forms. Pour off the excess water-glue mixture that doesn't adhere to the big gooey lump, aka Gick. Divide the Gick among the family and watch it ooze over your hand and form into long ropes. Roll it into a ball and bounce it. Blow bubbles into it. Take imprints off newspaper comics with it. Make rude noises with it. Gick will last for several months stored in the refrigerator in a sealed plastic bag. Let it warm to room temperature before playing with it.

Warning: Gick sticks to most fabrics and carpets. Wear old clothes, and use in an environment where it won't destroy furnishings. Borax can be found in the detergent section of the grocery store. It is toxic and should not be eaten. Parental supervision is required.

Botany

Brown Thumb Herbs

Linda Dobson, Saranac Lake, New York

If I can successfully grow herbs indoors with my brown thumb, you can, too. Clear a windowsill, then get seeds of your favorite herbs, small pots, potting soil, and pebbles for drainage. Indoor herb gardens are great for children because the plants grow relatively quickly enough to maintain the children's interest. Once the plants have grown, let your children help cook, using the fresh herbs. Your kids can pick more and hang them upside down to dry. Once dried, the herbs can be crushed and stored. Use the dried herbs to make potpourri or herb-scented candles.

Plant a Seed, Watch It Grow

Maria Hammer, Marshall, Illinois

For this activity, you'll need:

- 1 paper milk carton
- Green bean seeds
- Plastic wrap
- Rubber bands
- Potting soil
- Masking tape

Empty and clean the milk carton. Cut the top off the carton and cut a flap in one entire side so it can fold down completely; this becomes your "underground" window. With the flap folded down, stretch a few layers of plastic wrap across the opening and secure it with tape. Fill the milk carton with potting soil and plant a seed against the plastic so it shows. Bring up the flap and secure it with rubber bands. Each day, remove the rubber bands and fold down the flap to monitor the seed's growth.

Pick a Tree
Hope Ware, Peoria, Illinois

Pick a tree in your yard, or a neighbor's yard (be sure to ask permission), to observe. For my four-year-old, I made a simple book by folding several pieces of blank paper in half and then stapling the edge. My son drew a picture of a tree on the front and wrote, "My Tree Book."

Every few weeks, we recorded our observations in the special book. We divided the book into spring, summer, autumn, and winter. This tree, an ornamental pear, had a distinct feature that changed every season: flowers in spring, animals in summer, fruit in autumn, and it doesn't drop its leaves until December. My son did nature drawings each season. We even had a squirrel sit above us in the fork of a branch one summer day and throw down fruit at us after he had cracked it open!

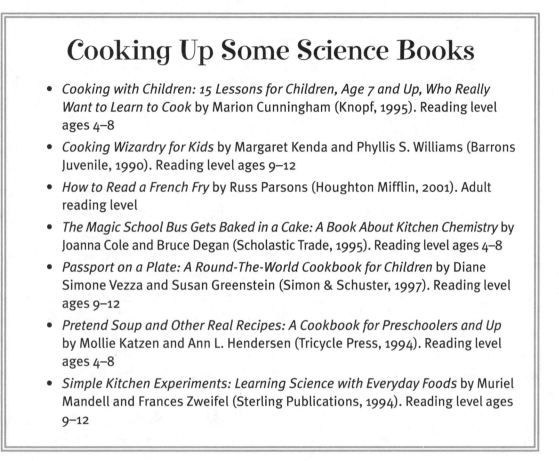

Cooking Up Some Science Books

- *Cooking with Children: 15 Lessons for Children, Age 7 and Up, Who Really Want to Learn to Cook* by Marion Cunningham (Knopf, 1995). Reading level ages 4–8
- *Cooking Wizardry for Kids* by Margaret Kenda and Phyllis S. Williams (Barrons Juvenile, 1990). Reading level ages 9–12
- *How to Read a French Fry* by Russ Parsons (Houghton Mifflin, 2001). Adult reading level
- *The Magic School Bus Gets Baked in a Cake: A Book About Kitchen Chemistry* by Joanna Cole and Bruce Degan (Scholastic Trade, 1995). Reading level ages 4–8
- *Passport on a Plate: A Round-The-World Cookbook for Children* by Diane Simone Vezza and Susan Greenstein (Simon & Schuster, 1997). Reading level ages 9–12
- *Pretend Soup and Other Real Recipes: A Cookbook for Preschoolers and Up* by Mollie Katzen and Ann L. Hendersen (Tricycle Press, 1994). Reading level ages 4–8
- *Simple Kitchen Experiments: Learning Science with Everyday Foods* by Muriel Mandell and Frances Zweifel (Sterling Publications, 1994). Reading level ages 9–12

An Apple a Day

Rebecca Rupp, adapted from *The Complete Home Learning Source Book*

After a weekend of apple picking, we decided—since we had bushels of material—to study apples. We read the story of Johnny Appleseed (two versions) and made a batch of pioneer-style dried apple rings. Then we made collage pictures featuring people with carved dried apple heads. (Results: wrinkled witches, wrinkled wizards, and a wrinkled Johnny Appleseed planting apples.) We then discussed why sliced apples turn brown and did an experiment to prove that the enzyme responsible for browning is pH-sensitive (squirt on some acidic lemon juice and the apple slice stays white).

We read about Isaac Newton and his gravity-demonstrating apple, and the Greek myth of Atalanta and the Golden Apples, drawing illustrations for both. We tried an experiment from *The Amazing Apple Book* in which two apples are hung about an inch apart on strings from a bar (we used the shower rod in the bathroom) and then the kids try to blow them apart. (No way: Instead the apples bump together, which led to a nice discussion about air pressure.) Eventually, one of the blown apples fell into the bathtub, which gave the kids the idea of bobbing for apples, which they tried—and then of experimenting with practically everything in the refrigerator to see what floated and what didn't.

Finally we read the story of William Tell, and the kids drew elaborate targets of a boy with an enormous apple on his head and set off for the backyard to practice with their bows and arrows.

- *The Amazing Apple Book* by Paulette Bourgeois (Addison-Wesley, 1990)
- *The Complete Home Learning Source Book* by Rebecca Rupp (Three Rivers Press, 1998)

Planets

Mars in a Dish
Fiona Bayrock, Chilliwack, British Columbia, Canada

This activity simulates the rusty, dusty surface of Mars. Place sand in a glass baking dish and cover the sand with water. Cut up steel wool into small pieces and press them underwater into the sand. Push the steel wool into the water every day until the water disappears, usually within a week. When it's completely dry, use a spoon to crush the rust and mix it with the sand.

And a Mission to Mars

Elizabeth Johnson, Philadelphia, Pennsylvania

I turned our basement into Mars by covering the floor with old couch cushions and foam mattress covers. I put red bulbs in all the light fixtures and lined one wall with the Mars landscape paper mural we made the day before. I also made a dozen pom-pom yarn balls and hid them around the basement as specimens to be collected.

I called a preflight meeting to discuss the mission and gave the children badges with the title of captain or lieutenant in front of their names. Each child was given a pair of boots and a flight suit of snow pants, a parka, gloves, and a bike helmet, and assigned the duties for the mission.

The captain (the older child) gets the walkie-talkie (I get the other one) to keep in contact with mission control (me). His job is to look for any life forms (a spider, the cat, etc.) and pick a place to plant the American flag (for example, atop the washing machine). The lieutenant gets a bucket and flashlight to collect specimens (pom-poms).

They blast off in a stove box we found and decorated to look like a space ship inside and out. While they're in space, they eat the special snacks we bought the day before—things that won't float around in zero gravity (Go-Gurt yogurt, Capri Sun Juice pouches, etc.).

When the mission is completed, we decontaminate the kids and conduct a postflight meeting where we discuss the mission and close with a ceremony that includes a certificate signed by "the president" and a pair of wings (cardboard badge) to wear proudly on a baseball cap or shirt.

They replayed the mission for several days afterward.

Meteorology

Head in the Clouds

Judith Waite Allee, from *Educational Travel on a Shoestring*

Let's Get Started

Keep track of rainfall for one month.

The next time you go on an airplane trip, make sure your child gets the window seat. It provides a great bird's-eye view, literally. As you take off, observe the different sounds that the plane makes, such as the wheels retracting or the flaps rising or lowering. Make sure you bring along a book about clouds to see if your child can identify them.

- *Educational Travel on a Shoestring* by Judith Waite Allee and Melissa L. Morgan (Shaw Books, 2002)

Weather Diary

Beverley Paine, Yankalilla, South Australia

My son, Thomas, designed his own weather diary. He tracked temperature, barometer readings, clouds, humidity, and wind speed every hour or so for more than a week. It became a full-blown science project, meticulously recorded.

Fundial

Shay Seaborne, Woodbridge, Virginia

Starting early in the day, I asked my younger daughter, Laurel, to stand on our patio that receives sun most of the day. Caitlin, the older child, traced an outline of Laurel's feet with sidewalk chalk. Then she traced the outline of Laurel's shadow on the pavement and labeled it with the current time. After an hour or two, Laurel stood in the same spot while Caitlin traced the new shadow and marked the time. They repeated this throughout the day, gaining a clearer understanding of time, the science behind sundials, and the earth's rotation.

Biology

Up Close and Personal
Fiona Bayrock, Chilliwack, British Columbia, Canada

Use a microscope to do the following activities.

- Compare the hair and fur of as many different animals you can find (including humans)

- Compare salt and sugar crystals

- Compare the wings and other body parts of the dead insects you find on the window sill or in lamp fixtures

Let's Get Started

Take your dog or cat to the vet; compare this with a visit to a physician.

- Demonstrate osmosis (water passing through a membrane) by observing what happens to purple onion skin when you prepare the slide with a salt solution rather than plain water

- Observe how the microscope reverses images by looking at a printed *e*

Oceanography

He Sees Seashells

Rebecca Rupp, adapted from *The Complete Home Learning Source Book*

When our boys were five, seven, and eight, they loved sorting, playing with, and studying our seashell collection. In the course of this, they learned to identify everything from a clam and a conch to moon snails, mussels, and sand dollars, and devised an elaborate shell-based fantasy game in which the wicked starfish kill the helpless oysters but are ultimately defeated by the brave murexes with their purple paralyzing poison.

We also read stacks of shell books, followed by ocean books, fish books, and Augusta Goldin's *The Bottom of the Sea*. The boys weren't too taken with the text, but they were interested in the descriptions of the topography of the sea bottom and the uses of echo sounders and fathometers. This led them to build a model sea bottom with clay in the bottom of a large tin dishpan, complete with continental shelf and slope, plunging trenches, volcanic islands (one erupting), underwater caves, and a toy submarine. We then flooded the model and "mapped" the sea bottom by measuring water depth with a ruler and recording the results on graph paper. (*Warning:* This takes a *lot* of clay.)

- *The Bottom of the Sea* by Augusta Goldin (HarperCollins, 1967)
- *The Complete Home Learning Source Book* by Rebecca Rupp (Three Rivers Press, 1998)

Physics

Beginner's Physics

Kim Weaver, Victoria, British Columbia, Canada

One of our favorite series of experiments is simple machines from Janice VanCleave, where we learned how anything that helps you more easily complete labor or work can be considered a machine.

Consider the following: A lever can lift a stack of heavy books using two pencils, whereas one finger can't accomplish the same. You can easily introduce physics terms, such as *fulcrum,* to your children's vocabulary this way, and tell them that a teeter-totter also works on a fulcrum. Balloons and small milk cartons can become jet boats, showing that air pressure can bend to move objects. A few marbles in the rim of a paint can or a row of pencils underneath a book can so effectively reduce friction that moving it seems almost effortless. You can illustrate the reduction in friction and effort needed to move a pile of books using pencil rollers by first taping an elastic band to the bottom book and measuring the stretch of the elastic—or effort to move the books—without the pencils. Then measure the stretch of the elastic *with* the pencils; the difference is quite dramatic.

Simple machines is a neat science fair topic as well, with lots of interest from visitors.

- *Janice Van Cleave's Machines: Mind-Boggling Experiments You Can Turn into Science Fair Projects* by Janice Van Cleave (John Wiley and Sons, 1993)

Rocket Science in a Bottle
Maria Hammer, Marshall, Illinois

Materials
- 2-liter (or 2-quart) soda bottle
- Cork that fits the mouth of the bottle
- Plastic lawn chair, overturned (or other suitable ramp)
- Basketball needle
- Bicycle pump
- Water

Fill the soda bottle one-quarter full of water. Pass the end of the basketball needle through the cork. Fit the cork into the bottle mouth. Attach the needle to the bicycle pump and lean the bottle against the overturned chair. Pump air into the bottle until the bottle takes off.

Make sure you do this on a warm day, because you *will* get wet. Set up in a large yard free of power lines and neighbors' windows.

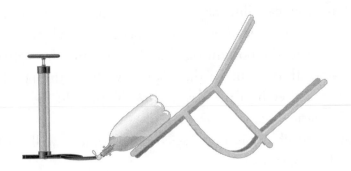

My son tried this with his dad, who hooked it up to an air compressor, and it sailed about 100 feet! I got this idea from *The Tightwad Gazette* by Amy Dacyczyn, and she additionally suggests that the kids experiment with fins to find out how it flies with them.

Giant Marble Maze

Hope Ware, Peoria, Illinois

Based on games where you set up a series of tunnels, loops, and jumps for marbles, we decided to make a maze in the front yard using anything we could, and then using a ball as the marble.

What a physics lesson. After we slid the ball *up* a slide, it had to roll across a jungle gym, through another slide sitting sideways to act as a tunnel, through the window of a playhouse, and drop into a bucket. I whooped and hollered when my ball actually made the journey. Of course, I also looked up to see my neighbor staring and laughing at me.

General Science

Flying Eggshells

Rebecca Rupp, adapted from *The Complete Home Learning Source Book*

When our boys were five, seven, and eight, we read—somewhere—about the first demonstration of the hot-air balloon principle, a two-thousand-year-old Chinese experiment in which eggshells filled with bits of burning tinder were made to rise into the air. Inspired, we cracked eggs and tried to make them fly. The boys tried different kinds of tinder, including paper scraps, a shredded cotton ball, and broken toothpicks; they tried poking different-sized holes in the empty shells. One kid tried blowing through a straw to direct more air into his shell; another created an elaborate series of fuses to ignite his tinder. One boy came up with a controlled experiment designed to pinpoint the optimal amount of tinder, testing everything from a teeny scrap to a solid handful. One kid tried adding a birthday candle.

Nobody got an eggshell to so much as twitch, but the experiment was still a rousing success. The boys did learn that hot air rises and that fire needs air to burn; but more importantly, they discovered firsthand how to formulate, test, and evaluate hypotheses. For days afterward, they were still discussing their experiences and coming up with new ideas.

For lunch we ate scrambled eggs.

- *The Complete Home Learning Source Book* by Rebecca Rupp (Three Rivers Press, 1998)

Go Fly a Kite
Merelee Syron, New Egypt, New Jersey

Every year there is a kite festival nearby, so we began a tradition of making our own kites to fly. Each year we get a little more adventurous and learn more about aerodynamics and flight.

- Wind Kites: 1-800-541-0314

Footlights
Maria Hammer, Marshall, Illinois

After reading a *Magic School Bus* book about light, we made an old-fashioned footlight. This one needs adult supervision throughout the project.

We used:

- 1-gallon plastic bucket
- Aluminum foil
- Play-Doh
- Votive candles

Line the bucket with the aluminum foil. Turn the bucket on its side. Anchor it with some Play-Doh to keep it from rolling, if necessary. Use more Play-Doh inside the bucket to secure three candles. You're ready to ask your child lots of questions!

- What if only one candle is lit—is there more or less light than if all are lit?
- Does light generate heat? What about enclosed light bulbs as compared to open flames?
- Would it be brighter or darker if the bucket wasn't lined with foil?

Take the shroud off a flashlight, if possible, and turn it on.

- Does this aim the light in one direction?
- Which way is better if you want to focus more light on a single area?

Look at a car headlight up close. Compare it to the flashlight and footlight.

Power Sources

Maria Hammer, Marshall, Illinois

At five years of age, my son thought monster trucks and race cars were terrific, so we spent an entire summer looking for things that *didn't* use fast, racy motors. We explored Styrofoam gliders, balsa wood rubber band–powered planes, air rockets, row boats and paddle boats, balloon-powered toy cars, steam trains, horses, and bicycles. He now knows that the people who had to make do without modern gasoline-powered motors are also to be admired for their hard work and ingenuity, reminding both of us that we have it easy these days.

To Fly

Rebecca Rupp, adapted from *The Complete Home Learning Source Book*

Our sons were always interested in the science of anything that flew, from flying fish and peregrine falcons to airplanes, rockets, and space probes. When they were seven, nine, and eleven, we spent weeks studying flight. The boys experimented with a battery of paper airplane models, testing them in a homemade wind tunnel (powered by my hair dryer). They assembled and inflated a model hot air balloon (which successfully got off the ground), and they built three different kinds of kites (ditto). They built parachutes and used these to drop things out the upstairs windows (varied results). We read about balloons, zeppelins, blimps, and the Hindenburg disaster; we read books on the history and science of flight, and biographies of the Wright brothers, Amelia Earhart, and Charles Lindbergh. The kids built models of the Wright brothers' *Flyer* and Lindbergh's *Spirit of St. Louis*. We read about Leonardo da Vinci's plan for a helicopter and made paper helicopter toys that spun nicely when dropped from the top of the staircase. We then digressed briefly into the behavior and biology of hummingbirds, which hover, and the boys made and hung hummingbird feeders, which—to everybody's immense delight—attracted hummingbirds.

We read the story of Chuck Yeager and the breaking of the sound barrier, and demonstrated jet propulsion with balloons, soda straws, and a string stretched across the living room. We read a biography of Robert Goddard and built and launched model rockets. Thrilled with this, the boys decided next to study outer space.

● *The Complete Home Learning Source Book* by Rebecca Rupp (Three Rivers Press, 1998)

Entomology

Beautiful Butterfly Garden
Jennifer Miller, Puyallup, Washington

A butterfly garden is a fun way to learn about plants and wildlife and make your yard gorgeous at the same time. The idea is to plant colorful flowers that attract butterflies and to provide food for caterpillars so that butterflies will lay their eggs there. You also want to provide some water for the butterflies. Your garden can be big or, if you lack the space, use a container or two for your plants and put them on your front step.

Once your garden is planted, it's time to enhance the experience. Your children could keep a daily journal, writing about the things they notice in the garden. What kinds of butterflies are attracted? How do the butterflies make you feel? How about drawing pictures of the flowers and the creatures that visit the garden? Remember, if they do nothing but enjoy the flowers and butterflies, a butterfly garden is full of valuable lessons.

Genetics

Play with DNA

Rebecca Rupp, adapted from *The Complete Home Learning Source Book*

When our sons were nine to twelve years old, they became fascinated—after several impassioned conversations at dinner—with the Human Genome Project. We read several books about genetics, including *DNA Is Here to Stay* and *Amazing Schemes Within Your Genes*; we studied photomicrographs of chromosomes and learned about karyotypes; and we extracted DNA (a sticky, but impressive, process) from an onion. We made two-dimensional DNA models from construction paper, using different shapes and colors for the four nucleotides (adenine, thymine, cytosine, and guanine) and the sugar-phosphate backbone, and built a three-dimensional plastic model of the DNA helix. We made model "chromosomes" with colored pop beads and used these to demonstrate DNA replication and to show how DNA functions to make RNA and proteins. We also typed everybody's blood (including that of both parents and an unlucky visiting grandma) and discussed the inheritance of blood-group proteins.

- DNA extraction kits, blood typing kits, and DNA models are available from Carolina Biological Supply Company; 800-334-5551; www.carolina.com.

- *DNA Is Here to Stay* by Fran Balkwill and Mic Rolph (First Avenue Editions, 1994)

- *Amazing Schemes Within Your Genes* by Fran Balkwill and Mic Rolph (First Avenue Editions, 1994)

- *The Complete Home Learning Source Book* by Rebecca Rupp (Three Rivers Press, 1998)

Conversation Starters

- If you had to lose one of your five senses, which one would you choose? Why?

- Is it important to keep the space program going?

- With a growing population, what can we do to make sure everyone has enough food and shelter?

- If you could live on another planet, which one would it be? Why?

- Which is more important, art or science? In what ways are they complementary?

6

It's a Big, Interesting
World After All

One of the very first maps my oldest child created was a result of a television commercial for Fire Prevention Week. Days later, without prompting or assistance of any kind, he presented me with a map of our home and the escape routes everyone should take should a fire occur at night. The map's accuracy was impressive, topped only by the sound planning behind the routes laid out for us all. This is the son who turned into a volunteer firefighter and emergency medical technician at a very young age.

Interest provided the impetus for patient, accurate creation, just as it can for your child. Once children know they can accomplish something like map making for one reason, they know they can accomplish it for others, whether those reasons include fun or necessity. Not only is a skill learned, but also children receive a genuine shot of self-esteem.

As you can see from the plethora of map activities that follow, they are a fun and easy gateway to the study of geography for young children. Because it's a true hands-on activity involving a big dose of creativity, it's no wonder that homeschooling families have let loose their imaginations to use maps in so many ways. They know the activity will bring forth questions just begging for answers. For example, while looking at or drawing a map of the United States, your children might notice that some western states have straight borders compared to the others. When they ask *why*, they have opened the door to a conversation about natural versus man-made borders. Okay, they say. What creates that squiggly border between Pennsylvania and New Jersey? Before you know it, you're onto the Delaware River, and why is it called the Delaware if it's between Pennsylvania and New Jersey? "Did you know," you ask them, "that a long time ago on Christmas Day, George Washington crossed the Delaware from Pennsylvania to Trenton, New Jersey?" Which will you first find out more about—Washington, Valley Forge, or the Revolutionary War?

Take a trip around the world in the way that best motivates your children. Perhaps your travel will center on the world's well-known arts and crafts. Your voracious readers might want to read their way around. Your culinary "experts" might find eating their way around a most enjoyable experience. Some kids will travel best through games and fun quizzes, others via the likes of Carmen Sandiego and other computer software travelers. Consider the different mathematical systems, or even the world's greatest inventions, as jumping-off points. (And wouldn't it be nice if you could actually *travel* around the world?)

Be sure to expose your children to the many types of maps for different uses—maps of roads, topography, population, demographics, climate, constellations, and so much more. While some children might find it fascinating to see how highways and byways wind around your city, others may become enamored with the ability to determine the elevation of their home, Uncle Bill's house, or their favorite park. Once your children are familiar with maps, don't forget to incorporate globes and note the connections and differences between the two tools.

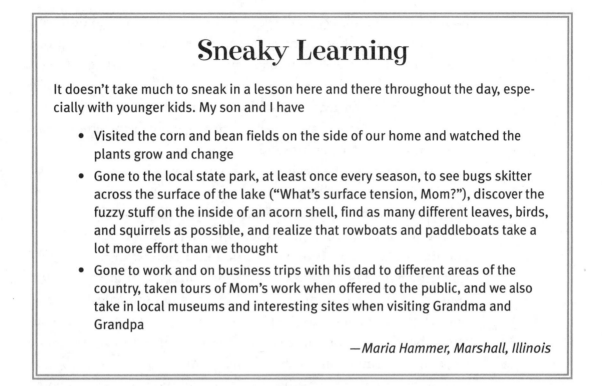

Sneaky Learning

It doesn't take much to sneak in a lesson here and there throughout the day, especially with younger kids. My son and I have

- Visited the corn and bean fields on the side of our home and watched the plants grow and change
- Gone to the local state park, at least once every season, to see bugs skitter across the surface of the lake ("What's surface tension, Mom?"), discover the fuzzy stuff on the inside of an acorn shell, find as many different leaves, birds, and squirrels as possible, and realize that rowboats and paddleboats take a lot more effort than we thought
- Gone to work and on business trips with his dad to different areas of the country, taken tours of Mom's work when offered to the public, and we also take in local museums and interesting sites when visiting Grandma and Grandpa

—Maria Hammer, Marshall, Illinois

Don't forget the study of our remarkable planet itself: how volcanoes, earthquakes, floods, glaciers, and more shaped the land on which we stand, why the landscape is different elsewhere, and how people make the most of natural resources available to them.

Social studies, however, is much more than maps and dirt, and, thankfully, also more than lists of countries' populations, languages spoken, and chief exports. It's also about people: their intimate knowledge of the places they live, the way their unique environment influences their lives and vice versa, and how they arrange everything from their government, politics, culture, and etiquette.

People do not stand apart from their history. Past events helped shape the hows and whys of their lives. Everything and everyone has a history, and you need not study it long to realize it can be the starting point of learning that can take your child down a thousand different roads, into scores of different subjects. History is an important piece of a picture that, as we begin to assimilate it, grows ever larger to become the world as we see it. To understand why a group of people become warriors instead of pacifists, conquerors and not the conquered, rich or poor, Muslim or Christian, is to help remove our own cultural filter toward true understanding.

So where does one begin in a subject as vast as humanity's history? Start at the beginning? Go backward to the beginning? Go strictly American or weave in world history at the same time?

Homeschoolers find that where one starts is not nearly as important as placing what one *does* study into context in the big picture. Enter time lines, history's great organizers. A time line allows your child to place anything historical in a chronological continuum. This can include all the presidents and world wars just as you remember from school, but you can also add inventions, discoveries, and great moments in literature, math, science, and architecture. What about natural disasters, the evolution of governments, and the rise and fall of nations? Let your child's interests guide what gets included, even if it means different time lines for each of several children.

Time lines take many shapes. Some folks like notebooks into which they can insert pages as necessary. Typically, each page has a time period written at the top, and that page is dedicated to that period's historical happenings. Other families create a real line that can hang across a bookshelf or clear across the living room. In this method, notable events may be written on cards connected to the line. Obviously, this approach is more finite than the notebook method unless your living room is as large as Madison Square Garden. A friend covered a large hallway wall with paper on which her children placed both dates and drawings of the events. Commercial sources include premade time lines that fill fat books, book series, posters, and lengthy wall charts. Whatever method you use, remember that the purpose is to keep history in perspective, and to enjoy the journey as you do so.

Maps

Zoo Maps
Therese Peterson, Milwaukee, Wisconsin

With our county zoo membership we receive a map each time we visit. It includes markings for the machines that make molded plastic animals and machines that squash your penny, imprinting it with the image of an animal. Since we are collectors, we use the maps and symbols to find those trinkets we haven't put in our collections yet. We visit frequently, so set limits as to how many purchases we'll make each time, ensuring that we have to go back again and again.

Homemade Playground Maps
Sandra Dodd, Albuquerque, New Mexico

When we went to a different city park each week, we made a game with a clipboard, a clear plastic report cover, wipe-off crayons, pencils, and some fast-food toys. I made a map of the playground and put it in the report cover on the clipboard. Then we took turns, singly or in teams with mom or a friend, burying in the sand half a dozen or so "McDonald toys" (which is our children's generic term for simple, small, or free toys), or hiding them on playground equipment, or maybe in the crook of a small tree. With crayon we marked each hiding place on the plastic map cover with an *X*. After all toys were found, we erased the *X*s and started all over again.

Story and Memory Maps

Rebecca Rupp, adapted from *The Complete Home Learning Source Book*

How about introducing map activities through your children's favorite storybooks? Our kids always loved making story maps, in which they invented maps of Treasure Island, Neverland, Oz, Hobbiton and surroundings, and many more. One of Caleb's first maps, based on *Little Red Riding Hood*, showed Little Red's house, complete with garden and doghouse, Grandma's house (with birdbath), the path through the woods (windy), the hunter's camp (tent), and a spectacular fortified wolf lair.

We also experimented with "memory" maps, during which the boys made maps of the houses and places where we've lived, with all the notable personal sites labeled: the place where Caleb fell off his bike, the tree house, the best blackberry bushes, our favorite picnic spot.

- *The Complete Home Learning Source Book* by Rebecca Rupp (Three Rivers Press, 1998)

Follow Mom by Road Map

Bobbi Jo Baumgardner, Cloverdale, California

I recently had an opportunity to travel by car across several states without my children. Every time I arrived in a larger town or city, I called the kids to tell them where I was, and described what it looked like. They used the road maps I left with them to follow my path.

During a return trip—when the children were with me—they recognized the places I had told them about and had a wonderful understanding of the route we were taking.

Reading Side Trips

Lisa Herring, Placerville, California, courtesy of *Right at Home* newsletter

When my son and I read about a city or country in a story, we take an extra minute to locate that place in our atlas. He enjoys finding it, and it gives him an understanding of where the story takes place, what the terrain might look like, and how far away it is.

Tracking Mail or Phone Calls

Kris Bordessa, Diamond Springs, California

Buy a large black-line map of the United States and some small sticky dots at the local office supply store. Suggest that your children keep track of mail or phone calls (incoming or outgoing) by putting a sticker in the state of origin. This can also be done with state maps; simply use your stickers to mark specific cities within the state you're studying.

Push Pin Geography

Meghan Anderson, Paradise, California

About once a month, my daughter holds a push pin in her hand, closes her eyes, I spin her around, and she places the pin somewhere in the large world map on our wall. Where it lands is where we plan and take our "trip" for that month. (If we have visited before and don't want to go back, she picks a new place.)

We learn about the currency, language, sites to see, customs, religion, history, and whatever else we come across. Our experiences also include searching out native restaurants, or recipes if that fails, costumes, putting on plays, listening to music, and learning folk dances. We're limited only by our imaginations. We've pinpointed some countries that we would like to visit in the flesh someday. When our trip is over, we stamp the "passports" we made previous to starting our trip program.

Puzzling World
Samantha Pearson, Manly, New South Wales, Australia

Have fun putting together a giant jigsaw puzzle map of the world, glue it together, and hang it on the wall where it's ready to refer to time and again.

Multipurpose Wall Map
Fiona Bayrock, Chilliwack, British Columbia, Canada

To increase a general understanding of world geography for almost any age group, trim the extra borders from an inexpensive wall map and glue it to a large piece of cardboard about eight inches larger all around than the map. (Your local appliance dealer should be able to give you large used boxes for free.) If you're short on space, glue the map on the cardboard so that two corners of the box are equal distances from the edge. Then it will stand like a science fair backdrop during the day and you can tuck it behind the sofa at night. There are many ways to use this map. Here are three:

- Every time you come across a new place name—from a book, the news, clothing labels, banana stickers, where someone travels or lives, anywhere—run a thread from the location on the map to the outside cardboard border, stapling the thread at both ends. Write the place name and significance for it on a small piece of paper under the border staple. An easy way to start is where family members were born. This will mushroom. You won't believe how kids will be looking for new places to add, and it's a great activity to get kids looking things up in an atlas.

- Read John Burningham's *Around the World in Eighty Days* and staple his journey on the map. An interesting debate is whether Burningham actually went around the world. Although he did indeed go 360 degrees around the globe, he completely missed South America. (Don't you love when there's no right answer?)

- Staple the journey of an explorer, such as Magellan or Columbus.

My Place

Sandra Dodd, Albuquerque, New Mexico

Any book with a map is fun, from Usborne puzzle books to the world atlas, but we especially enjoyed a book called *My Place,* about a town in Australia, with kid-style maps of over three hundred years of history. As new children move in or are born, they map their neighborhood while the town grows up, but the water and the big tree remain the same.

- *My Place* by Nadia Wheatley (Kane/Miller Book Publishers, 1994)

North, South, East, West

Annelieke Schauer, Avon, Connecticut

Each of my daughters, ages six and nine, owns a compass, and they often take the compasses with them on trips or even errands. By simply playing with them, letting me know whether I'm actually driving in the direction we want to go (sometimes the road we need actually goes east before it turns south, for example), they have strengthened their map skills and senses of direction. When we travel in territory unknown to us, we can be much more certain we're actually going in the right direction. The girls know exactly where our home is located and can confidently describe the location relative to other area towns.

I've also taken them to a field to locate "treasures" with their compasses. One day treasure may be lunch, and the next a particularly lovely wildflower or the swan's nest. I already know where the object is located, and I give them directions to follow, such as "ten steps east, then turn in a southeast direction" and so on. I give them some idea of what they're looking for, and we do a lot of detouring, too, just to increase the fun and practice. They really feel like explorers—I guess they really are.

Exploring the World

Flat Shayna
Aileen Aidnik, Shingle Springs, California

When my daughter, Shayna, was about seven years old, she "wanted to learn where the states are." We read Jeff Brown's book *Flat Stanley* and decided to perform a take-off on the idea with "Flat Shayna" (substitute the name of your child here). We made a paper doll that Shayna decorated in traveling clothes, wrote a cover letter explaining our goal, asked the recipients to take Flat Shayna on an imaginary tour of their area, and to send her back with notes of her trip—and maybe a very inexpensive souvenir of the journey.

We started with friends and family, then friends of friends and family. It started taking so long to get Flat Shayna back that we decided to make a dozen of her, and sent her to different regions of the country. This way we received letters back more frequently and the real Shayna didn't lose hope or interest. When a letter came back, we put a colored dot on the U.S. map, read a little about the state in various books, and played an inexpensive card game called Five State Rummy that I purchased at Wal-Mart.

We made a scrapbook from the letters we received, including some of the souvenirs. Some people really got into the spirit of the project and sent more, others did a wonderful job of taking Flat Shayna on tour, and still others sent her on to friends and wrote to tell us where she was!

We sent out the Flat Shaynas for several months, and we ended up covering thirty states before we were done. Not only was it fun, but the real Shayna indeed "learned where the states are!" We still have the scrapbook and enjoy rereading it and reminiscing.

Let's Get Started

Hang a world map in your child's bedroom.

Scrumptious Geography

Jennifer Miller, Puyallup, Washington

Have an international dinner once a month. Go to the library and check out a cookbook from whatever country you'll highlight. Choose some music from that country to play during dinner. Have the children make placemats featuring symbols of the country. Invite the grandparents or another family, and ask them to bring a food item from that country, too.

Postcard Exchange

Jennifer Miller, Puyallup, Washington

We join postcard exchanges when someone on one of our e-mail lists suggests it. List members receive addresses and send postcards from their area throughout the year. Then, to keep track of our postcards, we put a big map of the United States on our wall and tack the postcards up around the map. We used yarn to make a line from the postcard to the state on the map from which it was sent.

More Postcards
Jen Blake, Rapid City, South Dakota

Anytime friends and relatives travel, we ask them to send us a postcard from their trip. Combined with a little Internet research about the state, my eight-year-old daughter is able to learn on the sly. Research includes answering the following questions: When did that state become a state? What is one thing interesting about its history? What are the state flag, flower, and bird? All of this goes into a notebook, and I've witnessed my daughter going back through it when reading about other states.

Spin the Globe
Linda Dobson, Saranac Lake, New York

When the kids were out of ideas, we sometimes used a spin of the globe to determine what country we would next learn about. While many children know of the countries typically talked about in the news, movies, and television, they aren't aware of just how many other countries there are. A spin of the globe often brought their little fingers to a country that was foreign in every sense of the word.

Next, finding information on such countries became a treasure hunt and a big part of the fun. Traditional sources included nonfiction library books, fictional stories set in the location, encyclopedias, videos, and asking everyone they ran into if they had ever been there. Imagine the kids' surprise when they asked a librarian if she had ever been to Tibet. She hadn't, but her friend had, and was happy to talk with them about it.

Wynn Kapit's Coloring Book

Cindy Allas, Fairfield, California

This author who created the geography coloring book is the same one who wrote the more recognized *Anatomy Coloring Book*. It includes several maps of the continents, historic land empires, flags of the world, climate regions, ocean currents, major religions, official religion, vegetation regions, and major use of land, population distribution, and racial distribution. This activity is better for older children.

The Land Down Under

Jackie Clifton, Prescott Valley, Arizona

While struggling to come up with an Australia unit study for my seven- and twelve-year-olds, we invented a board game in which the players take on the role of specimen collectors for a new zoo featuring animals of Australia. The object is to travel to the different areas of the continent, collecting all the specimens, and return safely to the starting point. Along the way there were hazards that had to be overcome, like being chased by a crocodile, and geographical obstacles to conquer, such as mountains and deserts.

We created the board by taking a piece of poster board and making a Play-Doh model of Australia, complete with geographical features, to place in the middle. Around the outside edge we drew spaces for players to travel with game pieces. In order to collect at least one animal from each climactic zone and type of topography, it was necessary for the kids to research these. We also made it a requirement to stock up on "supplies" at each major city, allowing them to learn what those cities are and where they're located.

This single activity resulted in the children learning about the animals, landforms, climate, population, and major cities in Australia. If you want to, throw in a requirement to answer a few history questions before proceeding out of each city to work a history feature into the game.

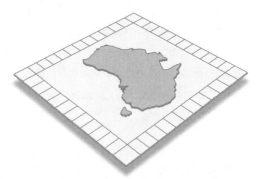

City, Province, or Country?

Kim Weaver, Victoria, British Columbia, Canada

We helped our daughter learn the differences between cities, provinces/states, and countries by using the money analogy of pennies for cities, dimes for provinces/states, and dollars for countries. For example, we live in Victoria, which is a penny, and quite a bit smaller than a dime. Canada has ten provinces, so dimes represent them. Canada itself combines the pennies and dimes into a country.

To help her remember the provinces, we cut out province and territory shapes and made a puzzle out of them. This active, hands-on learning experience helped her to get a feel for our country. Adding an interesting detail about each province and territory (its bird or flower) also helped her to remember and appreciate Canada's diversity and natural beauty.

Veggie Geography

Shay Seaborne, Woodbridge, Virginia

When shopping at a larger grocery store, I encourage each of my children to choose an unfamiliar fruit or veggie to try. We take the items home and look up what they are, how they grow, where they come from, and how to prepare them. This helps the children learn to use various sources of information, teaches them something about geography, agriculture, trade and culture, and reinforces the notion that it's good to try different foods.

Where Does It Come From?

Susan Dinkledine, Russiaville, Indiana

My fourth-grader and kindergartner enjoyed this geography game together, and two older boys joined in for it as well.

We went around the house looking at clothing, toys, appliances, and other objects. We found where they were made and located those places in our world atlas. We noted which countries made more clothing, which produced more electronics, more toys, and so on. They have since continued this activity by noting where other items are made. One will ask me, "Mom, my ___ was made in ___. Where is that?"

Cookie Geography

Fiona Bayrock, Chilliwack, British Columbia, Canada

Become familiar with a region, country, or even an entire continent by making a cookie map. An impromptu lesson in map scales occurs when you enlarge a map to poster size for the cookie pattern by making a grid on the map and poster board and drawing the outline onto the poster board one cell at a time. Doubling the cookie recipe is an instant fraction exercise, and using only four colors of icing provides a chance to practice the Four-Color Map Theory (all maps can be colored with four colors so no two areas of the same color touch).

If the pattern is larger than your baking sheet, cut the pattern into two or three pieces with a straight line from edge to edge. Cut and bake the pieces separately and reassemble before icing. Label cities, mountains, rivers, and other physical features with full-strength food coloring and a very fine, new paint brush. Add a flag and compass rose. Black food coloring paste is available.

Cookie Recipe

- 1 1/2 cups flour
- 1/2 cup sugar
- 1/3 cup shortening
- 1 tbsp. milk
- 1 tsp. baking powder
- 1/2 tsp. vanilla
- 1/2 tsp. salt
- 1 egg

Mix all ingredients together in a bowl. Wrap the dough in plastic and refrigerate it for two to three hours. Preheat the oven to 400 degrees Fahrenheit. On a lightly floured piece of aluminum foil, 10 to 15 centimeters (4–6 in.) longer than your cookie sheet, roll the dough until it's 1/8-inch thick. Tape the short ends of the foil to your work surface to keep it in place.

Place the cardboard pattern on top of the rolled dough. Use a small knife to cut the dough to the shape of the cardboard while holding the pattern in place with your other hand. (*Tip:* If the cutting motion distorts the shape, shorten the cuts.) Cut off the tape

and carefully lift the foil onto a cookie sheet. Bake 6 to 8 minutes until lightly brown around the edges. Cool on the pan.

Icing: Cream 2 tablespoons butter, alternately adding 2 tablespoons milk and $1/2$ to 1 cup of confectioner's sugar until you have several cups of very soft icing, stiff enough to stay where you put it but goopy enough to hide spatula marks.

Assemble the cookie on a large, foil-covered piece of plywood. Ice it and allow it to set for 8 hours before labeling it with food coloring. Then ask your friends to come and help you eat the world.

If you're really ambitious, try a whole continent of cookies. South America works well. Cut a poster map of the whole continent into countries and cut and bake each country cookie individually. Trim the cooled cookies to the exact shape of the pattern piece before assembling them jigsaw puzzle-style on the board.

Time *Magazine as a Resource*
Jeanne Faulconer, Stanardsville, Virginia

My mother-in-law gives us *Time* magazine for Christmas each year, and it is truly one of our windows to the world. My boys have always picked it up and read from it, and it has led to incredible discussions about what is going on in the world and the background that got us to this point.

The photojournalism is very good, which is often a grabber for preteen and teen boys. Of course, there are sometimes articles or pictures that are graphic or sexually explicit, so I generally get hold of the magazine first. But I've found that even some of this content, such as articles on AIDS, has generated excellent discussion about issues I want my children to be knowledgeable about. I think one reason my children like *Time* is that it's a magazine for adults; it's not dumbed down. Having *Time* in our home has given my children good reading experiences as well as good oral language experience, as they formulate questions for me and begin to express their own opinions about complicated issues.

People of the World

People Make the World Go 'Round
Kim Weaver, Victoria, British Columbia, Canada

We have learned as a family about parts of our world's cultures by first "adopting" a foster child, Karla, in Guatemala through an international aid agency. Our foster daughter is similar in age to our children, and we write letters back and forth through an agency interpreter. It has inspired us to learn all we can, age appropriately, about Guatemala, its festivals, economy, seasons, and so on in relation to our lives in Canada.

We have also hosted international students for short periods of time, which inspired us to learn about other countries and cultures and to learn a few welcoming words for our visitors. The personal contact makes learning very relevant and fun.

Native American Experience

Elizabeth Johnson, Philadelphia, Pennsylvania

It helped us to get into our roles knowing that some of our ancestors were American Indians. On Day 1 we started by sitting on a rug in a circle as I told a story of a young boy on his first vision quest. I briefly mentioned that Native American names were usually based on something in nature and described the personality of the person. Then each of us chose a special place around the house or yard to sit quietly and wait for a name to come to us. When we were ready, we came back to the circle and announced our new names. We made a fire with brown construction paper logs and orange, red, and yellow tissue paper flames and held a ceremony, complete with drumming, making the names official.

On Day 2 we rose with the sun. We avoided modern conveniences like electricity or watches. My daughter wore a Native American tunic she made the day before. We went to the local nature preserve and spent the entire day outdoors marking trails, observing nature, tracking wildlife, and identifying plants and birds. It began to rain lightly and we found shelter. My daughter got a small scrape and her brother found jewelweed by the stream and applied it to her wound. We ate turkey sandwiches, berries, popcorn, and tortillas and drank water. We left when the sun began to set.

Doll-Sized Longhouse

Merelee Syron, New Egypt, New Jersey

Last Thanksgiving we made a dollhouse-sized Indian longhouse out of sticks and bark. The exterior was created from a piece of plywood with dowels screwed in from the bottom. On to these we tied sticks then glued on bark. We left one side open to see inside. We added faux fur bearskin rugs, clay pottery, polymer clay corn, small sticks heaped up with orange paper fire, and dried herbs hanging from the rafters. It made a great Thanksgiving table centerpiece.

For some great ideas, see *More Than Moccasins* by Laurie Carlson.

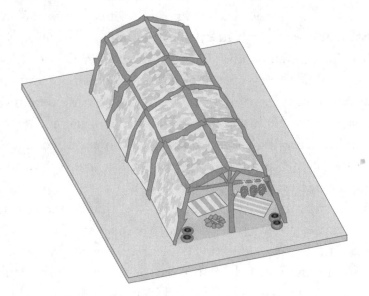

Hosting a Foreign Visitor

Aileen Aidnik, Shingle Springs, California

We've hosted foreign exchange students for short-term visits, usually three to four weeks. From them we've learned about different countries, and because of homeschooling, my daughter was available during the day to go on tour with the groups the visitors came with. She even served as an English tutor when the exchange students were in formal morning classes. As a result, she has developed a strong interest in Japan and hopes to travel there as part of a 4-H program, and she applied to be a People-to-People Youth Ambassadors delegate this summer with an eye on travel to Australia.

A Friend Is in the Navy Now
Jeanne Faulconer, Stanardsville, Virginia

When a homeschool friend of ours joined the Navy, we sat around the kitchen table cutting up magazines with red, white, and blue pictures. Using fingernail-size clippings and gluing them to cardboard, we made a large mosaic of the American flag.

During this art time my children and I talked about what it means to be in the service, why people and governments fight wars, what might be worth sacrificing your life for, and why people disagree over issues surrounding war and peace. They also had the chance to express their fear for our friend's safety, and I had a calm window of opportunity to explain what his experience might be like.

We mailed the flag to the new recruit, along with a letter telling him and his family that we had talked about him as we glued these hundreds of pieces of paper in place. It was a valuable lesson in citizenship and friendship.

Government

Discuss Politics with a Politician
Jeanne Faulconer, Stanardsville, Virginia

We all learned a lot when a homeschool friend of ours ran for state office. When she was in our area campaigning, she stayed in our home and we had great discussions about politics and government.

Amnesty International's Children's *Urgent Action* Monthly Newsletter

Call Amnesty International at 800-AMNESTY or go to the Web site at www.amnesty usa.org and ask to be placed on the mailing list to receive the children's edition of the *Urgent Action* newsletters. This edition is written for children, shows maps of where human rights violations have taken place, and describes what has happened.

The newsletters include instructions on how to address, write, and mail letters in support of children whose human rights have been violated. Sometimes the children receive a letter back from the government official to whom they have written. Letters arrive from all over the world (although you never write to the country in which you live).

—Linda Spaulding, Pattersonville, New York

Hands-On Government

Julie Swegle, Colorado Springs, Colorado

When you study how our electoral system works, get involved in the campaign process. Call the office of a local candidate and ask what you can do to help. Stuffing envelopes is fine, but even better is being involved in the door-to-door campaigning. Children can pass out flyers at each house and say, "Vote for _____" as easily as an adult can. Most people you meet will be very excited to see your child taking an active interest in the community.

Learn to Lobby

Linda Spaulding, Pattersonville, New York

Contact any local environmental group and tell them you'd like to help; they will put you to work! My family's work with the Citizens Environmental Coalition (CEC) has led us to lobby state legislators and be part of press conferences and protest rallies.

The CEC meets with newcomers ahead of time to review talking points and lobbying techniques. A team leader is assigned to go with the novices, but everyone in the group is encouraged to talk about something. It doesn't get any better than this for learning about the workings of government, and you can establish contacts with legislative staffers or the legislators themselves that come in handy when pursuing homeschooling issues.

Don't Know Much About History? Don't Worry!

How People Lived

Cristina Ramos-Payne, White Plains, New York

Many children's history books available in the library are full of simple projects to demonstrate how people lived in times past. History grows more interesting when children can make a Trojan horse, a pomander that a medieval person would carry, or butter just like a colonial family. After reading a children's biography about the philosopher Diogenes by Aliki, my children walked around outside with bare feet while carrying a walking stick as they became Cynics for the day.

Let's Get Started

Using a world map, globe, or atlas, look for a country for each letter of the alphabet, A to Z.

Yum, Hardtack

Jeanne Faulconer, Stanardsville, Virginia

We mixed flour and water to make hardtack and discussed how this was a main staple of the sailors' diet during Columbus's voyage to the New World. We also made wooden boats with sails and took them to a nearby creek. It was amazing to hear the boys discuss how hard it must have been for the explorers to travel in the huge ocean as they launched their own crafts—exactly what I had hoped for.

Historical Reenactments

Linda Spaulding, Pattersonville, New York

Your local paper usually announces where and when historical reenactments take place near you. As a rule, they're free and often have hands-on elements that appeal to kids.

The Graveyard Shift

Norma Young, Pennsburg, Pennsylvania

This activity can be modified for various age levels. We went to a local cemetery and walked around looking at gravestones. My daughter and niece had the mission to "choose a person you want to know," with the stipulation that the person had died at least fifty years ago. We then took snapshots of the headstone and they copied the wording on the stone into a notebook.

At home they explored various aspects of their person's life: What was going on in the country/world during his lifetime? What kind of music was popular when he was a teen? An adult? What kind of music would he sing to his own child? What books were new then? Are those books still read today? Who was president during his lifetime? What kinds of diseases did people get then? Are those still a threat now? What would he have done for entertainment? Can you figure out what job he might have held? What has been invented since he died? Did he have brothers/sisters/wife/children (any other relatives)? This may take another trip back to the cemetery!

One of the girls liked to write little stories about her person at various stages of life, an activity that integrated and personalized various subjects. They both developed a new appreciation for the personal histories behind those rows of headstones.

Set up a talk show interview. One person interviews the child who is "in character" as her person. Research different time periods. Historical cemeteries are great resources.

Native American Activities
Linda Spaulding, Pattersonville, New York

Don't miss local Native American activities like powwows to which the public is invited. We've participated in the powwow dances, drumming, and stories, sampled Native foods, and looked at the handicrafts. Spend a day; take your time. Talk with participants.

History Fair
Bobbi Jo Baumgardner, Cloverdale, California, courtesy of *Right at Home* newsletter

My homeschool group has an annual history fair. The local museum's curator has been helpful in setup and offering space for two weeks in the rotating display area. Children may base their projects on any time period, but the chosen event or time period must be verifiable by two different sources.

After researching their project, the children create displays using models, backboards, and/or descriptive tags. The organizer sets up a delivery time during which the projects can be dropped off, and then the curator sets them up.

While the projects are on display, we have a cookies-and-punch reception for the children, some of whom attend in period clothing. A parent announces each project, its creator, and presents the children

The Social Studies–Literary Connection

Care to try a history-centered learning experience? Start looking here!

- Beautiful Feet Books: www.bfbooks.com; study guides with literature packs
- Carol Hurst's Children's Literature: www.carolhurst.com; under "subjects," books listed by period, theme, and grade level
- Historical Fiction: falcon.jmu.edu/~ramseyil/historical.htm; Wow! Bibliographies, unit plans, award winners, and more
- Historical Fiction for Children: www.marysmoffat.co.uk/bibliography/cont.htm; extensive bibliography by century
- Historical Fiction Resources: www.vinton-shellsbury.k2.ia.us .tms/eventh /rdg7/hf/hftoc.html, categorized by period
- Historical mystery fiction for kids and young adults: members.tripod.com /BrerFox/Kids_YA/historicalmystery.html, searchable by time period or author

with participation certificates. This has been so successful that we may need to limit attendance or find another location next year.

American Girl Classes

Cindy Allas, Fairfield, California

Based on the book series of the same name, our co-op creates American Girl classes with biweekly meetings for girls ages six to thirteen divided into three age groups. Each three-month session is about one of the American Girls. For class they read the next book in the series, complete workbook pages from the teacher's guide, make crafts and food from the time period, and earn extra credit by doing book reports, wearing costumes, and having items to show and share. Participating in these activities earns them trading cards that they love to trade with each other in an attempt to collect the set.

Each session ends with a play for the enjoyment of all parents.

Think Close to Home

Sandra Dodd, Albuquerque, New Mexico

Really local history helped my children grow interested in more distant ideas. What used to be where the 7-Eleven is now? What was in that building before it was a thrift store? Where were our cars built? What kind of cars did we drive before they were born? When was Wyoming Boulevard the very edge of town? When was our house built? Why did their grandparents come to New Mexico? History that could and has touched them created a foundation for adding to their personal bigger pictures.

Mummies

Jeanne Faulconer, Stanardsville, Virginia

While studying ancient Egypt, my children mummified dead insects and buried them in decorated matchboxes. They also constructed dirt and sand pyramids in the backyard. I can't say I had anything to do with this; they just did it as they were synthesizing what we were reading.

Pyramid Dig

Diane Keith, Redwood City, California

The crowning jewel in our study of ancient Egypt was inspired when my son wished out loud that he could go on an archaeological dig. We had read a great deal about archaeologists' discoveries of pyramids and the buried treasures they held. I decided to indulge his fantasy. I bought air-drying modeling clay at the art supply store and suggested to each of my sons that they construct a pyramid, complete with buried treasure as a gift for the other. (Christmas was only two weeks away!) They constructed the pyramid using seven layers of clay. As they made each layer, they embedded it with treasures, which included small feathers, stones, coins, rings, and seashells. Plastic action figures substituted for the pharaoh and his entourage. They used hieroglyphic rubber stamps to imprint a message on the outside walls of the finished pyramid. Then they waited for their pyramids to dry (about ten days).

On Christmas, each presented a pyramid to the other, along with a small hammer, chisel, and brush. They decoded the hieroglyphic message on the outer pyramid walls and proceeded to begin their "dig." They discovered the cache of treasure buried in each layer and were impressed with the "fossilized" imprints of seashells, feathers, and coins in the broken clay. This simple, inexpensive experiment satisfied their need for a hands-on dig experience and enriched their understanding of archaeology.

- Hieroglyphic rubber stamps are available in a kit called *Ancient Egypt/Book and Treasure Chest* by George Hart and James Putnam (Running Press, 1994). Not only does it include the stamps, but it also contains papyrus and other artifacts that teach about the rituals and customs of ancient Egyptian society.

Notebook Time Line

Jennifer Miller, Puyallup, Washington

In a spiral notebook, draw a line on every page and write the beginning and ending years represented by each page along the line. Whenever you read about an event in history, print a picture or photocopy something to paste in the notebook. Write a little note about the event.

The Time Line Game
Shay Seaborne, Woodbridge, Virginia

I made cards on which were written important inventions, eras, and people, then hung a string horizontally across a bookshelf. I gave the children the cards and clothespins and let them arrange and re-arrange them until they felt they had put them in correct chronological order. Then together we looked up the actual dates, added them to the cards, and made the few corrections necessary. This helped my children to see how history included many elements, and gave me a good picture of how much they already knew.

Journals with a Child's Perspective
Scott Stevens, Paris, Tennessee

Dear America is an excellent series of books that are journals of historical events written from the perspective of children. Currently we are reading *A Line in the Sand: The Alamo Diary of Lucinda Lawrence,* the fifth such journal that we have read. On December 10 we will read Lucinda's entry for the very same day, then talk about what she wrote and explain any unfamiliar words. We also talk about what happened the days before in order to recall any information that might be relevant to the current day's entry. The books are historical fiction but are very accurately written and include historical information about the subject at the end of the journals. By reading the journals of others, my own children receive help expressing their thoughts and ideas in their own journals. Historical fiction is a great way to get interested in a historical subject, children enjoy it much more, and therefore probably learn more than they would from a history textbook.

Genealogy and Grandparents

Jean Reed, Bridgewater, Maine, courtesy of *The Home School Source Book*

Let's Get Started

Trace your family tree using the Internet.

Knowing that five of our ancestors came over on the *Mayflower* sparked a real interest in the history of that time. A Civil War sword passed down through the family did the same thing. Talking with grandparents about what life was like for them when they were growing up can do more than introduce a history lesson. Speaking with them about changes they have seen transforms history from something dry and abstract to something alive. For a cheap, enjoyable project, top it off with a collage from magazine pictures that illustrate the changes.

Test the Parent

Calandra Johnson, Elgin, Oregon

Have your child create a history test and key for her parents, have her administer the test and then grade it. It's fun for both parents and child!

Make It Yourself

Cindy Allas, Fairfield, California

Make wampum belts on a loom using pony beads and a strip of cardboard with notches cut in each end on which to wrap the yarn. From researching wampum belts, we knew that the choice of colors and designs would tell a story. As we studied Colonial America, we made quill pens and strawberry ink, cross-stitch samplers, and weather vanes. The weather vanes did double duty with science lessons.

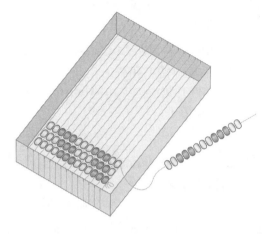

Pick a President, Any President
Maria Halloran, Winfield, Missouri

I recently bought decks of cards, one with all the states and several items of interest on the back, and one with all the presidents, complete with pictures and information about them. Each day we draw one card from each deck. We find the state on a map and color it in, and then I read aloud the information on the back of both cards while the children color or practice handwriting.

Sometimes we spend the whole morning talking about our president of the day, and when history-buff Dad is home, our president discussion really takes off!

A Presidential Notebook
Merelee Syron, New Egypt, New Jersey

We made a book about presidents in a three-ring binder full of clear sheet protectors that open at the top. Every day we fill out a sheet with the next president's biographical information to add to the binder. As we learn more, we add interesting facts to the sheets.

We also slip in brochures of places we visit related to that president and his time period, articles, and pictures that we photocopy. It has turned into an impressive piece of work that we still add to now and then, as well as use for reference.

Do you know which president was the first to use a telephone? We do!

Figuring Out the Transcontinental Railroad
Ann Israel, Catonsville, Maryland

To demonstrate how difficult it would be to start on opposite ends of the country and have a railroad meet in the middle, I had my boys get out all of their old Brio and Thomas the Tank Engine track. They each started on opposite ends of the house and were told that their goal was to construct a track that would meet in the dining room. I built obstacles for them out of blocks and other materials along the way (obstacles representing mountains, rivers, and lakes). The boys had a meeting and then went their separate ways. When they each ran out of track on opposite sides of the dining room table, they realized that this wasn't easy. Because we already had the track, this was a good, cheap lesson, as they realized they had to tear down some of their work and use better communication to accomplish the task.

Get Arrested
Shay Seaborne, Woodbridge, Virginia

When my daughters asked to learn more about woman suffrage, I created a unit for our little "play and learn" group. First we staged the 1848 election in which the "men" (boys in our group) were allowed to deliver their ballots, but the "women" were barred from voting. Pretending to be in Rochester, New York, in 1872, when Susan B. Anthony and thirteen others were arrested for attempting to vote, the children made their own placards and held a protest. The girls were "arrested" by the boys.

We also viewed photos of suffragists on parade and in protest and created a time line showing the relevant events that transpired between 1776—when Abigail Adams asked that the Continental Congress "Remember the Ladies"—to the passage of the Nineteenth Amendment in 1920. (But being arrested was their favorite part!)

Historical Museums' Endless Offerings
Cindy Allas, Fairfield, California

When our local museum held a pioneer/Gold Rush Day, we made butter in lidded containers with cream and a BB. The BB provides the agitation as you shake the container for about an hour while walking around. (A baby food jar and marble also work, but you have to be careful not to shake the jar so hard as to break it with the marble.) We also used a scrub board and bar laundry soap to wash towels, panned for gold (BBs) in a trough with gold pans, took the haul to the "surveyor's office" to see how much our gold would have purchased, wrote with quill pens and walnut ink, watched Navajo rug weaving, listened to an old-time band play a saw as an instrument, and heard a local author read from his book about a girl's journey west. Whew!

Dress-Up Friday
Tara Hall, Colliersville, Tennessee

When studying a certain period of history, we spend each Friday looking up dishes and clothing for that country and try to duplicate what life was like then. It's also fun to play games that were popular at the time (such as Tabula from ancient Rome). Find these by searching on www.google.com.

Where the History Is

Lillian Jones, Sebastopol, California

Some of the most valuable resources around are the guides and docents who work at educational exhibits, museums, and historical sites. Crowds often just file right past these treasure-houses of information and enthusiasm, but if you ask questions, you'll find that they can go on and on in fascinating depth about the exhibits and background details of history.

We see docents at exhibits light up when we take the time to ask questions, and having parents present thoughtful queries provides a good model for a child to grow up with.

Stir Interest with Good Flicks

Sue Patterson, Wichita Falls, Texas

My favorite way to teach and learn history is through movies. Whenever you want to spark interest in a particular period, think about the movies that might help convey the material in a dynamic way. If, for example, you're thinking about medieval times, how about *Ivanhoe* or *Robin Hood*? Historical fiction, biographies, documentaries, and Public Broadcasting System specials are all available at the library for backup, as are videos designed for classroom use. These often show segments on the geographic region associated with the time period as a bonus. Isn't this better than dry textbooks that only elicit a desire for a nap?

Dioramas and Models

Jean Reed, Bridgewater, Maine, courtesy of *The Home School Source Book*

Dover Publications offers inexpensive dioramas and models. (Some of the more complicated ones can be tricky to put together.) Usborne also has great historical models that aren't too difficult. Ambitious children can mount them on plywood and use cheap material from the model section of Wal-Mart to create more complete scenes with grass, trees, more people, and animals.

- Dover Publications: 31 East Second Street, Mineola, New York 11501; fax 516-742-6953; store.doverpublications.com
- Usborne Books: EDC Publishing, 10302 East 55th Place, Tulsa, Oklahoma 74146; 800-475-4522; www.edcpub.com

Heads Up

Cindy Allas, Fairfield, California

We made pre-Columbian Olmec heads with plaster of paris. We added coffee grounds for color, made a square block in a cutoff milk container, and then carved away.

Can You Dig It?

Linda Spaulding, Pattersonville, New York

Someone gave us a flyer from the local historical society indicating that visitors were welcome to watch a dig there. When we asked if my daughter could help, there were some questions about tetanus shots and insurance, but the folks in charge were fine with her pitching in. She did everything the archaeology students did and learned

Books for Active History Lessons

- *American Kids in History* series (John Wiley)
- *Ancient Greece! 40 Hands-On Activities to Experience This Wondrous Age* by Avery Hart and Paul Mantell (Williamson, 1999)
- *Who Really Discovered America? Unraveling the Mystery and Solving the Puzzle* by Avery Hart (Williamson Publishing, 2001)
- *Colonial Days: Discover the Past with Fun Projects, Games, Activities, and Recipes* by David C. King (John Wiley, 1997).

a great deal from talking with the teachers and students—a wonderful hands-on experience. Most communities should provide opportunities for at least observing an archaeological dig. Check your local paper.

Legos Can Be Anything
Cindy Allas, Fairfield, California

Use Legos to make Viking ships, reenact scenes from the American Revolution, re-create the battle between Cortez and the Aztecs, and anything else you can think to make.

Conversation Starters

- Find an interesting court case in the newspaper and pretend you're on the jury. Which way would you vote?

- Use one of the many Web sites to find interesting historical tidbits from "This Day in History" listings. Pick one: www.yahooligans.com/docs/tdih or www.historychannel.com/thisday

- If we were going on a trip to _____, what would be the best things to take along? Why?

- How many of the state postal codes do you know?

- What past decade would you like to visit? Why?

7

Art from the Heart

As most homeschoolers understand, on some days you know within ten minutes of waking up that things just aren't going to go smoothly no matter what your best intentions are. On days like these, simple things like construction paper, glue sticks, colored pencils, scissors, and all of the recycled materials saved for artistic endeavors are life savers. Give most young children a few art supplies and they contentedly transform into busy, intent artists. This type of creative expression, along with study-related projects once in a while, supplies plenty of satisfaction as a creative outlet, at least in the early years.

Provide a creating place, be it a corner of the kitchen, a nook in the attic, or a reasonably comfortable basement or garage, and keep an array of art materials at the ready for those moments when inspiration strikes. The walls of the same area can serve as a gallery when the refrigerator door gets full. If an interest in art continues, older children appreciate a place of their own where work will be safe from the younger ones' "whoops" moments.

Activities often referred to as crafts are also staples of home-centered art education. You can share with your children a skill you already possess, or you can learn a new one right by their side. The list of possibilities is endless, but here are a few to whet your interest: batik, basket weaving, beadwork, book binding, candle making, crocheting, dioramas, enameling, fabric painting, family albums, flower pressing, jewelry, knitting, latch hook, leather work, macramé, mobiles, models, murals, needlepoint, origami, painting, paper making, photography, pottery, printmaking, quilting, sculpting, sewing, stenciling, stone carving, tie-dyeing, tin work, weaving, or wood carving. Such projects take time and focus so they give children the opportunity to stick with a project and learn patience.

Time-period or culturally related art activities serve as perfect lead-ins to topics of study, providing time to introduce and discuss the topic in a relaxed manner.

Art, like beauty, is in the eye of the beholder, so education includes developing an eye—and an appreciation—through exposure to and study of the work of others.

Beyond Visual Art

Don't stop with the paints and crayons! Beyond visual arts, the family can make and enjoy music together by singing or playing instruments or both. While some of the research remains controversial, a lot of folks believe that acquiring musical skills aids children in grasping concepts useful in math and science. As with any other accomplishment, success inspires confidence and bolsters self-esteem. You can fill your home with music whenever you desire and take the family to musical performances ranging from light comedy to heavy orchestral works.

Movement through dance improves coordination and increases an understanding of one's body and its place in space—and children love to move! Dance lends itself to experimentation at home—just let the music move you. Teach the kids the dances you enjoyed as a teen. Besides folk and ethnic dances, it's fun to try waltzes, tangos, and cha-chas. Even the youngest children can perform simple square dances and appreciate the "professionalism" of

To TV or Not to TV

We have found that limiting television viewing is the single most effective tool for getting the most out of homeschooling. Try limiting TV watching, video game playing, and Internet surfing to one or two days a week or to an hour a day. Such rules cause fewer hard feelings, are easier to enforce, and are less draining than negotiation on a day-by-day basis.

Try a one-month sabbatical. If you conduct the experiment during the summer, it won't seem like a punishment associated with homeschooling, and most of the shows are reruns then anyway. If necessary, to avoid temptation or enforcement problems, store your television(s) at a friend's home or in your attic.

—From Homeschooling on a Shoestring *by Judith Waite Allee and Melissa L. Morgan (Shaw Books, 1999)*

their own performances. Moving and enjoying it are the important things.

Children don't need a whole lot of prodding to pretend, so why not exercise those vivid imaginations through dramatic performances? Productions can be tiny and performed in the living room, or larger and involve other families gathering at the library, church, or community center. Allow the children to be involved in all aspects of the dramatic presentation, from the story choice (don't forget the possibility of plays written by your children) to scenery, costumes, lighting, and direction. All provide wonderful opportunities for attention to detail, real-life problem solving, public speaking, and that vital self-discipline.

Since schools have cut back time and funding for the arts, it's more important than ever to create your own opportunities for both creation and appreciation. Art has universal appeal across continents, cultures, and time. It's a gift you don't want your child to miss.

Creating Art

Ornamental Color Fundamentals

Amy DeRusha, Somersworth, New Hampshire

To help our girls understand colors and where they fall on the color wheel, we buy plaster Christmas ornaments to paint. We start with primary colors, mix those, then explain that we now have secondary colors. If we then mix secondary colors with primary colors, we create tertiary colors.

Bathtub Colors

Jane Powell, Bowie, Maryland

Take small to medium plastic containers such as Tupperware, ladles, spoons, medicine droppers, and food coloring and place them in the bathtub. Add a few drops of food coloring to a few of the containers and fill them with water. Let the children play with the colors. For younger children, talk about which colors are which, then check to see how much they are remembering by pointing to different colors and asking the children to name them. For older children, point out that blue and yellow make green, red and blue make purple, and so on.

Zoo Art

LeCee Galmiche Johnson, New York, New York

We bring paper, paints, and crayons to the zoo, and the children sketch the animals and foliage. Our inspiration came from an adult art class doing this very thing. My triplets asked if they too could draw.

Helpful Art Books

- *Story of the Orchestra: Listen While You Learn About the Instruments, the Music, and the Composers Who Wrote the Music!* by Meredith Hamilton (Black Dog and Leventhal, 2000)
- *Kids Make Music! Clapping and Tapping from Bach to Rock!* by Avery Hart et al. (Williamson, 1993)
- *Classic Tunes and Tales: Ready-to-Use Music Listening Lessons and Activities for Grades K–8* by Tod F. Kline (Prentice Hall Trade, 1999)
- *A Drawing Book That We Start and You Finish* (Klutz, Inc., 2001)
- *Cooking Art: Easy Edible Art for Young Children* by Potter Kohl and Roseman-Hall (Gryphon House, 1997)
- *The Little Hands Art Book: Exploring Arts and Crafts with Two- to Six-Year-Olds* by Judy Press (Williamson, 1994)
- *101 Music Games for Children: Fun and Learning with Rhythm and Song* by Ger Storms and Anne Griffiths (Hunter House, 1995)
- *Music Mind Games* by Michiko Yrko (Warner Brothers Publications, 1997)
- *Start Exploring Masterpieces: A Fact-Filled Coloring Book* by Steven Zorn (Running Press, 2001)

It's art. It's biology. It's environmental studies. It's good to be out in the fresh air. It's fun!

Create Symmetry

Linda Dobson, Saranac Lake, New York

Here's an easy way to explain symmetry to your children. Fold a piece of paper in half. Have your child draw half a picture on one half of the paper. When she's done, have her outline the half picture with black crayon, pressing as hard as she can.

Next, fold the paper against the first fold, take a *warm* iron, and press the paper. The half picture will melt onto the other side, creating an exact copy of the first half, showing symmetry. To complete the picture, use water colors or crayons.

County Fair

Merelee Syron, New Egypt, New Jersey

Art Info

- Learning Through Art (video series): L & K Concepts, 113 Linden Street, Woodmere, New York 11598; 516-374-3963
- Math and Music: Wildridge Software; 888-244-4379; www.wildridge.com

Every year my children make projects for the county fair, and we always come home with a feeling of great satisfaction from having our projects displayed all week and hearing the comments of people walking by admiring our creations. This year we ordered molding material that we poured on my daughter's foot. When it dried, we filled the foot mold with plaster of paris, painted it a skin tone medium with painted toenails. It came out incredibly accurate, and when we put it in a shoe box, it was mistaken for a real foot!

- Art materials from: Nasco Arts and Crafts catalog: 1-800-558-9595

Coffee Filter Art

Jane Powell, Bowie, Maryland

Take a paper coffee filter (wide-bottomed ones work best), markers, a spray bottle filled with water, and a sheet of white paper. Flatten the filter. Ask your child to decorate the filter with the markers, but decorate *sparingly* and not in big globs or shapes.

Take filter, paper, and spray bottle outside, into the bathtub, or any other safe spraying place. Place the filter on the paper and spray.

The colors will blend and move, making art on the filter as well as on the paper behind it. If the child just uses two colors to decorate, she can see how yellow and blue make green, and so on.

Juried Art Show

Linda Clement, Victoria, British Columbia, Canada

When my two children played school with a schooled friend last summer, they made up twenty-four classes, with each of them teaching a third of them, assigning work and marking it.

When they were finished, they wrote category signs and ID tags and taped up the work along the walls in the laundry area and basement hall. (I'd have forgotten about this but some of the work is so good I just can't take it down!) They handed out judging forms to everyone in the house and announced winners at an award ceremony.

Some of the art assignments included making a picture out of natural materials gathered in the yard, drawings made with charcoal, poems, graph paper drawings, drawings or painting of particular subject matters, and a category called "surprise art."

At the ceremony, they received prizes of everything from books to Barbies to art supplies to do more of the same category of art. The ceremony took nearly thirty minutes, and the kids had a great time opening up the sealed paper bags that held their prizes. The audience applauded and they blushed and made short speeches, usually about how they made the decisions about the piece. I know they learned a lot, although I'd be hesitant to categorize what it was they learned.

Let's Get Started

Draw pictures that become greeting cards for friends and family.

Paper Bag Puppetry

Diane Keith, adapted from *Carschooling: 500 Games and Activities to Turn Travel Time into Learning Time*

We turned paper bags into puppets to conduct plays in the car. I kept a stack of small lunch bags in the glove compartment. Whenever the kids got travel weary, I'd suggest they put on a play. They drew faces on the bags and decorated them with whatever we had handy in the car. Torn strips of paper were taped on for hair, aluminum foil became jewelry and armor, and fabric scraps were fashioned into capes and clothes. The kids liked to perform familiar fairy tales and mythological stories using the paper bag puppets to act out the scenes. We really enjoyed our impromptu, mobile theater.

- *Carschooling: 500 Games and Activities to Turn Travel Time into Learning Time* by Diane Keith (Prima Publishing, 2002)

Mirror, Mirror

Linda Dobson, Saranac Lake, New York

What child doesn't like looking at himself in a mirror? Take advantage of this and along with the mirror provide a piece of paper and colored pencils or crayons and he can create a self-portrait. Have your child create one a couple of times each year, and date the creations. Over time, the collection will reveal a lot about your child *to* your child.

Junkyard Wars

Maria Hammer, Marshall, Illinois

My son and I frequently play our own version of the popular The Learning Channel show *Junkyard Wars* with Legos on the sidewalk. I give him a certain number of Legos in various sizes and tell him to use only those to make a car, plane, seesaw, anything I can think of.

Shoe Box Puppet Stage and Puppets

Ann Lahrson Fisher, Carson, Washington

Turn a sturdy box such as a shoe box on its side and voilà! You have a miniature stage for simple stick or finger puppets. To make the puppets, draw and cut out paper puppet characters that suit the story. Make sure they're of a size that will fit proportionately to the stage box. Glue the characters to art sticks or tongue depressors and set them aside to dry. In the "stage floor" of the box, cut two or three slits (depending on the size and sturdiness of the box) through which the puppets can move on and off the stage. If you want to use finger puppets instead, cut a single and larger slot that is big enough that the characters can pop on and off the stage without having their limbs accidentally ripped off.

Now let your child decorate the stage to suit the play, using paint, paper, markers, or whatever materials suit the story. A simple outdoor scene of trees, hills, rocks, bushes, and flowers on the three walls will work for many stories. A generic indoor setting, with windows, curtains, pictures on the walls, and even some cutout cardboard furniture, can provide a backdrop for indoor settings. If your story requires both settings, make a box stage for each scene. Cut out furniture from stiff paper or cardboard and paint or color with markers.

Dig into your fabric scrap bag for materials suitable for a stage curtain. Cut out two rectangles, string them on heavy cord or a stick, and fasten to the front of the box. For a final touch, see if you can adapt a lamp or flashlight for "stage" lighting.

Now sit back and enjoy the show!

You've Got a Clue
Merelee Syron, New Egypt, New Jersey

We made a game of Clue using family members for people and places we've been instead of rooms. Make three piles of 8 index cards. One pile has pictures of family members, one pile has places, and one pile has weapons. We made pictures on all cards for non-readers. Along the edge of a piece of posterboard we made squares, using all 24 things on the cards, plus squares that said things like, "Vacation—go ahead three spaces."

We added funny captions under each person's picture on the gameboard, such as, "Has no alibi" and "Blood samples taken for DNA." It's much more exciting to find out that Grandma did it with a baseball bat at the Empire State Building than to learn it was Colonel Mustard in the conservatory.

Art Appreciation

Art Museum Scavenger Hunt
Jennifer Miller, Puyallup, Washington

To get the children *really* looking around, make a list of objects they can find in paintings, such as a red shoe, a sunflower, an apple. Have the children mark off each item they spot. The hunt can get more complicated as the children grow older.

Appreciating Architecture
LeCee Galmiche Johnson, New York, New York

We study the fabulous buildings in New York City by touring them. We take pictures of them and then draw and/or build them with papier-mâché. This is so fun and inexpensive and can be done anywhere.

Reviving the Masters
Jenny Reynolds, Coffs Harbour, New South Wales, Australia

We've been studying Vincent Van Gogh, and I wanted it to be something more. I found a calendar of masterpieces for two dollars at a bargain center, so I bought it. I love *The Irises*, so we chose to study that one first. I thought it would be nicer to frame it rather than pin it to the tack board, but we have limited resources. I rounded up the family and went to the local recycling center, where we all hunted for old picture frames.

For two dollars each we bought some very old and musty frames with dreadful prints displayed and took them home to begin the transformation. We pulled them apart, discarded the old print, washed and then sanded the frames, and cleaned the glass until it sparkled. Using acrylic folk art paints, we painted them in colors that would highlight the new print that would be housed within. If the frames were larger than the print, we used colored cardboard as a border for the print.

It was a Saturday's work for the entire family, and the results were wonderful. We now have some beautiful "paintings" adorning our schoolroom and home.

Everyone's an Art Critic

Rebecca Rupp, adapted from *The Complete Home Learning Source Book*

For this homemade game, our kids used a stack of index cards on which they drew symbols to represent either their personal opinion of an artwork (a gold star meant "I love it;" a black *X* meant "I hate it," a yellow sun meant the painting seemed happy or cheerful) or a description of the artwork (a tree for landscapes, a stick figure for portraits, a squiggle for abstract art, etc.). After they'd created a good-sized stack of cards, we worked our way through our collection of art prints and postcards, choosing symbols for each painting—which gave us a chance to discuss Rembrandt, Cezanne, Kandinsky, Van Gogh, Millet, Winslow Homer, Grandma Moses, and many more. The boys were so tickled with this one that they began drawing and critiquing their own pictures. We ended up with our own homemade art gallery in the hall.

- *The Complete Home Learning Source Book* by Rebecca Rupp (Three Rivers Press, 1998)

Performing Music

Months of Music Making

Calandra Johnson, Elgin, Oregon

As a former public school music teacher, I'd like to share an easy way to do music at home with the younger set. Buy or make a small drum, triangle, maracas (shakers), two sticks, whistle, tambourine, sand blocks, jingle bells, and so on. You're just creating different percussive sounds, so you could even use two pieces of silverware, pots, a box of rice or cereal to shake, a pan with a wooden spoon, or even a crystal glass to "ting." Small rhythm instruments box kits are available at your local musical instrument store.

Helpful Internet Art Sites

- Children's Art Activities Online: www.thegalleriesatmoore.org/actvitities/colorbook.shtml
- Children's Museum—World of Wonder: www.wowmuseum.com/Exhibits/Music.htm
- Children's Music Archive: judyanddavid.com/cma.html
- Crayola: www.crayola.com
- Education World: Visual and Performance Arts Center: www.educationworld.com/arts/music.shtml
- Freeware Humpherlinks: www.humph3.freeserve.co.uk/activities.html
- KinderArt: www.kinderart.com
- Meet the Masters: www.MeetTheMasters.com
- Music Activities: www.ecewebguide.com/music_activities.htm
- Pasta Play: www.pastaplay.com

What to do: Choose a nursery rhyme, folk song, or other favorite. Choose a special word in each phrase or sentence and have one special instrument play on that word.

Example: "Twinkle, Twinkle" could be the triangle playing on each syllable of the two words (total = four strikes). The rhyme is chanted or sung the entire time. "Star" and "are" could be the tambourine, "high" and "sky" could be a drum. Again, you strike the instrument for each syllable in the special word(s). Strive for precision and crispness. Create a small poster with the rhyme written out, and put a different colored box/line/triangle/squiggle/shape around or under the special words to make a visual map for the children to use.

The next step is to create a form or entire piece suitable for performing for visiting grandparents or Dad when he gets home. To do this, simply sing or chant the whole rhyme a certain number of times and do different combinations. For example, if you were doing your song five times in a row, the form could be as follows: first time, sing/chant the entire rhyme with no instruments; second, sing/chant with instruments playing on special words; third, mouth the words silently while playing instruments on special words; fourth, sing/chant while playing instruments on special words; fifth, sing/chant the entire rhyme with no instruments. The form of this arrangement would be ABCBA. A pause of silence at the end puts the musical finish on it, and you'll find yourself hearing delighted applause.

Search for books about Carl Orff's musical method to learn more. In Orff you actually do body sounds before transferring to the instruments. Usually snap, clap, pat thighs, or stomp foot on the special words. This also adds another option for your form arrangements: First time, sing only; second time, sing with body sounds on special words; third time, sing only; fourth time, sing with instruments on special words; fifth time, silently think or mouth words while playing only body or instruments on special words; sixth time, recorder plays melody with assigned instruments on special words. You could do this for months and months building repertoire, difficulty, and student input/ideas for your arrangements.

Homemade Rhythm Band Instruments

Ann Lahrson Fisher, Carson, Washington

Kids love to make music, singing and marching to tunes on favorite tapes and CDs, and playing simple instruments. Try making these simple rhythm instruments with them, and then get ready for a parade!

Oatmeal Box Drum

Turn the box upside down, poke two holes, about an inch below the bottom, on opposite sides, and string a cord or ribbon through the holes so that your child can wear her drum around her neck. Help your child decorate the box in any way that pleases her.

Beat the drum using hands or beaters. Listen for different sounds. Does the drum sound the same or different with the lid on the bottom or off? Turn the drum on its side and it becomes a log drum.

Drum Beaters

Anything will do—spoons, pens, pencils, Lincoln logs. Try them all out for different sounds and effects. A very nice beater can be made with a Superball and a piece of ¼-inch dowel. Using a drill bit that is slightly smaller than ¼ inch, drill a hole partway into the ball and jam a drumstick-length piece of doweling into the hole.

Sandpaper Blocks

If you have a couple of sandpaper blocks, go get them! If not, get a couple of pieces of wood that will fit in your child's hands comfortably and staple sandpaper to the wood blocks, scratchy sides out.

Sandpaper blocks can be brushed together to make a "shh-shh" sound reminiscent of a snare drum. They can also be clacked rhythmically while marching around the room. With practice, you can get both sounds, a "clack" followed by "shh."

Bottlecap Tambourine Sticks

Bottlecap tambourine sticks have a surprisingly pleasing sound and are fun to make. For each stick, you need three to five metal bottle caps, such as are found on beer bottles these days, nails of two sizes, and a stick. We used six- to eight-inch lengths of sticks cut from yard prunings that were about $1/2$ inch in diameter. You could also use a 1-inch square piece of wood that has been sanded smooth. The caps must first be flattened with a hammer, a job that your young child can help with. When the caps are very flat—flatter caps make a better sound—toss them on the barbecue and let them get very hot. This tempers the metal and improves the sound from a thud to a tone. Later, when the caps have cooled completely, take your larger nail and pierce each cap in its center. Then, using a smaller nail with a wide head (so the caps won't fly off the stick), nail the caps to the stick, making sure that they can move freely on the nail.

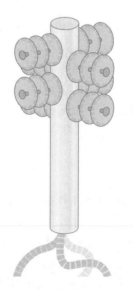

Leave it natural or decorate the tambourine stick as you wish, perhaps with colored electricians' tape, ribbons, tiny jingle bells, or streamers. Then march and shake.

Rubber Band Box Guitar

You'll need rubber bands of various sizes and a sturdy box about 4 to 6 inches across. Just stretch rubber bands of various sizes across the box. Each band can be tuned by tightening or loosening it. Large boxes are good for stretching bands tightly for higher pitches, but be careful or the rubber bands may snap.

Although this homemade instrument fits right into the rhythm band, it can be enjoyed on its own as well. Kids can explore the various tone qualities of different widths and sizes of rubber bands. They can make notes high and low by stretching and loosening the bands. They may enjoy trying to tune each band to tones on a real instrument. The rubber band guitar gives kids a chance to freely explore the rudimentary science of sound and string vibration.

Ankle Bells

Marching legs can make music, too. Sew the ends of a strip of elastic in a loop. Make the loop big enough so that it will stretch to fit over your child's shoe. Purchase some jingle bells from a craft store and help your child sew them to the elastic strip. Make one for each ankle.

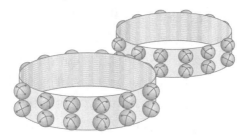

The "No Practice" Method

Jeanne Faulconer, Stanardsville, Virginia

My boys had a very negative experience with a piano teacher who wanted them to fill out practice records. She gave them candy when they practiced a certain number of minutes per day. This may work for some children, but my boys quickly lost interest in piano and became very anxious about the lessons. I found a new teacher who understood our goals for piano lessons: for the boys to be exposed to music and learn to enjoy it. We agreed there would not be pressure for practice. She even said that if they didn't practice at home, she would show them some good practice techniques during the next lesson.

One of my sons returned to lessons and flourished under the no practice method; after a few weeks he was playing at home all the time! We've moved to another state now, and I had to find another no practice teacher, but now that it was clear what I was looking for, it wasn't really that difficult.

The current teacher is a very accomplished musician and teacher who has some very advanced students. He doesn't pressure my son to practice. My son has discovered that when he practices more, he makes more progress and gets to enjoy more new music. He's also discovered that I will almost never call him to clean up the kitchen if he's playing the piano. At age thirteen, my oldest son sometimes has busy weeks when he doesn't practice as much, but he doesn't dread going to his lessons because now he won't be berated. Instead, he accepts that practice time ebbs and flows. If he chooses to try to become a stand-out musician, he will have to become more disciplined, and he recognizes this. If he continues to choose to play as a hobby, he will still get the benefits of what he is learning—which includes decoding written music, developing his ear for right and wrong notes, recognizing and appreciating culturally significant composers and music, brain development that may help him with spatial and mathematical skills (so the experts say), further development of fine motor skills, and an appreciation for the talent and skill it takes to achieve accomplishments in music. Not a bad consolation prize!

Musical Feelings

Jamie Miller, Roseville, California

Often it's easier for children to express themselves by drawing than by talking. To help children ponder the effect of music on emotions and, therefore, on how they feel as they listen to Mozart or Beethoven or another favorite, have them draw how they feel on big sheets of newspaper or the newsprint that you picked up at your local paper's printing facility.

Let's Get Started

Compare and contrast three different styles of music.

Family Music Night

Linda Dobson, Saranac Lake, New York

Will your family music night come in the middle of the week, or provide fun on the weekend? Find one of the many sources for making cheap instruments out of household items (many are described earlier in this chapter). If you play the banjo or the oboe, dust it off and join in. Recorders are a popular choice for children's first instruments, and younger children love keeping rhythm. Don't be surprised when everyone can't help but start singing and dancing, too.

Music Appreciation

Background Music: A Learning Tool
Hope Ware, Peoria, Illinois

For the very young there are the obvious action and nursery rhyme songs. We sing these every day in our circle time. However, we also use music in many other ways. For instance, when studying the letter *J*, the song "Jam and Jelly" became our theme song for the week. (And, of course, we also ate jam and jelly sandwiches every day for lunch.)

When our focus was South America in a two-week-long unit study, we borrowed tango music from our local library. When doing art or worksheets or having quiet play time, we listen to teaching songs that feature the sounds of the letters, days of the week, or months of the year. During reading time, we may select from a number of classical artists.

My boys have formed definite preferences for and opinions on their likes and dislikes. We try a variety to keep it interesting. When they get older, we'll study specific artists and styles, but they have already learned *so* much by hearing music in the background during our learning time.

More Background Music Ideas
Calandra Johnson, Elgin, Oregon

Switch to different radio stations for different types of music or choose a channel on your satellite dish (we love the Hawaiian and Latin channels). Put on a CD and choose the Repeat All feature. As soon as Mom is sick of that disk or has a free moment, switch the disk to something new. Put an older child in charge of the background music for a day. Thrift store records and record players are a cheap way to build your listening library, and at that price, you can set your kids free to explore for themselves.

Performing Arts

The Family Variety Show
Jennifer Miller, Puyallup, Washington

Our children like to plan variety shows for which my husband and I are the audience. We've also invited grandparents to watch our talented children perform. They've done everything from comedy routines and magic shows to poetry readings and dancing. They love to design tickets and posters promoting their upcoming show, and for the big night they get all dressed up.

Lights, Camera, Action!
Cristina Ramos-Payne, White Plains, New York

When my two children knew the story of *The Three Little Pigs* inside out, as well as many variations, they put together their own play that I recorded on our camcorder. Costumes were as simple as hats (to distinguish one pig from another when an actor played dual roles), construction paper rolled into a cone shape and tied with string for the wolf's nose, and one egg cup cut out of a carton for a pig nose. Add a playhouse, a pop-up tent, and a pile of sticks for the houses. The children enjoyed watching the play and showing it to family. For variation, I put music on and taped them dancing for their own music video.

Let's Put On a Play

Linda Spaulding, Pattersonville, New York

For the past six summers we've enjoyed producing and acting in our Home Educators Enrichment Group and Friends' productions of Shakespeare plays. The group had held book discussions for several years, and while reading *A Midsummer Night's Dream* one spring, my then eight-year-old daughter suggested we do it as a play. We got an abridged version by Leon Garfield and went from there.

We perform at one of those wooden fort playgrounds with built-in bleachers (although we did take some parts of *Midsummer* into the adjacent wooded area for the forest scenes and then back again). The process has evolved to where the children perform all aspects of the play, from acting to costuming and scenery. Homeschooled children get first dibs at the parts, then we allow friends to fill in. Everyone is required to memorize all their lines. We practice about once a week for the first six weeks, then two to three times each during the last two weeks. We invite parents and friends to attend, and last year some of the children played in a recorder ensemble prior to the beginning of the play.

Shakespearean Delight

Holly Furgason, Houston, Texas

My children, ages eight to seventeen, love Shakespeare! We introduced them to comedies first. We didn't teach them any vocabulary, discuss the plot, or read through the play first. Shakespeare was a playwright and his works are for "watching." We just found a good-quality video production of *The Taming of the Shrew*. The kids laughed all the way through! We actually had to limit the amount of time they could spend watching it.

One by one we added the other comedies. Before long they spoke fluent Shakespearese and translated for me. They soon grew interested in Shakespeare's histories and tragedies, too.

Bring Theater Home

Sandra Dodd, Albuquerque, New Mexico

Get videos of *Cats, The Nutcracker, The Pirates of Penzance, Cinderella* (the newer Disney musical, with dancing), *West Side Story, Singing in the Rain,* and *Little Shop of Horrors.* Follow up with live performances, as some children will be more interested in the staging than the story, some will care more about sound and lighting and curtains. Remember, as they get older, they may not want to go to the theater with Mom (says the mom of teenaged boys), so do it while they're young!

Find Free and Inexpensive Performances

Linda Spaulding, Pattersonville, New York

Attend local college orchestra and choir concerts; they're good and usually free. Attend plays and dance or music performances such as those at The Egg in Albany set up for school groups ($5 per ticket, one parent free). We also enjoy free concerts at the Troy Music Hall Music at Noon series, sitting in the expensive box seats eating lunch! Look in the local paper for notices of these events, talk with people in the community, and notify other homeschoolers through an e-mail list.

Let's Get Started

Find stencils related to one of your child's interests. Redecorate her bedroom walls.

General Art and Music

Quick Guide to Art and Music
Luz Shosie, Guilford, Connecticut

Get real materials and instruments, lessons and practice (if the kids choose), or just let them mess about with piano, recorder, ukulele, drum, clay, paint, seeing art and artists, acting, listening to music, dancing, and playing along.

Mixing Art and History
Jean Reed, Bridgewater, Maine, from *The Homeschool Source Book*

Our kids really enjoyed relating period art with their history reading. Period art coloring books are available from Bellerophon Books; they're sometimes slow to ship, so plan ahead.

- Bellerophon Books, P.O. Box 21307, Santa Barbara, California 93121; www.bellerophonbooks.com

Conversation Starters

- Are pictures really worth a thousand words?
- Actors spend their time being "somebody else." Would you like to do this? Why?
- If you could have dinner with a famous artist, past or present, who would you choose? What would you discuss?
- What are some examples of symmetry in nature?
- How many countries' national anthems do you know? What do you like or dislike about them? How are they similar or different?

8

Because Life's Important
Facts Aren't
Just Academic

Having spent our own compulsory time in the school institution, many of us, as eager, energetic young adults proclaiming independence from family to make our own way, couldn't wait to get into the real world. While we spent our time in school dutifully exposed to geometry, modern world history, and chemistry, how many of us walked away knowing how to do our own laundry, change our car's oil, or invest our money? If you picked up these and 1,001 other necessary skills for real-world survival as a child in your home, consider yourself lucky. Many more of us entered the real world lacking numerous useful skills.

While the media continues to share news about homeschooling primarily through stories of impressive academic performance, the children are learning other lessons that are at least equally if not more valuable as they grow up in the real world. As you move closer to education mind, remember that a child's life isn't just about good report cards and getting on the right sports team. It's also about becoming a polite, honest, thinking adult capable of independent thought, word, and deed. Not only does this serve the individual and society in the long run, but it's the direction in which children's natural inclinations point them.

The urge for independence grows right along with children. I believe that many of the troubles experienced by children in middle and high schools are induced by the schools. That is, the external forces of control and constant state of dependency on others directly contradict the internal forces pushing in the opposite direction. This is a recipe for frustration, the same frustration that allows a trapped animal to chew off its extremity to escape a snare. Add to this the fact that necessary life skills are all but ignored, and you can throw inability to handle the frustration into the mix.

I was not at all surprised to see how many of the ideas submitted under the "life skills" category related to becoming a better person. Even though I know homeschoolers spend a lot of time in the kitchen and enjoying housework with their offspring, they were obviously more eager to share ideas about learning kindness, responsibility, volunteering, cooperation, manners, sense of community, and going the extra mile. In addition, we've included several ideas to help improve listening skills, as the ability to understand the other person's side of an issue also contributes to character.

Here you'll find household ideas, including cooking, sewing, and carpentry. Also included are tips about physical education and health and safety issues. Because computer and library use are integral aspects of a lifetime of learning, we've collected some great ideas about them. Finally, although it may not typically be considered a life skill, we've thrown in a couple of fun ways to improve memory skills (which I will be sure to highlight in my own copy of this book!).

Especially during the early years, children watch you very closely as you go about taking care of business at home. Seize an opportunity—take a few minutes to include your children in whatever you're doing, talk about it, and answer any questions as you work together.

You are, after all, their first teacher; by example, you will also become their very best.

Becoming a Better Person

Powerful Cooperation Illustration
Shay Seaborne, Woodbridge, Virginia

Find two similar transparent containers and some glass "jewels" or other small, attractive items. Put about half the jewels in each container. Call or label the containers You and Me. Transfer jewels from the Me container while talking about positive things you do for the child. When the container is empty, show the child there are no more jewels to give. Depending on the child's ability, ask the child to think of things she could do to put jewels back in the Me container, or use some examples, such as helping to set the table or doing your morning chores without needing a reminder.

The Extra Mile
Sandra Dodd, Albuquerque, New Mexico

When we pick up our trash after a movie or in a clear-your-own-table restaurant, we pick up extras, things that someone else left, too.

When we go into a store, we push in a shopping cart or two from the parking lot. When at the park, if stickers are growing, we dig them out and put them in the trash so little children won't get stickers later, or we pick up broken glass. Because it's become automatic, it's no sacrifice, and the kids have the satisfaction of knowing that other people's worlds are a bit nicer because they were there.

Earning Their Way

Colleen Senko, Terrebonne, Oregon

Let's Get Started

Help your child prepare and record interviews with neighbors about their work.

We don't buy toys for the kids. They earn money with extra chores: helping with yard work, baby-sitting, painting, and big cleaning projects. In addition, they have normal everyday chores, such as making the bed, brushing their teeth, and finishing all homework assignments, that bring them additional allowance. They get the most enjoyment from planning a purchase, and a toy is more than a toy when they buy it themselves.

Sniping Cessation

Sherry Dolash, Calgary, Alberta, Canada

When we find we're sniping at each other due to whatever reason, we stop and take the time to say five nice things about the other person or about each family member. This helps us see the other person or persons in a new way. Also, by the time we've thought about five nice things, the bickering or hard feelings have disappeared. My children have even reminded me to use this technique when I'm complaining about what someone else has done. It makes one stop and think.

Christmas Eve Tradition of Community Service
Athena Dalrymple, Columbia, Maryland

Each Christmas Eve, drop off gift-wrapped new or almost-new books at a nearby hospital for the children who happen to be there that day or the next to have a little something to read and be cheered up. Write on the gift wrap or on a separate list the approximate age for which the book is appropriate and maybe a little something about it (sports trivia, scratch-and-sniff, mystery, etc.), so the books can be well matched to the children.

Some hospitals allow the children who drop off books to visit the patients, but others will not, due to confidentiality and infection control. We've found hospitals that are *not* children's hospitals to be the better place to perform this service, as children's hospitals tend to get a lot for children at this time of year. Additionally, they have trouble deciding which twenty or thirty (or however many books you are donating) children to whom to give the books when they have hundreds of patients, where other hospitals often have very few children on Christmas Eve and thus will have enough to go around even a few days after Christmas.

Learning to Fly
Debbie Eaton, Rock Tavern, New York

For a different, albeit difficult, activity, consider the many benefits of "flying." Learning the flying trapeze is said to help people overcome fears, develop trust and self-confidence, and build athletic ability, including strength, agility, timing, balance, and rhythm. Children can continue to move on to higher and higher levels of practice if they choose.

- *Learning to Fly: Reflections on Fear, Trust, and the Joy of Letting Go* by Sam Keen (Bantam Doubleday Dell, 2000)

Soul Building

Colleen Senko, Terrebonne, Oregon

A ninety-year-old neighbor was being cared for full time by her daughter. The stress of not being able to ever leave even to get milk or run simple errands wore her to a frazzle. My son offered to "grandma sit," and the job grew through the years as he was able to handle more responsibility. Eventually, the daughter had more freedom and my son earned money and an irreplaceable spot in grandma's heart. Calibrating meds, health, and diet lessons were bonuses of the experience.

Responsibility for Furry Friends

Debbie Eaton, Rock Tavern, New York

One of the most fun things kids can do is care for animals if they want to. Homeschooling creates a unique environment in which the kids get to develop a relationship with their animals that couldn't happen if they were in school—at least not to this degree. Care of animals develops discipline and a feeling that the children are needed by something fairly helpless without them.

Children learn lessons about life as they watch the animal's stages of development, culminating in the animal's passing that helps them perhaps consider physical mortality. This can assist in mental, emotional, and spiritual growth.

2001 Top Ten Web Sites

Out of the millions out there on the Internet, I try to choose only the best Web sites for each newsletter. Here is my top ten list of favorite Web sites from 2001:

1. K–12 Teaching and Learning Center: www.k12tlc.org
2. Autodidactic Press: www.autodidactic.com
3. Math lessons: math.rice.edu/%7Elanius/Lessons
4. Kids Konnect: www.kidskonnect.com
5. The Green Frog News: www.thegreenfrognews.com
6. Sodaplay: www.sodaplay.com/index.htm
7. One World-Nations Online: www.nationsonline.org/oneworld
8. Absurd Math: www.learningwave.com/abmath
9. Enchanted Learning: www.enchantedlearning.com
10. How Stuff Works: www.howstuffworks.com

—*Carol Narigon (Ed.)*, Home Education Magazine Online News, *January 2002.*

They learn about feeding the animal to maintain optimal health, and veterinary care when the animal is less healthy. If the child chooses to sell offspring, this interest can become a small business. We compare the physical characteristics of animals and people, and study the history of the animal that is our pet. We learn about the different personalities of animals within certain species, and the different characteristics of animals from different species, as well as their unique needs. This, of course, can become a springboard to many areas of study.

Tithing

Tara Hall, Colliersville, Tennessee

To help show a young child how tithing works, have him put 10 percent of his allowance into a fund. Once it reaches a set amount, take him shopping to buy necessities for children—crayons, shoes, tooth-brushes, and so on. Arrange for him to give them to a family in need or a shelter. Have your child be on the lookout for ideas—you'll be amazed at how thoughtful he is and how he becomes sensitive to the needs of others.

Volunteer in a Soup Kitchen

Linda Spaulding, Pattersonville, New York

Often volunteers come from local religious organizations. Call one and ask if they participate, or call the Salvation Army to see if they sponsor a soup kitchen and hook up with a group that is already volunteering. Start your own group if they have need of an additional crew. As a volunteer, you help cook the meal, serve it, and clean up.

Some groups may be reluctant or simply not willing to allow children to do anything the adults do. That's what happened with the first group we joined, so we quit that and found another group that welcomed the kids. People who come to eat love seeing them there. We're on the schedule for once every six weeks.

Surrogate Grandchildren

Athena Dalrymple, Columbia, Maryland

Go to a nearby retirement home and offer to make weekly visits to a few residents there. Your child can read to the residents, play an instrument for them (so long as it's not too loud), do magic tricks, or just tell them about his activities of the past week.

Manners

Visitors from Another Culture
Luz Shosie, Guilford, Connecticut

Have you ever noticed how rude some folks can be when teaching children manners? John Holt's advice was to act as if children are visitors from another culture. They don't know all the rules, but they want to be like the grown-ups. If they're treated with respect and kindness, they'll learn to be respectful and kind. We never told our son to say "please" and "thank you" (or "say the magic words"), yet he grew up to be one of the most polite teenagers I ever knew.

Ladies Prefer Gentlemen
Hope Ware, Peoria, Illinois

When our son, James, was about three years old, my husband had a talk with him one night. My husband made it out to be a really, really, cool secret thing. He told James that there is something very special he can be when he grows up—a gentleman.

My husband proceeded to tell him all the cool things that gentlemen do, like sit up at the table and always chew with their mouths closed. They get to be pleasant to others. He gave him a whole list as if he were teaching James a secret code! He assured James that others would notice and say, "There's James Ware—*he's* a gentleman." James *begged* for more information on exactly what gentlemen were and what they do.

After the talk, when James did something ungentlemanly, we would just say, "James, a gentleman would never do that. Here's what a gentleman would do," and then explain the best behavior.

From Burkina Faso

Our move to West Africa, Burkina Faso, and our departure from Western Europe is for our family a huge learning experience. We moved here three months ago because it's not possible to home-school my children, ages two and five, in the Netherlands.

As we eat the local food, which is cheap, healthy, and nutri-tious, we learn how food is prepared. We learn through the people that work for us, the garden, and the climate. It is the month of Ramadan now, and that makes us talk about Islam and why people don't eat or drink during the day. We bought an African drum and will look for other instruments.

Because I'm a single mother with no friends or relatives here, the fact that we're left to our own devices is a great learning experi-ence. I tell my children about mistakes I've made, for instance, when I deal with people and situations. Even if we only spend a year or two here, we will have learned a great deal.

—Soline Weidema, Ouagadougou, Burkina Faso

For weeks James repeated the gentleman rules to me. "Mommy, I'm not going to do _____ because a *gentleman* would never do that!" He's nearly five years old now and we continue to use the same method, as it seems to be working very well.

Beyond Please and Thank You
Sandra Dodd, Albuquerque, New Mexico

We've taught our children the basics—introductions, thanks, re-sponses to sneezes and such—and they know that etiquette has to do with making other people comfortable and with maneuvering within social situations without making waves. But fancier things I show them by pointing out examples both good and bad when we're out and about, or watching movies, or reading books.

Younger Holly would often ask, "What should I have said when she said, 'I like your dress'?" or other such courtesy-stumpers. Discussing what could make real or imagined situations better has worked for us.

Physical Education

Share the Fitness Club

Andrea Hargreaves, San Antonio, Texas

We use our membership to a fitness club for physical education. The children are allowed to swim during certain hours of each day, and they're also allowed to use the racquetball courts. It saves me from having to pay for those things, plus I get to work out and use the free babysitting service, on some days saving my sanity.

Aikido

Debbie Eaton, Rock Tavern, New York

There are great benefits to aikido, a martial art that focuses on defending oneself but not injuring the other party unless it is absolutely necessary. A spiritual philosophy attends the practice if one finds a good teacher, and exercises are designed to improve alertness, being in the moment, and listening, among others.

- *The Spirit of Aikido* by Kisshomau Ueshiba (Kodansha America, 1998)

Shaving Cream Ice

Kathy Borsari, Plymouth, Massachusetts

Spray shaving cream all over the kitchen floor and let the children go "ice skating." This is how we often celebrate the first day of school.

Horseback Riding

Debbie Eaton, Rock Tavern, New York

If a child can control a horse, he can often acquire a higher degree of self-control. I studied the art of riding for many years and have fond memories of it. I was in a position to have my own horse, and I set goals for myself and achieved them. This kept me from involving myself with school activities that may have led to more unhealthy practices. I wasn't involved in drugs or drinking because I was an athlete. I also developed a relationship with the animal that I ended up exhibiting, and I had to be organized to accomplish these activities. I met many people outside my school and developed social connections. I also developed an inner discipline in caring for the animals because of my motivation to reach my goals. I enjoyed it and did it without prodding.

4-H is a good organization to belong to, for it assists children with learning about animals. These days, there is much information on the Internet and good Web sites on alternative health for animals.

Famous Fitness

Calandra Johnson, Elgin, Oregon

Let the kids choose songs and design exercise routines to them. Videotape them when they're done, and then use the tapes for winter workouts. Kids *love* seeing themselves on television. Encourage appropriate "costumes" and unusual environments for extra fun.

Try a New Sport Together

Linda Dobson, Saranac Lake, New York

While you may not have enough family members to create a football team, you can pick up a croquet set, volleyball and net, or horseshoes. Maybe you'd prefer swimming or tae kwan do or long jumping as a group. Research together a sport in which none of you have ever participated, then enjoy trying it for the first time as a family. If after a fair trial you find you like it, use all opportunities to find and read more about rules, techniques, methods, famous players, and so on. Find related Web sites and magazines, and watch for newspaper articles.

Play Chess with Armor On

Debbie Eaton, Rock Tavern, New York

We are now engaged in the art of fencing, which has been described by our instructor as "playing chess with armor on." It develops endurance, stamina, cardiovascular fitness, and reflex responses. Children can meet other children and practice with them.

- *Foil Fencing*, 4th ed., by Muriel Bower (Wm. Brown, 1980)

Household

Sewing Boards

Amy De Rusha, Somersworth, New Hampshire

To teach the girls how to sew, we cut cardboard into various shapes and, using colorful electrical tape, taped the edges to make them pretty. Around the edges we punched holes. I cut a long piece of yarn and taped one end to become a needle. Once the shapes have been sewn, the girls go through old magazines, cut out pictures they like, and glue them to the boards.

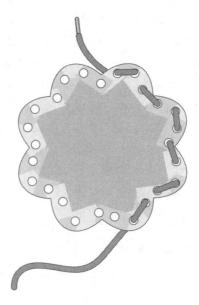

The Secret's in the Learning

Jennifer Miller, Puyallup, Washington

I bought my son a children's cookbook and told him that one night a week he could plan a meal and prepare it for the entire family. He loved that, poring over the pages of the book each week trying to plan the perfect meal.

He would write out his menu on paper. I asked him to make me a shopping list so I could be sure we had everything we needed for him to whip up his dinner. He checked the pantry to see what we had and then made a list of the things we needed. Many times he invited his grandparents over to enjoy his culinary delights. At just eleven years of age now, he's quite capable in the kitchen.

The Science of Laundry

It's interesting what you learn when you homeschool seven children. One of the lessons is that laundry never ends, and another is that there is a bountiful science lesson in every load.

My five-year-old daughter Jessica's knit top with ribs is dotted with dandelion "wishes" from a few days ago when we were blowing them (yes, our neighbors love us) and talking about seeds. Another shirt has a grass stain on the back from the day we lay in the grass looking up at the seeds that look like helicopters, thousands of them, adorning the maple tree. We talked about how, when they're at just the right readiness, they will float to earth to become little maple trees if they land in the perfect spot.

Then there's that other shirt, the white one with the peach stains. Jessica was on a roll that week, coming to me with the peach pit wrapped in her shirt. "Is this a seed, too?" she asked. We explored the working of a peach pit, why we couldn't grow a peach tree from that particular pit, and talked about our weather and the kind of weather peaches like. I hunted down the pictures of our family picking peaches, and we opened a jar of canned peaches from that trip last year. During the peach conversation, Jessica made the connection that the wishes, helicopters, and the pits were all seeds, different but equally important.

Yep, there is science in the laundry. This week it was botany. Next week? I'm hoping it isn't about exploring the invertebrates that fit into pockets. I know Jessica will lead me to something though.

—*Mary Lamken, Bothell, Washington*

Extended Baking Experience
Ruth Dunnavan, Moultonborough, New Hampshire

I tried baking with my children when they were little, but their attention waned long before the baking was done. I found that if I fixed the dry ingredients with them one day, the wet ingredients the next, and assembled the ingredients on a third day, we completed the project with ease.

Cook Up a Christmas Gift

Colleen D. Williams, Toccoa, Georgia

Starting in September or so, contact all of your relatives and ask for their favorite recipes. Have them sent to you by a deadline, say by October 31. Take these recipes and sort by type. We used main dishes, appetizers, desserts, and sweets (this was a biggy!).

We typed all the recipes into a readable format and credited the contributor after each one. My oldest son used Paintbrush software and designed a cover of a Christmas tree with all the relatives' last names inside a decoration ball and hung it on the tree. As a gift for every family, we printed and mailed a copy of the eight-page cookbook. Over the years it has become incredibly handy because *all* the family favorites are in one book.

Themes for cookbook collections are endless: birthdays, Hanukkah, major U.S. holidays, Fourth of July picnic ideas, and so on.

I Can't Believe It's Butter!

Jennifer Miller, Puyallup, Washington

My kids love to make the butter for Thanksgiving dinner. We put whipping cream in a mayonnaise jar with a marble to help churn it. They take turns shaking the jar, jumping up and down with it, doing a little dance, and a while later after plenty of exercise, we have butter.

We put the butter in a cookie press and press out cute shapes onto waxed paper and refrigerate them. Before dinner we cut out little squares and put the pads of butter on a fancy plate. They love presenting their contribution to the family gathering.

How Much for the House?

Athena Dalrymple, Columbia, Maryland

Give your children a real estate magazine and have them look at the photo of the house and read the description, then guess the list price.

Let 'em Help!

Pam Jorrick, Korbel, California

Letting kids help when they're at the age when they actually *want* to may take more time and patience in the beginning, but it makes them feel important and forms the habit of pitching in. I'm convinced that in the long run, it's a lot easier than trying to force them to learn chores when they're older.

Real Tools

Jeanne Faulconer, Stanardsville, Virginia

We set up a workbench and got real tools, even for our youngest son. All the boys helped us with basic household projects. We helped them with building simple items like a birdhouse and a toolbox. We salvaged scrap lumber from the builder who built our house and got even more scraps from him as he began building in another neighborhood.

Household Finances

Athena Dalrymple, Columbia, Maryland

While making it clear what is confidential so that the child doesn't announce the family income in passing, share all household financial information, and explain why certain mortgages were picked over others. We gave our son the printouts of certain year terms with certain interest rates and pointed out what each would mean in total interest likely to be paid if the mortgage actually went full term and wasn't paid off early. We discussed why you pay off credit cards in full each month (or why you don't), how we picked the amount of life insurance on each parent, and how we picked the retirement investment funds and other investment funds and how often we contribute what amount to which funds. We also note where the money is going over a weekly/monthly/annual basis. Quicken is good software for printing this out and seeing pie charts, bar graphs, and the like.

Recycling

Pennie Rowland, Lake Oswego, Oregon

Recycling information is as close as a drive around town. As we drive, we look at the environment and discuss landfills, junkyards, and how trash is disposed of. This gives the children an open-eyed approach to trash, and they learn how important it is to take recycling seriously.

Health and Safety

You Are What You Eat

Maria Hammer, Marshall, Illinois

This project goes well with a study of the food pyramid. You will need

- Construction paper (one piece for each person)
- Food stickers or colored stars (available at teacher and office supply stores)

Label each piece of paper with a person's name, then write "Breakfast," "Lunch," "Dinner," and "Snacks" down the left side. For whatever foods are eaten for that meal, place one sticker for each serving. Older children can add "Water," "Exercise," and "Sleep" for added focus on general health. Whichever type of stickers you use, be sure to post a key for your children's reference.

This opened our eyes to what (and how much!) we were really eating.

JAMES

Breakfast ☆☆

Lunch ☆☆☆☆

Dinner ☆☆☆☆

Water ☆☆☆

Track Food to Its Source

Linda Dobson, Saranac Lake, New York

While you're at the grocery store, choose one each of a processed and a fresh food. With your children, trace each product back to its source, perhaps charting the steps required to get the food from farm to table. What happens to the food at each step? Which food takes the longest to get to you? Which is healthier? Why? A lot more questions can be asked.

Let's Get Started

Let your child help in the kitchen as much as possible.

Battle Wounds

Dotchi Baker, Ten Mile, Tennessee

Mixing together petroleum jelly and red food dye we made pretend battle wounds by laying a piece of tissue paper on the skin and dropping this wound goo on the tissue. We then practiced first aid on our imaginary injuries.

We measured the bandage tape to see which size fit over the wound best. We measured the ingredients for the wound goo and figured out how much one-third of the wound goo was (there were three of us), and my son pointed out all the sight words he knew from the first aid manual. The best part came when my youngest son really did cut himself on the foot one day and his six-year-old big brother knew exactly what to do while I was still running to the scene of the accident—he even measured the tape to the optimum size for the bandage.

Home Inventory

Edventure's Technological Literacy News, November 16, 2001

Have children make a list of items in the home that they perceive as having a medical application. Examples are toothbrushes, vitamins, massagers, and so on. Respect privacy issues regarding prescription medicines, but encourage the children to get creative on other fronts. For example, is "dandruff shampoo" a medical technology?

Review and discuss the lists. Extend the activity by separating the medical technologies you've identified into categories. What disciplines were required to invent, design, and produce these technologies—biological, mechanical, electrical, other?

Neighborhood Vexillology

Diane Keith, Redwood City, California

Vexillology is the study of maps. When my children were about six and eight years old, they loved to ride their bikes up and down the sidewalk in front of our home. As they gained skill in bike riding, they wanted to expand their boundaries. My husband, Cliff, agreed that they could ride around the block without crossing any streets. He photocopied two maps of our neighborhood (one for each boy) and highlighted the approved route and boundaries to show the boys where they could ride their bikes safely. He took them in the car and drove around our very long block, pointing out the street names and landmarks, and again showed the boys where each of these things were on their maps. Then, referring to the maps frequently, he rode a bike along with them to show them the new route.

As the boys grew older and became proficient bike riders, they occasionally asked for their boundaries to be increased. Each time, my husband repeated the procedure he initially developed. He and the boys would agree on safe parameters, and then he would show them how to map out their approved bike-riding boundaries, and explore the new route with them. Eventually, their boundaries increased to within a one-mile radius of our home, then a five-mile radius, and eventually we eliminated boundaries and simply agreed to certain routes, depending on where they were going. The reason my husband initiated this process was twofold: he would always know where to begin to look for the kids in case of an emergency, and he wanted to teach them how to use maps and landmarks to find their way. The result? Both boys are adept map readers and have an uncanny sense of direction.

- www.maps.com: free, printable, custom-tailored maps to suit your geographical needs

What If?

Judith Waite Allee and Melissa L. Morgan, from *Educational Travel on a Shoestring*

As a young girl, Judith's daughter, Nancy, loved to play "What If" during car trips. While the game was entertaining and thought provoking, the subject matter was serious: What could Nancy do if there was some kind of emergency? Both mom and daughter came up with new what ifs all the time, and over the years the game triggered many thoughtful discussions on difficult topics.

The game can be played while standing in line, waiting for tickets, or during hours in a car, train, plane, or bus. Here are a few what ifs to get you started:

- What if we get separated (including where would we meet)?

- What if a stranger asks you for directions?

- What if we get robbed?

- What if you find a strange package?

- What if you get lost in a strange city?

- What if someone wants to take your picture?

- What if someone threatens to hurt you or your parents if you tell anyone what he or she did?

- What if we have a car accident? What would happen next?

Parents cannot anticipate every possible scenario, but we can help our kids rehearse some of the more common situations that they might encounter and help them develop problem-solving skills.

- *Educational Travel on a Shoestring* by Judith Waite Allee and Melissa L. Morgan (Shaw Books, 2002)

Listening Skills

Listen
Luz Shosie, Guilford, Connecticut

How do you teach your children to be good listeners? Listen to them! Take time to give your undivided attention and simply listen—without correcting, arguing, trying to "teach" anything. You'll learn a lot.

Legos for Listening
Linda Dobson, Saranac Lake, New York

Give two children the same number and sizes of pieces of Legos or any other building set with lots of duplicate pieces. Have them sit back to back or in another way in which they can hear but can't see each other. Ask one child to build something from his pieces. Now the fun begins.

This child must give directions to the other child so that she can build the same thing—no peeking! Have the children take turns building and giving directions. Watch them try hard to figure out what went wrong, and communicate better the next time.

As the children grow and/or get better at the game, you can set a time limit and/or add more pieces to build a more complex model.

Computer Use

Combining Language and Keyboarding Skills
Fiona Bayrock, Chilliwack, British Columbia, Canada

Help your child find an e-mail buddy with whom she can correspond. Most kids love to send and receive mail, and e-mail is no different. When she's writing to a friend, suddenly she has a need to spell and punctuate correctly. Proofreading can be a real drag, but if you do it early, talking about what you're doing and why, soon she'll understand what to look for and get in the habit of doing her own proofreading.

Combining Socialization and Computer Literacy

Jeanne Faulconer, Stanardsville, Virginia

We had a more computer-savvy homeschool friend help our son set up his own home page—computer skills and socialization in one step!

Getting Ready for Databases

Ruth Dunnavan, Moultonborough, New Hampshire

When my children were preschoolers, we made a database of all of their friends. For several days we collected information on their stuffed animals, Barbies, fast-food toys, and whatever else we found. We set up database fields for the toys' names, heights, hair colors, and "favorite foods." We spent lots of time discussing what we should enter, and as a bonus, the kids practiced measuring the dolls with a tape measure.

Research Race

Athena Dalrymple, Columbia, Maryland

If you happen to have side-by-side computers, race to see who can most quickly find the answer to a pending question. This doesn't need to be limited to finding a Web site that has an answer, but could also include finding someone to whom to send an e-mail if she is able to quickly get back with the answer or where the answer may be found.

The Essential Internet

Cindy Allas, Fairfield, California

Whether it's looking up materials from the library, doing a search for lesson plans and activities for a unit study, finding book lists for good reading, discovering interactive or printable worksheets, finding answers, or building our reference material, the Internet is indispensable.

If They Don't Like to Write It Down . . .

Shelly Wilson, Cameron Park, California

Our six-year-old enjoys playing Reader Rabbit's Math (ages 6–9) game. One of the activities involves adding money, but the concept stumped him, especially as the amount grew larger or involved carrying. My pencil-and-paper explanations helped him see the whole concept and arrive at the correct answer. However, he isn't inclined to write things down, so his frustration grew.

I purchased a few packs of magnetic numbers that included all the function symbols at the dollar store. I showed him how to set up the problem on the table next to the computer, and by manipulating and seeing the numbers, he could get answers without my help.

Remember to keep magnets away from the computer, or simply remove the magnets. They're not strong, but there's no reason to take any chances.

Tons, Tons, Tons of Information

Jane Powell, Bowie, Maryland

Having a computer is just about a *must* for homeschoolers.

- Looking for information? Try about.com, or go to google .com and see what Web sites can help.

- Need lesson ideas? Go to familyeducation.com and look around. They supply recommended reading lists, ideas for teachers, TAG tips, ADD tips, and more.

- Looking for community? My favorites are ivillage.com, parentsoup.com, and homeschool.com. Those women are savvy, smart, and some of the most creative and dedicated minds I have ever come across. They offer message boards where you can post ideas, questions, offer advice, and they supply archives (they keep all the great information) and search features (you can type in a word you're looking for and find everything that's ever been written about it).

- Try nickjr.com and pbskids.org for teaching ideas and program listings. PBS is known for quality programming, and this site will help fuel your viewing choices, which you can tape and view at your convenience.

- Free e-mail addresses are available from hotmail.com, ivillage.com, excite.com, onebox.com, yahoo.com, and more. Be sure to read the terms of use, storage limits, and how long your messages are retained when you sign up. Sometimes it's handy to have a separate e-mail address to receive newsletters and other nonurgent mail where you can read it when you get a chance versus crowding your regular address with everything.

- Efax.com offers free fax service. They provide a local phone number where you can receive faxes, they send e-mail notification that you have a fax, and then, after downloading their software, you can read it. They charge a fee for sending faxes.

11 Evans News
Stasia Penkofflidbeck, Essex, Connecticut

Our sixth-grader, Anastasia, records her own educational progress by producing a biweekly newsletter called *11 Evans News* on the computer. Each curricular subject is chronicled, as are special events and field trips. We parents have our own column in which we highlight our daughter's progress and achievement.

She uses a digital camera to include images of her doing things, how-to photos in science labs, and artwork from a homeschool art class. She uses Adobe PageMaker, but you can also use Microsoft Word or AppleWorks.

Along the way she learned how to turn an interview into a profile piece, how to catch a reader with good headlines and "gotcha" opening paragraphs, and how to use visual layout techniques for text, graphics, and images. She has honed her writing and editing skills and learned how to meet a deadline. She uses the computer, digital camera, scanner, and the Internet with increasing acumen. Finally, the newsletter is a running record of progress and a part of her portfolio that can be shown to others.

Using the Library

Decipher the Dewey
Calandra Johnson, Elgin, Oregon

Each child chooses one to three library books from the nonfiction section. While

Let's Get Started

Visit your library weekly.

you temporarily cover the Dewey Decimal System number, the other children look at the book and try to guess its Dewey number as closely as they can. They can score points for closeness. For example, if a book's number is 609.43 and the closest guess was 605, that person's score is 4.43. Low score wins. Of course, the kids can add, subtract, and use decimals, also making this a math lesson.

Location of Learning Materials
Ruth Dunnavan, Moultonborough, New Hampshire

My daughter was a library aide one summer. One of her jobs was to "adopt a shelf." Each week she was expected to check her shelf and rearrange any books that were out of order. She quickly learned the location of many materials.

Memory Skills

How Do I Get There?
Lisa Herring, Placerville, California

Between classes, errands, and field trips, we spend a lot of time in the car. To help my first-grader work on both directions and memory skills, I have him tell me how to get to our next destination. As a result, he remembers the difference between left and right easily, and he's very aware of the layout of our town.

Bear Hunt Game
Judith Waite Allee and Melissa L. Morgan, from *Educational Travel on a Shoestring*

This game is a fun way to develop memory skills. You may know it in a different version, because it's as old as the hills. The first person

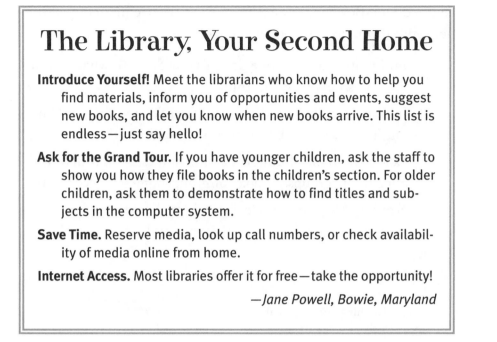

The Library, Your Second Home

Introduce Yourself! Meet the librarians who know how to help you find materials, inform you of opportunities and events, suggest new books, and let you know when new books arrive. This list is endless—just say hello!

Ask for the Grand Tour. If you have younger children, ask the staff to show you how they file books in the children's section. For older children, ask them to demonstrate how to find titles and subjects in the computer system.

Save Time. Reserve media, look up call numbers, or check availability of media online from home.

Internet Access. Most libraries offer it for free—take the opportunity!

—Jane Powell, Bowie, Maryland

says, "I'm going on a bear hunt, and I'm bringing . . ." and he names a serious item, like a sleeping bag, or a silly item, like a jump rope. Each person says the same thing, including the items already added, and adds one more. Children do get better as they practice.

- *Educational Travel on a Shoestring* by Judith Waite Allee and Melissa L. Morgan (Shaw Books, 2002)

Helpful Organizations

Lone Scouts and Independent Girl Scouts

Kimberly Goza, traveling somewhere in the U.S.A.

Here are a couple of little known facts about scouting. You can join either Boy or Girl Scouts organizations and *not* belong to a troop, if you so desire. Boy Scouts are a bit more restrictive in their qualifications, but if you homeschool, you qualify.

- Information about Lone Scouts (Boy Scouts): www.scouting.org/factsheets/02-515.html
- Information about Independent Girl Scouts: www.girlscouts.org/faqs/parents_guardians.html#members_notroop
- Yahoo group for all Boy Scouts who homeschool, with or without a troop: groups.yahoo.com/group/homeschooledscouts
- *Scouting Magazine* article about Lone Scouts: www.scoutingmagazine.org/archives/0110/a-lone.html

4-H

Aileen Aidnik, Shingle Springs, California

4-H is based on hands-on learning, so it really fits in with homeschooling! The children can take any project they want and learn as much as they want. Keeping the 4-H record book involves English, spelling, and grammar; keeping track of expenses associated with a project is math; and the various projects fit into fine arts, science, math, and social studies/geography. Leadership skills are a big part of the program, as is learning to do presentations or demonstrations in front of a group, something a homeschooled child could miss out on otherwise.

Last year my daughter, Shayna, raised rabbits (science and math), made Ukrainian eggs (fine arts and Russian history), participated in international cooking (math, science, home economics), did square dancing (physical education and history), was a junior leader for "Chocolate, Chocolate, Chocolate" (leadership skills, planning meetings, and learning goals). The cooking project sparked her interest in creating chocolate desserts, and she ended up taking several classes from professional chefs at a local cooking store/school.

She is also heavily involved in community service activities, initiated a project in which our county clubs participated, and, as a result of that, arranged to volunteer on her own at a local convalescent hospital for four to eight hours each week. That experience taught her skills and gave her a glimpse of her potentials she never realized were there.

Conversation Starters

- Where would you like to live when you grow up? What's nice about this place?

- What are the important things in life?

- Is it better to put money in a savings account or to invest it where it can possibly earn more interest—or be lost?

- What are you good at doing? What occupations would allow you to best use your skills?

- Over humanity's history, how has cooking changed? How do you think you might prepare food when you're a grandparent?

9

Especially Cheap,
Exceptionally Quick
and Easy, or Great
for Groups

Among the top ten questions continually asked about homeschooling, the one about money remains near the top: How much does it cost? Using school mind, the questioner's assumption is, of course, that there is a correlation between what public schools spend to educate a child and what one must spend at home to educate the same child.

Ever-increasing chunks of your school taxes support the system, not education. Education is no more expensive than it is complicated. Even so, because they are only human *and* often live on less, homeschooling families love a bargain when they can find one, and you've just found dozens!

The activities included in this chapter cover the gamut of academic learning. Those in the first section are notable as low or no-cost ways to combine fun and learning. Many are ways to make your own educational resources instead of running to a store where you'd pay top dollar for them. Not only does the do-it-yourself approach save money, but you and your children can lend your own brand of originality to your creations.

Here you'll also find leads to materials that are free for the taking, tips about what not to buy (with suggestions for replacement), and the programs of nonprofit organizations that are chock full of learning.

Once you really get into the learning-at-home-is-fun mode, you'll realize that just like books, there are far too many activities to try than there will ever be hours in the day and night to complete. To help you pack as many into your allotted time as possible, the second section contains a collection of activities homeschoolers have found exceptionally quick and easy. (You'll be happy to discover they're also really inexpensive ideas as well.)

Interestingly, homeschoolers often find it's just these types of activities that pack the most learning punch while growing into family favorites. Sometimes it's because they're uniquely created, at other times thought up on the spur of the moment to fill a specific and current need. Often, such as with the multipurpose cassette recorder, it's because once the children are presented with the necessary tools, they instinctively go about putting them to the best use to learn what they want to know.

Finally, group gatherings are a staple among home educators, so we've also gathered ideas to help you keep the fun going when children congregate. These activities may take only one afternoon, or they may continue on a long-term basis when you know the same group will repeatedly come together. Let the pursuits included here spark ideas for even more that are fine-tuned to what your children and their friends hold as common interests. Are there sports they all love? Cartoon or video game characters? Do they enjoy Legos or other building materials? Hot Wheels or Nascar races? Use it all!

Remember, a group can be two or twenty-two. It can be gathered inside to avoid a rainy day or congregate in the yard because the

Home Learning Habits

Some habits really help in homeschooling. I continually use any opportunity to teach. If we take a walk, we talk about the trees we pass, why some lose their leaves, what happens in spring. I try to give my kids a "wonder in the moment" that catches their interest and will encourage them to pursue more information on their own. Of course, that means some odd occurrences, like keeping an aquarium of crickets in the house for a week, or consoling one of my twins because his Sunday school teacher wouldn't let him keep the dead wasp he found on the windowsill. I teach very conversationally and I teach whoever is there—that means kids in the neighborhood are always coming to get me when they find a new plant or animal or nest. Yes, this interrupts my schedule, but it keeps my children's interest high and they are learning volumes. I'll sacrifice a perfectly organized house for their wide-eyed interest.

—Cindy Watson, Levittown, Pennsylvania

summer sun beckons. It can be all the kids in the neighborhood or a few siblings assembled in the playroom. What counts, and what is sure to be remembered, is that everyone learned together.

Especially Cheap Arithmetic

Back on Track
Meg Grooms, Orlando, Florida

Open a file folder, then draw a train in the lower left corner and tracks in the upper right corner. Connect the two by drawing game spaces in a winding fashion. You may wish to include bonus game spaces, such as a railroad crossing. The object is to get the train back on the track. Each time your child answers a question right, he moves a designated amount of spaces.

A few ideas for moving: Draw analog and digital clocks on flash cards. If your child can match the times (or can tell you the time), he rolls a die and moves that many spaces forward. If he answers incorrectly, he moves backward. Make game spaces with phrases such as "move ahead three spaces" or "move back one space." This helps with basic addition and subtraction.

Getting into Shapes

Jane Powell, Bowie, Maryland

Cut shapes out of felt, construction paper, old clothing, bedding, and so on. Ask your children to identify them. Once they've mastered that, create several of the same shape and play Concentration games with them. Ask them to give you two squares, two circles, and so on. If you use monochromatic shapes, you may also ask them to give you the red square or yellow circle. Extend it by asking, "What shape is the peanut butter jar? Bedroom door? The CD case?"

Versatile Coins
Jane Powell, Bowie, Maryland

Have your children count how many coins they have (physical count, not value). Then teach the value of each piece. You can also play a game where they keep the coins if they can correctly tell you their value. Move on to adding how much money they have once you give them a few coins. You can teach them how to count by fives, tens, or twenty-fives, and the game of keeping what they get correct can be extended to this level as well.

Especially Cheap Language Arts

Alphabet Match Cards
Meg Grooms, Orlando, Florida

Cut twenty-six unlined index cards in half. On one half write a capital letter, on the other half write its corresponding lowercase letter. Show the child one half and have her find the matching case. This can also be played like a memory game.

Letter Sticks
Meg Grooms, Orlando, Florida

You need thirty-one large craft sticks. Use a small nail to punch a hole in the bottom of each stick. On the top of each stick write a

Let's Get Started

Arm everyone with a dictionary, then race to find words. See who can open the dictionary closest to a given word, find words representing different parts of speech, and find a synonym or antonym for a given word.

letter. Make two of each vowel and mark them "Short" and "Long." Take a long piece of yarn, about four feet, and string it through the holes with the sticks in alphabetical order. Make sure there's enough slack in the yarn to allow the child to arrange the letters. Tie the ends of the string together.

The next time your child asks how to spell a word, tell her to try to sound it out with her letter sticks! As her skill improves, you can add doubles of each letter to spell more complicated words.

Spell It with Sign Language

Barbara Bowles

My son is a great speller, but any routine bores him. To hold his interest, we use simple sign language letters as a way for him to spell his words to me. He finds it fascinating and he has learned sign language at the same time. We use it everywhere, especially when we're waiting in lines. He gets a kick out of people not knowing what we're talking about.

Strolling Grammar
Cristina Ramos-Payne, White Plains, New York

When my daughter was five years old, we did our best learning while taking walks. One of her favorite games, the Noun/Verb Game, is loosely based on the familiar I Spy. We would decide if we were looking for nouns or verbs and take turns pointing them out as we walked. For greater challenge we looked for adjectives. I helped her with questions if she couldn't think of them, for example, "What do you think that tree feels like?" "Yes, hard!"

Sight Word Flash Card Game
Meg Grooms, Orlando, Florida

Write one sight word (see list) on an index card. Draw a corresponding picture for each word for a child who is just beginning to learn. Show the card to the child, have her spell the word, say it, spell it again, then use it in a sentence. As the child's skills improve, she can begin to make sentences from the cards and you can add more words. Gradually switch from cards with pictures to cards without pictures. When your child is ready, begin writing the words on paper and have the child read them.

Frequently Used Sight Words

The	Of
Was	From
Any	Many

Could	Would
Should	One
Two	Says
Said	Some
Come	There
Their	Other
People	

Phonics Game Even Three-Year-Olds Can Play

J.D., St. Louis, Missouri

Whiz Kids (Discovery Toys) is a wonderful phonics game that can be played by the entire family and is especially good in the car. Devise a similar game with index cards. It consists of two decks of cards. One contains letters, the other contains the names of items. For instance, pull a card that says "B" from one pile, and a card that says "color" from the other. Possible answers are blue, black, or brown. Even prereaders, when the letter card is picked, can be asked what starts with "buh" and is the name of a color.

Sandpaper Letters

Maria Hammer, Marshall, Illinois

After researching methods used to teach little ones to write, and seeing some of the outrageous online and catalog prices for them, I decided I could make my own version of the Montessori sandpaper letters with materials from the local craft store.

You will need

- Felt letters: These come in bags of capitals only and lowercase only and have more than one of each letter (share the cost with a friend and save even more!)

- Glue: Puzzle Saver glue was great. It's white glue on a brush
- Poster board or cardboard

Cut the poster board or cardboard into uniform-sized cards about the size of an index card. Draw a line in pencil about one-third of the way up from the bottom of each card. This will be your child's reference line so he can see where the letter will land on the lines of the paper. Glue the felt letters on and let them dry thoroughly. Your child's finger acts as his pencil as he traces the letters.

Esperanto, Anyone?

Judith Waite Allee, from *Homeschooling on a Shoestring*

All you need for a free ten-lesson correspondence course in Esperanto is a stamped, self-addressed envelope for every lesson. Learning Esperanto, a "generic" language, opens the door to communicating with a network of thousands of people worldwide by letter, on the Internet, or in person—people who want to further world

Let's Get Started

Have a book exchange day with fellow book junkies. Have everyone bring along fiction and nonfiction for children and adults.

peace by creating an easy way for people from all countries to talk with each other.

Learning Esperanto helps a child grasp English grammar and learn other languages at an estimated 15 to 50 percent faster. In 1987 more than six thousand people attended Esperanto's one hundredth anniversary congress—with no interpreters.

- *Homeschooling on a Shoestring* by Judith Waite Allee and Melissa L. Morgan (Shaw Books, 1999)

For Reading Out Loud

Cristina Ramos-Payne, White Plains, New York

We talked librarians at two local libraries into allowing our eight-year-old to assist during the toddler/first-grade story times. She usually picks out a book the week before and practices by reading it to her brother. I give pointers in keeping animated, being loud without shouting, and involving her audience.

Personal Journals

Beverley Paine, Yankalilla, South Australia

A journal is a personal history of ideas and activities. We use unlined, hardcover books to allow for illustrations and space to paste in photos, clippings, and pictures. My kids love to illustrate and decorate their writing pages, or doodle creatively around the words, which encourages art as much as writing.

Encourage the children to see the journal as a record of their lives and thoughts, a place to write, draw, make diagrams, and paste anything from dried flowers to concert tickets. The children love the increasing bulkiness as things are added.

Especially Cheap Science

Recycled Seeds Garden
Pamela Jorrick, Korbel, California

Plant a small plot or container garden. Instead of buying seed packets, save a few from the foods you eat, such as dry beans, pumpkin or other squash, and different kinds of melons. Children have fun experimenting by changing conditions, such as soil, water, light, and containers.

An outside garden will probably contain pests, giving more opportunities for study, experimentation, and learning about other life forms. Collect a few of the pests in jars with a sampling of food and watch them interact. How do they eat, sleep, and play? There's a lot to learn when you get your hands dirty, and you may end up with a few plants, flowers, or even some food when you're done.

Free Programs with a Purpose
Dawn Scagnelli, Vineland, New Jersey

My daughter is participating in our state's Audubon Society's Bridges to the Natural World, a program for prekindergarten through sixth grade. She is given a passport and has to visit at least ten of fifteen suggested habitats over the course of four years. She journals each habitat by drawing, although you may use words or photography as well, and then the naturalist stamps her passport. When the requirements are completed, she will be awarded the New Jersey Audubon Society's Junior Naturalist Award.

New Jersey Audubon Society
Department of Education
P.O. Box 693
Bernardsville, New Jersey 07924
www.njaudubon.org/Education

(Author's note: Search the Internet for a program in your home state.)

She is also a volunteer for Frogwatch USA, which is run by the U.S. Geological Survey. She helps monitor the declining amphibian population, learning to identify the amphibians in our area, not only by sight but by sound.

- Frogwatch: www.mp2-pwrc.usgs.gov/frogwatch

Our state parks also run bird counts that we will participate in next year!

Free Experiments
Linda Spaulding, Pattersonville, New York

Robert Krampf's Experiment of the Week provides fun and easy experiments using everyday household materials. Offering good explanations of why things work and don't work, the lessons arrive via a free weekly e-mail list.

- To receive experiments send an e-mail to Krampf@aol.com.

Especially Cheap History

Make-Your-Own Time Machine
Scott Stevens, Paris, Tennessee

When given a chance, kids still love to cut, paint, create, and imagine in a plain brown box. Check with your local appliance store for a large refrigerator box that can become a great place for history lessons. My children and I turned one into a time machine. We painted it, cut a door, and put knobs and gadgets all over the outside and inside. We made a time line and time meter on the outside, then let our imaginations send us back in time.

When your time machine is ready, choose a place in time that you want to visit. Go to the library and find several good books about the subject and place them in the time machine. Create a ceremony and/or special clothing that you need for time travel (helmet, gloves, period clothing, etc.). Set your time machine for the proper date and begin your journey.

Let's Get Started

Create and draw the "perfect animal" by combining features of other animals into a new one called a _____.

We traveled first to the dinosaurs, so I decorated the inside with pictures and various dinosaur toys we found around the house. My youngest daughter, six years old, was so caught up in the trip that she was a little afraid she wouldn't make it back! Upon entering the time machine, read your books to each other and use your imagination, as we did when we also traveled to pirate ships and castles.

Letterboxing

Debbie Varrell, Glastonbury, Connecticut

Letterboxing is a hobby that people of all ages can enjoy. It's like a treasure hunt where you follow clues, ranging in difficulty from extremely simple to incredibly challenging, to find a sealed plastic container with a rubber stamp and booklet in it. You collect stamp images from the letterboxes you find and leave in the booklet an image from a rubber stamp you bring along with you to show that you've been there.

While searching for letterboxes in our area, my family has visited historic places, beautiful parks and trails, small towns, and even businesses whose owners give a wink and a smile as you reach for the letterbox hidden in their establishment. Thanks to the creative clues, we've become adept at using a compass, identifying trees and plants, understanding geologic terms, and using deductive reasoning. We've also enjoyed glorious sunshiny days, fresh air, and exercise as we follow the clues.

Folks are encouraged to plant their own boxes and post the clues on a Web site, www.letterboxing.org, so if there aren't any letterboxes in your area, you can plant them and invite others to join the fun. Letterboxing is one of those rare gems of an activity that is accessible to all, touches on an enormous variety of topics and skills, can be done anywhere, and is free!

Creative Movement—Free and At Home

Julie Swegle, Colorado Springs, Colorado

Creative dance classes are fun, but if you don't have the time or money for classes outside the home, make up your own. If you danced at school dances as a kid, you can teach your children a creative movement class. Remember the Hustle? How about the Monkey, Mashed Potato, or Twist? Or (now I'm really showing my age) the Shorty George?

Every Friday night we have a family dance party. Dad plays the tunes he's downloaded from the Internet, and we teach the kids a "new" dance and practice some that we've taught them before. They love it, even our teen, who delights in showing everyone the latest swing moves.

If you've never danced before, don't be shy. There are lots of instructional videos available for a variety of dance styles. Rent a video and learn right along with the kids.

I Didn't Know That!

Colleen Senko, Terrebonne, Oregon

Go somewhere really fun, on a nature hike, to the zoo, a museum, it really doesn't matter where as long as the place is on your child's list of picks. Give him a tiny notebook. The challenge is to write down ten things he did *not* know before the outing. I especially enjoy the honesty of my son searching and saying, "No, I already knew that."

Junk Mail No Longer

Jane Powell, Bowie, Maryland

Tired of all those direct mailings? Don't know what to do with Sunday's sales circulars or those magazines you've already read? Here are a few ideas:

Increase Vocabulary

Cut out a variety of pictures. Get a piece of paper and a glue stick or white glue. Place a few of the pictures on the work surface at a time, and ask your child to choose one at a time to glue on the paper. As he glues, ask what the pictures are.

Begins With

Ask your child to pick pictures of things that begin with the letter ___ (fill in the blank). You could also ask her *not* to pick things that begin with ____ (fill in the blank). Add a few letters to your selection of cutouts; ask her to recognize them and tell you what sound they make.

Numbers

Ask your child to recognize numbers, put them in order, add, subtract, and so on. With the older children, give them a circular and ask them to pick out what they'd like and ask how much it would cost to buy them all. Perhaps ask them to add tax?

Learning on the Road

Judith Waite Allee and Melissa L. Morgan, from *Educational Travel on a Shoestring*

Learning can just as easily take place in the car as in a classroom. In a classroom, you can talk about land and rock formations and various terrains. In a car, you can observe them.

- *Educational Travel on a Shoestring* by Judith Waite Allee and Melissa L. Morgan (Shaw Books, 2002)

Holiday Little People

Jean Reed, Bridgewater, Maine, courtesy of *The Home School Source Book*

We had hours of fun creating a terrarium full of small plants from around the house and then using the Fisher Price Little People to act out holiday events. For a Thanksgiving scene we made Indian headdresses, pilgrim costumes, and lots of other props out of construction paper. The kids had hours of fun playing with what they'd created.

Saving *More* Cash

Forget the Sandbox

Shay Seaborne, Woodbridge, Virginia

After spending a ridiculous amount of money on building a large, durable sandbox, we discovered it wasn't such a good idea. The heavy cover, necessary to keep out debris and neighborhood cats, made it inconvenient to open the box, so we didn't do it often. When Caitlin and Laurel *did* play in the box, they played *in* the box and got covered with sand that they inevitably tracked into the house.

Later we placed on the patio an old baby bathtub filled with sand and covered with an old window screen. Now it was accessible to the children, and its smaller size discouraged the girls from climbing, so they tracked less sand into the house. The old sandbox didn't go to complete waste. I now have a beautiful raised-bed herb garden.

Free Paper
Jean Reed, courtesy of *The Home School Source Book*

Check your local print shop or newspaper office for the end of rolls of newsprint. Make sure to ask about scrap paper left from trimming various print jobs, too.

Books for a Song
Cindy Watson, Levittown, Pennsylvania

I make frequent stops at the Salvation Army or other thrift stores for books. Sometimes I find nothing, other times I walk away with five or six books I will need during the next year.

Mega Bookstore Teachers' Discount
Linda Spaulding, Pattersonville, New York

Take advantage of the 20 percent teachers' discount at stores such as Barnes & Noble and Borders. With proof that you're a homeschooler, they give you a card to be renewed each year. Musical and other tapes don't qualify, but almost everything else does, although the clerks sometimes quiz as to whether it's "educational." (What isn't??)

Author's Note: Many independent booksellers also grant similar discounts. Just ask.

Don't Buy Puppets

Shay Seaborne, Woodbridge, Virginia

Caitlin and Laurel hardly ever played with the nice, furry store-bought hand puppets we had. The girls were much more interested in puppets that they made themselves out of mismatched socks, wooden spoons from the dollar store (for stick puppets), pom-poms, sequins, pipe cleaners, yarn, wiggle eyes, and other odds and ends from around the house. These puppets possess great character and have a long history of use by the children.

- *The Muppets Make Puppets* by Cheryl Henson (Workman Publishing, 1994)

Book Chapter of Free and Almost Free Learning Resources

Jean Reed, Bridgewater, Maine, courtesy of *The Home School Source Book*

The Home School Source Book, by Jean and Donn Reed, contains a chapter devoted to free or almost free resources, most for the cost of a stamp, paper, and envelope. It also contains sections that review magazines and catalogs containing other good learning resources.

When Nothin' Is Going Right

Beach Bummin' It

Debra Kurtz, Atlantic City, New Jersey

On those days when nothing is going right, and weather permitting, my three sons and I head for the beach, a short five-minute walk away from our house. With plastic bag in hand we go on a nature walk, collecting anything that looks interesting—sea glass, seaweed, interesting looking litter, shells, and so on. I especially like to do this during the winter, when most of the tourists are gone. It seems there is more of a selection of seashells then.

We usually come home after an hour, hungry, ready to eat lunch or just chill out for a while. Our finds are rinsed with a hose, laid out to dry, and the kids periodically comment on the materials as they pass by them. They sometimes afford us the chance to check out a sea life book to learn more about what we brought home.

Let's Get Started

Play spit ball archery. All you need are straws, paper, and a homemade target. Let the kids establish the rules before they begin.

Make a Special Day
Dianne Rigdon, Bakersfield, California

When things start getting a bit stale, or we're getting burned out, instead of just taking the day off, we have a craft day, a reading day, or a computer day. We still get "some" schoolwork done, but it's spent making a spur-of-the-moment science project or reading together several chapters in books that relate to our history of Bible studies. Just for fun, we get out all of our computer programs and look for the sections that teach math or other subjects relating to what we've been learning.

Quick and Easy Arithmetic

Seeing 100
Kate Ward, Austin, Texas

We banded together groups of ten Q-tips. I handed my four-year-old one group at a time, saying aloud, "10, 20, . . . , 100."

Use that Extra Check Transaction Booklet
Cristina Ramos-Payne, White Plains, New York

To show how math is used in the real world, and to teach a little money management too, we gave our seven-year-old daughter an allowance on the condition that she keep track of her money. We gave her that extra check transaction booklet everyone seems to have lying around. We explained how to use the debit (subtraction) and credit (addition) columns and to check that the amount she recorded was actually how much she had. She also writes down where she gets the money—allowance, birthday gift—and how she spends it—toy, charity. She thinks it's fun to do math in her booklet.

Math Facts Jump Game

Jane Ferrall, Darien, Connecticut

Write the numbers from 1 to 20 on sheets of notebook paper, and line them up on the floor in two rows. Then call out math problems; the child jumps onto the paper with the right answer. It gets messy, as you have to keep rearranging the papers, but this game kept all of my kids amused for at least thirty minutes. Make the math problems harder for the older kids.

Lots of Roads to Roman Numerals

Athena Dalrymple, Columbia, Maryland

Roman Numerals on the Road

Using the Roman numeral system below, call out the values of road signs if all the Roman numeral values contained in it were added (or multiplied). For example, "Lovely Lane" would be worth 155 using the addition method (three *L*s for 150 plus one *V* for 5 more). Whoever yelled out "155" first would get the points, or just one correct answer if you keep score that way.

I = 1, V = 5, X = 10, L = 50, C = 100, D = 500, M = 1000

Reverse Roman Numeral Game

One player gives the other players a point value, and whoever comes up first with a word that adds up to that total wins that round. For example, I gave the value of 1,051 and my son said, "Blimp." (He used the *L* for 50, *I* for 1, and *M* for 1,000, for a total of 1,051.) You can give points per round won or just play for fun.

Roman Numeral Word Challenge

How many words can you come up with that have all seven Roman numerals? (We never came up with any.) Or six different numerals? (Our son came up with "exclaimed" and we came up with one other, but there might be more.) Or five different numerals? You can make this tougher by not allowing a repetition of any numeral, too.

Roman Numeral Value Challenge

What is the greatest value for one word using Roman numerals? We found one worth 4,000 using the addition method and then sort of gave up on that game, but this could be longer-lasting fun for younger children.

Quick and Easy Language Arts

The Multipurpose Cassette Recorder
Shay Seaborne, Woodbridge, Virginia

My children have spent many hours playing with a cassette recorder. They've read stories aloud, reenacted scenes from favorite movies, and produced their own shows and commercials. Sometimes we leave the recorder on and go about our daily lives. While most of the tapes weren't that interesting, we did manage to capture the moment when Cait lost her first tooth! Someday I'll organize and edit the cassettes and transfer them to a single tape.

Ziploc Books

Debbie Michael, Woodland, California

Good for even the youngest learners, take freezer Ziploc bags (which are sturdier than plain sandwich bags) and put in pictures, letters, flowers, or anything else you want in a book. Materials may be inserted vertically or horizontally, and you can make two pages per bag.

Punch holes equidistant from the edges on each bag above the zipper part. Use whatever ribbon or yarn you like to thread through the holes to bind the book. (I use hemp twine because I know it's natural and safe if ingested or mouthed by my daughter.)

When she was less than seventeen months old, I used an entire box of bags for pictures of babies from magazines. She spent at least twenty minutes once or twice a day looking at her "book." The idea can grow with your child for all types of materials, including scrapbooks of favorite interests or family mementos.

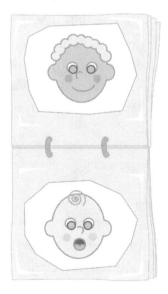

26 Letter Pick-Up

Theresa Doolan, Riva, Maryland

The game starts with a deck of alphabet cards (purchased or home-made index) and permission for your child to make a mess! Throw the cards on the floor, scatter them all around the room, and while Mom sits in a chair attempting to finish a cup of tea, she requests the child to bring her the card with the letter that makes the "buh" sound, the "sss" sound, and so on.

While we so often tell our kids to "clean up, clean up, clean up," this game allows them to enjoy a mess, and they don't even realize that while they're learning, the mess gets cleaned up automatically!

We've also played matching uppercase and lowercase letters, or just letter recognition with this game.

Homemade Magnetic Letter/Word Board

Roxanne Meredith, Nanaimo, British Columbia, Canada

We got a cookie sheet and a few light-colored magnet sheets from the dollar store. With a permanent marker, we wrote letters and common words on the sheets and cut them out. The letters and/or words stick in place on the cookie sheet. Make up words or sentences for your child to read; give her a turn to make a word or sentence for you.

Musical Phonics

Joanna Simpson, Dallas, Oregon

Put letters written singly on paper in a circle face down and play music. The children walk around the circle until the music stops. They grab the letter closest to them and say its sound and a word that starts with it. We do this until all the letters are gone. The winner is the one who got the most right.

For Kids Who Like Workbooks
Elizabeth Brett Crews, Fairfax, Virginia

When we read a book, I buy the activity papers or workbooks at the teaching store that go along with it. The children love the activities, and we usually finish them up the same day. This is easy because I don't use a formal curriculum. I also try to find some sort of performance of the story as a finale to our studies.

Quick and Easy Social Studies

A Personal Boston Tea Party
Kathy Joyce, Buchanan, Michigan

Take a few clean Cool Whip containers and empty a few tea bags into each one. Pile them on the back porch. Now go inside, get out your face paints, and get in character. Have the kids take off their shirts and start painting themselves up as Indians, all the while grumbling about King George and his taxes. Add in all the information you can about what the Colonists were thinking and feeling at the time. They'll pick up on all of it and enthusiastically join in with complaints and boasts about what you're preparing to do about it.

Now go out the front door and climb off the porch into your rowboats. Row around back and climb onto the British ship (don't use the steps!). While you guard the British lookouts the kids have rounded up and trussed, they can dump the tea over while whooping like Indians to convince the British who is doing this deed. Then you can all row back.

It takes less time to do this than it does to write about it. It doesn't take any preparation either. You could probably do it right now provided you keep face paints around.

Beginner's Mapping
Jean Reed, Bridgewater, Maine

Learning to use a ruler and measurement is easy when you begin with a scale drawing of a familiar room, including various simple furnishings like a table or bed. Beginners can start with one inch equaling one foot, and future maps can get more challenging by changing the scale. Drawing a map of the path from your house to a friend's is another way of introducing maps and symbols without buying anything except a ruler.

Quick and Easy Art

Seeing Doubles?
Cindy Watson, Levittown, Pennsylvania

I always get doubles of my photographs printed because grandparents and others always want some. Even when distributed, though, I still have extras. I give them to the kids with paper, scissors, and glue. They cut out their own shapes, glue them to the paper, then draw a picture around them.

Duncan may draw a rocket ship, and we now can write a story about him being an astronaut. Colin, of course, draws himself riding on a dinosaur. They love this craft and, because they can really "see" themselves, have amazing adventures on paper!

Mixing Bowl Colors

Hope Ware, Peoria, Illinois

When teaching my sons about secondary colors, we got out a large, clear glass mixing bowl. They took turns cranking an old hand mixer to mix two or three primary colors of food coloring. They guessed what color would result before we began the mixing process, then we talked about the actual result. In the clear bowl, everyone could see the results at the same time.

Miscellaneous

The Many Moods of the Homeschool

Calandra Johnson, Elgin, Oregon

Fight off burnout quickly and inexpensively by changing your environment. At home you can play background music, fill the air with a yummy or stimulating aroma, change or be creative with the lighting (turn on lamps only, use colored light bulbs, or put tissue paper over a window).

For a more drastic change, consider using an unusual room or another building to learn in. Don't forget to get outside as much as possible. It's a good way for Mom to fight seasonal affective disorder (S.A.D.).

Create a Tradition

Elizabeth Brett Crews, Fairfax, Virginia

On the Wednesday before Thanksgiving, we always go see Virginia's governor receive a tribute from the Native Americans in lieu of taxes at the capitol in Richmond. Then we hit some of the museums and shops. You can create any tradition at any time of the year.

Great for Groups

Set Up Teams for National Contests

Linda Spaulding, Pattersonville, New York

Lots of learning takes place when you set up teams so that home-schoolers can participate in national contests like the Scripps Howard National Spelling Bee and Math Counts. Check with your local or regional sponsor to get all the information you need to get started.

Share Talents

Linda Spaulding, Pattersonville, New York

Share knitting, crocheting, sewing, and gift-making talents with a homeschooling group. Have a show-and-tell day!

Telephone Pole

Hope Ware, Peoria, Illinois

When our co-op studied Johnny Appleseed, we talked about the differences between truth, rumor, lie, and a tall tale. To demonstrate the point, the boys lined up and we whispered a simple sentence into the first boy's ear. The first whispered the same sentence to the second and so on down the line until the last boy said the sentence aloud for all of us to hear. As the results were always hilariously different from the actual starting sentence, the boys learned a lot about the importance of never repeating something you've heard about another person because it might not be the truth.

Monthly Book Club

Cindy Allas, Fairfield, California

Each month our book club has a theme. Each child reads a book with that theme, makes a project, and gives an oral report or presentation. They write their reports first, then read them, as this gives them more confidence because they already know what they will say.

Group Quilt

Linda Spaulding, Pattersonville, New York

Have someone with quilting experience organize a group quilt and let everyone, kids and adults, contribute a patch. Put the squares together with a border, having the group decide on border colors.

Poetry Get-Togethers

Ruth Dunnavan, Moultonborough, New Hampshire

Get together several homeschooling families for a poetry recitation. In our group each child memorized a poem and recited it for the group. The youngest children needed prompting, but the experience was good for them, too. Afterwards we enjoyed refreshments.

Group Valentine Visit

Linda Spaulding, Pattersonville, New York

First a volunteer coordinator from the local nursing home came to speak to us. For Valentine's Day each family made cookies at home, then we got together as a group to nicely wrap them before taking them to the home, along with all the Valentine cards we made the week before. We passed out everything and chatted with the nursing home residents. They loved being with the kids, and we all had a great time with the project.

(Author's Note: You can use this idea for any holiday, or not even wait for a holiday at all! Some homes may require you to have certain immunizations if you visit on a regular basis.)

Homemade Geoboards

Shay Seaborne, Woodbridge, Virginia

A fun project for the family or a small group is making geoboards, typically a wooden board with equally spaced nails in rows, 6 by 6, 7 by 7, or however many are necessary to fill your board. Make a template out of paper and photocopy it enough times to give one to each participant and have a few extras in case of need. Tape a template on top of the board and drive a nail through each point on the template. When all the nails are in, remove the template. Wrap different colored rubber bands around the nails to make geometric shapes and learn about area.

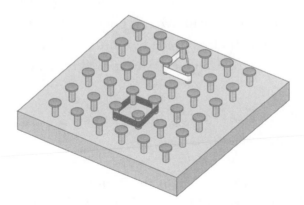

Moms Can Be a Group, Too

Linda Spaulding, Pattersonville, New York

How about monthly homeschooling mothers' meetings? I highly recommend doing it at night around a campfire with coffee and cake—and no children or husbands allowed. There's no need to have a particular topic for the evening; just see what comes up.

Better Than a Party

Shay Seaborne, Woodbridge, Virginia

For a memorable and meaningful birthday celebration, let your child choose an educational adventure, such as a trip to a special museum, zoo, farm, or historical reenactment. Let her take a friend or two along. Be sure to take the camera and a picnic lunch with a related theme, if appropriate. Your child's birthday will be remembered.

History Festivals

Holly Furgason, Houston, Texas

We do history festivals every year as part of a conference, but a support group or several families can easily create them. The festivals are not for learning about the culture, like building a pyramid with sugar cubes. The learning comes during the preparation. The actual festival is to experience what it was like to go to a party during a particular historic time.

We start by researching dress, food, music, art, dance, and games. Most of the materials we use for costumes come from thrift stores or garage sales, things like sheer curtains for Egyptian clothing or white sheets for tunics and togas. Food is usually readily available, since most was simple and unrefined, like eggs to apples in Rome, with some chicken wings, stuffed grape leaves, and baklava thrown in the middle. For Egypt there are dried or fresh fruits and nuts, roasted meat, and hummus and wheat pita bread. Folk music is usually available at the library, and we try to get as close to the original as we can. We decorate the room with art such as mosaics created with paper or Fima tiles from Rome or Egyptian drawings.

On the day of the festival, everyone dresses up and comes to enjoy food, games, dancing, and fun!

Don't Have a Group to Share With? Start One!

Jeanne Faulconer, Stanardsville, Virginia

We set up a homeschool co-op that meets once a week. Since some of the boys are also in Boy Scouts, some of our projects are on topics that will help them earn merit badges. So far this year we've covered financial management, tracking animals, and mammal study.

- Homeschooling Scouts: www.geocities.com/cherokeegs/Scout School

Sugar Cube Building Blocks

Helen Hegener, Tonasket, Washington

One morning when I was little I woke up to a most amazing creation: a perfect miniature sugar cube igloo. My mother had created it with a couple of boxes of sugar cubes and vanilla frosting. Using the frosting as "mortar" between the cubes, she'd built the igloo from a twelve-inch base into a perfect replica of an Eskimo house, complete with an entry crawlway. It was enchanting!

Since that time, my kids and I have built sugar cube towers, bridges, aqueducts, houses, and even fantastical castles, sometimes adding architectural details with small candies, licorice, and so on.

We've learned that a thick royal icing works best as mortar (most cookbooks will have a recipe for it).

Conversation Starters

- Play Twenty Questions.

- Figure out how many seconds, minutes, hours, days, weeks, months, years are left in the day, week, month, year, decade, century, millennium.

- Find someone knowledgeable in a subject of interest to your child, then barter your own or your child's skills in exchange for lessons.

10

These Hints Aren't from Heloise

Organization, Homeschooling Style

If you could see my desk right now, you'd laugh that I'm even addressing organization! But in this Information Age, organization is the name of the game. Experts now have it down to a science, with books specializing in straightening out everything from your kitchen, closet, office, attic, or junk drawer. In this chapter, homeschoolers are going to share their secrets in the very specialized field of organizing the homeschooler's home.

The first and most important secret, one that will save your time and sanity, is to accept that you cannot live the learning lifestyle with children and get your home on the cover of *House Beautiful* at the same time. I always kept a little saying on my refrigerator to remind me: "Cleaning the house while kids are growing is like shoveling snow while it's still snowing." How true. Even while you're clearing out one spot, it's piling up in the spot you just uncovered.

This said, it doesn't mean you have to live in a pigpen. To keep your home at a happy medium on the cleanliness scale, this simply means you need some help. I'm not talking about the paid kind either. You see, school mind tells us that the institution is *the* place for learning, and only those subjects taught there are important. So in many homes, either all or a large majority of the tasks included in the term *housework* are completed by Mom. (Is it any wonder working mothers often feel as if they never get any time to themselves?) Education mind, on the other hand, helps us realize that children of all ages are capable of more pitching in than we adults typically require or expect of them.

Sure, at first having little helpers means a job will likely take longer, but soon enough your child will be able to complete the task independently, and time spent today will be returned many times over in time saved tomorrow. As a bonus you receive three other significant rewards for your patience.

1. Your children learn the skills they can use for a lifetime.

2. Your children grow up realizing that Mom isn't a maid for the family, but rather that the family is a unit that works together for the mutual benefit of all.

3. You get to spend this additional time with your children working together, even as it frees up additional time for life's pleasures.

For more of the secrets that will increase your peace of mind and save your family time and energy, read on.

Let's Get Started

Get rid of or put away everything you haven't touched in the last six to twelve months.

Wednesday Cleanse Day

Jeanne Faulconer, Stanardsville, Virginia

Our Wednesdays include about half a day of vacuuming, dusting, mopping, cleaning out the refrigerator, toilet cleaning, and laundry. I have a typed list of all that needs to be done to help keep us on track. On Wednesday nights, we watch a special TV show together and eat popcorn to celebrate our accomplishments.

Get It in Writing

I've found it very useful to record some aspects of our home learning progress and program. From this I've derived so much confidence that I can't overstate how useful a tool recording is. It underpins all my planning and serves as a platform for many learning activities.

—Beverley Paine, Yankalilla, South Australia

Stock Up on Socks and Underwear

Linda Dobson, Saranac Lake, New York

Wait for a good sale, then make sure all family members have plenty of socks and underwear. This will help prevent the need to do laundry only because someone is out of essentials.

Leave Struggle Behind

Shay Seaborne, Woodbridge, Virginia

My best advice for those struggling through any particular aspect of homeschooling is to remember, "If it's torture, it's not worth it. Try something different."

Room for Art!

Tara Hall, Colliersville, Tennessee

Because my two youngest children like reorganizing my cork boards, I came up with the idea of using pipe cleaner "hooks" (red, white, and blue at the moment) on a string across the top of our wall. We attached the ends by making a loop and screwing in a ³/4-inch screw. We painted clothespins to match, making three with glitter all over them. These are for our "shining pictures of the week," one for each child, six, three, and two years old.

All of our artwork and special pieces go here. If you make the line taut enough, it won't sag. We've had over twenty-six clothespins on it for our specially made alphabet and it held up fine.

Finding Books Made Easy

Ruth Dunnavan, Moultonborough, New Hampshire

I keep each of my children's schoolbooks, workbooks, and note-books in a large box with the top edge reinforced with duct tape. Inside I place a metal file sorter that can be found in the desk accessories section of any stationery supply store. The file sorter keeps the books upright so they are easily located, and the box keeps everything together.

Real-Time Grocery List

Linda Dobson, Saranac Lake, New York

Keep a dry erase white board in the kitchen where everyone can reach it. When family members either use up a product or see that it's almost gone, they can add it to a list on the board. It saves a lot of time when you don't have to go through all the cupboards prior to every grocery shopping trip.

Organizing Literacy

Shay Seaborne, Woodbridge, Virginia

Best covert literacy tip: Go to the library and grab a stack of books, saying, "I'm getting this for myself." Then leave them lying around where they'll be noticed, like on the sofa. Children (and husbands) will sometimes pick up the books and start reading. A sneaky trick: start reading aloud from the book and, after a while, "get tired" and set the book down. This recently resulted in my husband reading his first classic novel.

Reducing Paper Clutter

Ruth Dunnavan, Moultonborough, New Hampshire

When possible, I have the children complete math lessons out loud. If they have to do short calculations they use a 10-by-16-inch dry erase white board. This saves on paper clutter and they like the feel of the

Let's Get Started

When you or your children find a great educational Web site, write its name, address, and a brief description on an index card. File the cards in a box by subject or as individual children's favorites. Browsing and return trips are encouraged by the presence of the cards near the computer.

board. The dry erase pens have a chemical smell so I don't use them for longer projects.

Square Planning
Rene P. S. Bane, Bowie, Maryland

Since to do lists just don't work for me, I bought a 3-by-4-foot dry erase white board that I marked off into sixteen squares, four by four. Obviously you can use other media such as large easel pads or blackboards.

Each square is something to do, and I make sure that all subject areas have *something* there. For instance, one square might have "Math: 10 lessons," another might be "*David Copperfield*: 10 chapters." When dealing with a number, I actually write out the numbers 1, 2, 3, 4, and so on and cross them off as they are done. Another square might say "Do electronics kit."

Some squares are for fun things like "Play date with Lillian" or "Field trip to natural history museum," especially when the kids suggest them.

A few more squares are for things I want to do around the house: "Put recent photos in album" or "Mail stuffed gorilla to California." (Yes, that was a real one and I'd put it off far too long!) The kids know Mom has stuff she's gotta do, too.

With sixteen squares, there's a lot of flexibility about what to put in, and being large and obvious is important, at least in my household! The point is that all the squares must be checked off (I draw big check marks through completed squares) before I erase them and put in a new set. This avoids problems I'd been having, like doing only the fun things and not finding time for the rest, or coming up with a great idea and then forgetting to actually do it in the bustle of everyday life. I've had *David Copperfield* around for a long time, and after reading *A Christmas Carol* to the kids, I thought it would be a good book to read next, but I kept forgetting it because there are so many good books to just pick up and read!

It's probably a good idea to have some time frame for checking off the boxes, but for me it took a while to figure out how much could be done in a given time period. I'm flexible—if we finish everything but half the chapters of a book, perhaps I need to put in fewer chapters the next time. Conversely, if I put down two chapters and they're a breeze, perhaps I should add a few.

	Mail thank-you letters ✓	Clean kitchen	
David Copperfield 5 chapters 1 2 3 4 5			Field trip
		Math: 10 lessons 1 2 3 4 5 6 7 8 9 10	
Play date		Do science project	

Best Times to Go on Field Trips to Museums, Zoos, and Historic Sites

Shay Seaborne, Woodbridge, Virginia

Mondays, the week after school starts, the week after Thanksgiving, the week after New Year's Day, the week after public school spring break—these are times when school groups are least likely to visit.

Keep in mind that most school groups head back from field trips by early afternoon. If a school group does come through while you visit, hunker down to the side for a few minutes and hang on until the group goes on. The school groups must move through quickly, because they have to get back on the bus.

Best Value from Annual Memberships
Shay Seaborne, Woodbridge, Virginia

Purchase only one—or at most, two—memberships to museums, historic sites, or other attractions per year and make that one or two the center of your focus for the year. Visit once a month or more often, being sure to go on special event days.

Bulk Food Containers Recycled
Kris Bordessa, Diamond Springs, California

When I discovered that my local grocery store discards their bulk food containers when they're empty, I asked if they would save them for me. We use them for small pieces and parts, organizing art supplies, and more. If your store sells nuts and candy in bulk, find out if they reuse the containers or if they're replaced with new ones from the distributor each time they're emptied. (Does this seem like an amazing amount of waste to anyone else?)

Where, Oh Where, Can My Library Books Be?
Linda Dobson, Saranac Lake, New York

It happened one too many times. I'd ask the kids to gather up their books because we're off to the library. Two hours later, when we were "only" missing three of them, we finally walked out the door. Talk about frustrating!

That was it. I cleared an entire bookshelf and dedicated it as the library books' home away from home. A box or basket works as well, just as long as it's for library books exclusively and the kids get in the habit of returning the books there when they're done reading them.

A cheap spiral notebook also sat on the shelf in which to record the titles and due dates as the books came in. As they went out, names got crossed off. The notebook did double duty as a place to record the names of books and magazines I wanted to look for when we quickly got out the door on our next trip to the library.

Log Book

Cindy Watson, Levittown, Pennsylvania

A simple notebook serves as my school log book. The front of the page has the day, such as "Day 45," in red ink; next to it is the date that I fill in when it happens. So if Thursday was an insane day with sick kids and doctor visits and we didn't get much work done, I'm not committed and we make it up at another time.

The next line contains each child's name, and under each name appear the day's assignments. At the bottom of the page, I write the topics covered by everyone, like fire safety or some science topics. After assignments are finished, I cross them off in red. When we don't quite get to everything, I circle it and add it to the next day's assignments. On the back of each page, I list all books finished that day and any outside activities, like homeschool choir or field trips.

Get the Best of the Zoo

Shay Seaborne, Woodbridge, Virginia

Buy an annual pass and go often during the year. Focus on only one or two areas each time, perhaps letting each child choose one area to visit. Zoos can be wonderful places for children to learn geography, biology, and Latin (names of the animals). Read the signs and discuss the differences in the animals' natural diet versus what they eat at the zoo.

Take advantage of any zoo programs, such as hands-on tables, scheduled trainer talks, and regular animal feedings. Also be on the lookout for unusual activities, such as keepers who are tending to the special health needs of an animal. Often they're willing to answer questions and give insights into their jobs, the animals, and the special care required by the animals. On days when the zoo is busy, head for the less popular spots, such as the invertebrate exhibit or reptile house. Very early mornings can be wonderful times to visit the primates, as they are more inclined to interact with visitors when the area is quiet and visitors are respectful.

Organize Pens, Crayons, Scissors, and More

Tara Hall, Colliersville, Tennessee

Cut out old pockets from pants or jeans and glue or sew them onto a sheet or piece of fabric. Hang it on the wall or, as I did, on a curtain

rod using pipe cleaners as the rings, and you have a window covering in which the kids can store their own supply of goodies.

Use zippers, buttons, and colorful ties to make it festive. You can write the children's names or initials with paint pens and let them decorate!

Organizational Aids

Sandra Dodd, Albuquerque, New Mexico

Here's what we use:

- Clear plastic bins
- Free paper boxes with lids from Kinko's
- Nails and pegs on walls
- Lots of shelves
- Old plastic silverware trays for markers, crayons, pencils, and parts

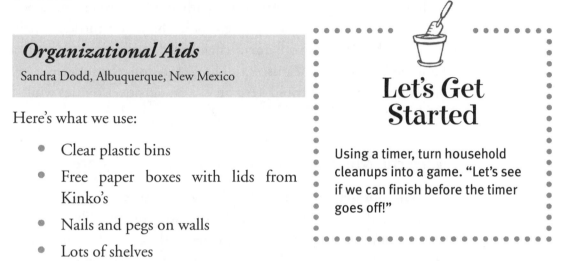

Let's Get Started

Using a timer, turn household cleanups into a game. "Let's see if we can finish before the timer goes off!"

General Tips for Organizing Your Home Around a Rich Learning Life

Ann Lahrson Fisher, from *Fundamentals of Homeschooling: Notes on Successful Family Living*

Work with Your Space, Not Against It

For example, put the art center near a water source such as laundry, bath, or kitchen. Alternatively, set the center up over a floor that is easy to clean. Perhaps you have a long-range plan to replace that floor and can live with stains for now. You might lay plastic or painting drop cloths under the art table if flooring needs protection.

Take Advantage of Unique Features of Your Home

Do you have a bay window? What a nice reading area that could make. An oversized hall closet, a butler's pantry, an enclosed porch, a space in an outside building can all be adapted to meet your particular homeschooling needs. An infrequently used bathroom could be a darkroom, a science lab, a dressing room, a home for turtles. A hallway may be wide enough for a chalkboard, art gallery, or even a bookshelf. Our home featured a sliding-glass door that offered a full view of our yard, so I could keep an eye on outside activities while I worked at my desk.

Vary the Materials and Projects in Your Centers

The kinds of materials in my family's favorite space were mixed, according to the kinds of projects we were working on. The activities and furniture arrangement changed regularly as the kids grew and changed. About the only thing that stayed the same was the paper/craft supply (paper, paint, markers, crayons, pens, scissors, glue—that type of thing). It was generally a mishmash including games of all kinds—craft projects, books, experiments-in-progress, science resources, dictionaries, an electric typewriter, a computer, pets, bulletin board, chalk board.

Keep Parent and Child Activity Centers Close, When Possible

Our family kitchen was ideal when the girls were young. If preparing food or cleaning up, I was available if the girls needed me. Writing or bookkeeping projects found me at my desk or the computer table nearby. My occasional sewing projects and even my volunteer phone work centered around this area. Learning is a family activity when children are young, and they want to be with you anyway.

There is a compelling reason to work closely with your children when they're young that you won't fully appreciate until they're older. When students are older, they may not want or need your assistance or help with their studies and projects, but you'll have ample excuse to rub shoulders with them frequently, giving you a chance to keep tabs on them without prying. You have a long established precedent of togetherness set when they were young. After all, your projects are already set up right there beside theirs. Parents can be so sneaky!

- *Fundamentals of Homeschooling: Notes on Successful Family Living* by Ann Lahrson Fisher (Nettlepatch Press, 2002)

Basic Routine

Jeanne Faulconer, Standardsville, Virginia

I've got a typed list of the children's daily responsibilities, like eating breakfast and cleaning up after themselves, making beds and straightening rooms, and so on. Additionally, one of my older boys serves as "house man" and one as "kitchen man" for the week. House man has specific daily responsibilities for keeping the house straightened up, such as helping our little one pick up toys, putting away things that get scattered, and so on. Kitchen man is responsible for keeping the kitchen going for the week—loading and unloading the dishwasher, wiping counters, setting the table, helping with dinner, and so on. At the end of the week, the jobs are rotated.

Supporting Homeschooling Shut-Ins

Linda Spaulding, Pattersonville, New York

Set up support strategies for shut-in members of your homeschooling community. We had a mom who was on seven-month bed rest for a pregnancy, and we all pitched in with cooking, cleaning, outings for the other children, and other needs. Arrangements were made through a Web site, e-mails, and phone calls. This could be done for any member in need of some support.

Organizing Informal Field Trips Close to Home
Mimi Dempsey, Fredericksburg, Virginia

I have found many field trips to be a bit too formal for my family, and with children ranging in age from two to nine, it's hard to find something that's good for everyone. I decided to call around town and visit local folks on an informal basis at places we would normally go anyway.

During nap time one day I called the post office, grocery store, vet clinic, and fire station, and off we went on our trips. I asked our guides if they could speak to the young children, as most field trips are geared for older kids. Though they did just that, they also spoke with respect and kept everyone's attention, even the adults'.

We got to see parasites and a kitty fetus at the vet office. We scanned items at the grocery store and learned about professional cake baking. We saw a local firefighter suit up, complete with oxygen tank, and learned what happens to a letter after it is dropped in the mailbox. Great learning took place, all in our own neighborhood.

Organizing the After-Field-Trip Thank You
Shay Seaborne, Woodbridge, Virginia

Bring a blank thank-you note or card with you on the field trip. This may be the only time you have these particular people together in one place! Encourage group members to sign the note before leaving the premises. Note who has taken photos and ask for their phone numbers so you can obtain a photo to send with the note.

Child-Size It!

Tara Hall, Colliersville, Tennessee

Place children's artwork, as well as other furnishings, at their eye level. Imagine how uncomfortable it must be for them to crane their necks to see what is in a picture. We turned over a tall bookcase to provide more sitting space and storage space for our children and their books. We put pillows on top and they read on top of the bookcase! It takes some thought but you'd be amazed how much more interesting the room is to children when it's "their" size.

Conversation Starters

- What can each of us do to keep the house neater?

- What is meant by the saying, "Inch by inch, life's a cinch, yard by yard, it's hard?"

- Let's figure out three simple things Dad (or Mom or kids) can do to help Mom (or Dad or kids) get household chores done more quickly.

- Discuss problems or topics that family members have throughout the week written down in a notebook kept available for this purpose.

- Do we have papers lying around that could go into files to make them easier to find? How should our files be arranged?

11

Across the Curriculum

Congratulations! You've made it through hundreds of activities and you're still looking for more—you must be having fun!

I consider this last collection of ideas very special, perhaps because I know them so well. You see, I've contemplated all of them over and over and over again in an attempt to classify them in any of the previous chapters. Finding this impossible, they got a home of their very own.

While in true homeschooling fashion many of the previous activities address more than one subject or topic at a time, the ideas in this chapter *really* cover the gamut. They are truly explorations of the world at large. These projects are included here because they give you a good idea of how you can bend and shape just about any activity under the sun to fit your child's learning needs and desires.

Included is an activity to help your children get the juices flowing in figuring out what they'd like to learn. You'll see that you, too, can turn fruit—yes, fruit!—into a starting point for learning about art, vocabulary, science, math, language, and penmanship. Your children don't like fruit? Switch to vegetables or motorcycles or toys or anything else that will capture their imagination. While you're at it, don't forget to hang on to some of those magazines, newspapers, and junk mailings you were going to recycle and turn them into even more fun projects.

Here you'll find out about learning during meals, with a mentor, while watching TV, at the mall, or on a late night walk under a full moon. We remember the importance of play as a child's most important work, and explore learning with jokes, Boy Scout activities, favorite games—played as intended or with little twists—and even while digging a hole in the backyard.

One mom explains how you can set any learning material to music for no-muss memorization, and Jean Reed joins me in celebrating the painless learning that accompanies hanging interesting information on the walls of your home.

As you revisit all of these activities from time to time, looking for just the right way to spend some precious moments on any particular day, remember that while these have been successfully accomplished in other homes just like your own, the countless contributors experimented and tested different approaches until they found the ones that worked best with their own unique children. Have fun doing the same at your house.

You can use one, many, or all of these activities to help your children to find the experience of *flow*, a term coined by Mihaly Csikszentmihalyi, a prolific author, professor, and former chairperson of the Department of Psychology at the University of Chicago, who has devoted his life's work to the study of what makes people truly happy, satisfied, and fulfilled. This Year 2000 Thinker of the Year describes flow as "being completely involved in an activity for its own sake. The ego falls away. Time flies. Every action, movement, and thought follows inevitably from the previous one, like playing jazz. Your whole being is involved, and you're using your skills to the utmost."

What greater opportunity could you present to a child you love? What better place than at home? What better guide, facilitator, adviser, and colearner to be there to see it than you?

Happy learning . . . always.

Play

Parents seem to believe that a child's life needs to be completely organized and supervised by people who are supposed to be "experts in child development." My wife and I do not believe that at all. In fact, we can make a strong case for the exact opposite: Leave children alone to decide what they'll do, with whom, when, and how, and not supervise or interfere unless they ask for it, and then only minimally.

What I'm suggesting is to let the children play. As our society becomes more psychotic, stressed, pressured, and fearful, what's missing is freeform living—spontaneous, unplanned activities such as we did when we were young and simply left alone with a friend or two or more. I believe that many people are unable to cope with today's demands partly because they didn't get enough independent play while they grew up. Too much organization has made them conformist instead of creative and self-assured. A friend, a graduate of Harvard and Oxford, has made a long study of play and found it to be one of the absolute essentials for a happy and productive life.

One of today's great tragedies is that most public schools have eliminated recess, my favorite class in school, for children above the fourth grade. This limits children's opportunities to interact freely with each other and/or with kids of different ages from themselves. They are stuck indoors all day with those of the same age and same abilities and similar backgrounds, as schools classify and sort them and "assign" them all activities. It's synthetic, coercive, and unnatural.

Need proof? Watch all animals as they grow up—playing and being left alone. Play is imperative training for successful life. Nothing can take its place.

—Ned Vare, Guilford, Connecticut

Dig a Hole

Luz Shosie, Guilford, Connecticut

When Cassidy was about six years old, he found a shovel and we set aside a corner of the yard for digging. My first thought was, "You'll get all dirty!" (I must have been channeling my mother.)

But I relaxed and remembered that children are washable and bathing can be a fun and educational experience, too. So the hole grew deeper and the resulting dirt pile grew bigger. It became Cassidy's and his friend Ken's favorite activity, more attractive than Ken's fancy climbing gym.

They found bugs, roots, rocks, worms. They made roads, tunnels, castles, rivers. They said, "Let's betend," and became race car drivers, space warriors, zookeepers, and chefs for a few hours. Were they learning biology, math, geology, physics, art? Fortunately, in our state of Connecticut, we're not required to document our "educational experiences," so we didn't have to squeeze hole digging into a subject category.

Mall Games
Janell Wolfinger, Bristol, Indiana

My son has always gotten bored while riding in the car or walking around a mall, so we've played simple games that help him learn. When he was four years old, I would go through the alphabet and he would name words that began with each letter. Now that he is almost six, I give him arithmetic problems or say a word that he sounds out and spells for me.

Long on Learning
Merelee Syron, New Egypt, New Jersey

I wouldn't be caught homeschooling without my 36-inch wide, 1000-foot roll of white paper. I have one wall covered with it for a time line. Sometimes we roll some out to trace our bodies and fill in the bones. We make maps corresponding to our history units.

Right now we have a 6-foot long piece on the wall with the states east of the Mississippi. Union states are outlined in blue, confederate states in gray. Battles are labeled in the color of the winner. Each side's generals are listed at the bottom. We did the same for the American Revolution.

We have also rolled out a sheet to see how long a blue whale is, and to mark relative distances between the planets.

- Order paper from Nasco Arts and Crafts catalog: 1-800-558-9595

Best Advice for Those Whose Young Children Are Not "Getting" Reading
Shay Seaborne, Woodbridge, Virginia

Just keep reading with them. Point out signs and read them aloud. Read books. Read cereal boxes. Keep magazines, books, newspapers, and other printed matter around the house and let them see you use them. Take them to interesting places and allow them to be involved. Let them use the produce scale at the grocery store and the stamp dispenser at the post office and the copy machine at the copy center. Read the words on them all as your child uses them. Most of all, be very patient, and listen to your heart.

Unforgettable
Ritzya Mitchell, Herndon, Virginia

Anything set to music, that is, made into a song, is easier to learn and almost impossible to forget. You can use a known tune or something original. My children all knew their names, address, and phone number, including area code, by the age of three. It goes like this:

(Key of C major just for ease. It can be sung beginning on any pitch.)

"My name is Robert Mitchell. I live at 5555 Elmtree Road
   a   c   c dd   e c, a c c ddde   f e   d

Smithville, Virginia. My phone number is 755-755-1234."
   d   d   g f c. a   c   d d e ff d e eef g g d e c

You can use the same technique with days of the week, months, states, capitols, presidents, scripture—anything. I'm sure some of these are already published, but so far I've just made up my own.

Memorable Posters

Linda Dobson, Saranac Lake, New York

Is your child having trouble remembering something? Whether it's multiples of 7, tricky spelling words, word definitions, or anything else, get out the poster board, markers, stickers, glue, and anything else that helps your child create a memorable poster. By turning the elusive facts into a work of art, your child will proudly display them where he sees them throughout the day. Before long, the facts will be committed to memory.

Animal Role-Playing Game

Ann Lahrson Fisher, Carson, Washington

This free-flowing activity entertained our very young children and their friends for hours on end. Any number of children can play, and there is no competition.

We usually played in the living room, with me sitting in my favorite chair, taking a much needed break. I called out an animal, and the kids had to make themselves look, act, or walk like that animal until I called out the next animal. Sound effects were definitely part of the game, and they marched around the room "being" the named animal.

Calling out "Snakes" would have everyone lying on their bellies, wiggling and hissing; giraffes usually reached their arms up tall and stood on their toes; elephants swung their arms as trunks and plodded with big heavy steps; horses tossed their heads, whinnied, reared, and cantered. Well, you get the idea. Other animals that kids enjoyed acting out included crabs, cats, dogs, fish, whales, bulls, bears, lions, frogs, grasshoppers, monkeys, and penguins.

By mixing up the animals, housebound kids could really get a lot of wiggles out on rainy indoor days. We also played this game outdoors, on the trampoline, and I'll bet it would be fun in water, too. It's especially fun after a trip to the zoo. Sometimes they played without me, each taking turns being the caller.

This game calls on the child's thinking, memory, visualizing, creative, and physical skills.

Let's Get Started

Visit a town or city you've never seen before.

Figuring Out What to Learn

Jerry Mintz, Alternative Education Resource Organization, Roslyn Heights, New York, from *My Life as a Traveling Homeschooler* by Jenifer Goldman

One of the first things we did when we got back home was a question class where Jerry asked me to just brainstorm any questions that came to mind. Then I rated the ones I was most interested in, and we studied them first. Here are the questions I came up with; the numbers are my rating on a scale of ten. It took about half an hour.

- What's the point of this? 7
- How does a television work? 5
- Why are kids mean to me? 8

- Who invented the lamp shade? 5

- Who thought of putting pockets in pants? Who invented the zipper? Buttons? 7

- Who invented the computer? Who invented the mouse? Who invented the name Apple? How come Apple and Macintosh are related? 8

- Who invented the cellular phone, answering machine? 7

- Why doesn't my father live closer to me? 8

- Who built the first house on earth? 7

- Why can't people get along more easily? 8

- Who invented the piano? (Is that science or music?) 7

- Who invented written music? Who was the first person to write music for the piano? 7

- Who invented the desk, the table? 7

- How can I make more friends? 7

- Why don't I like to use the left hand in piano? (I know the answer a little bit.) 6

- Why do I dislike my artwork and other people always like it? 6

- Who wrote the first map? 7

- Who thought of having a leader for the first time? Where did it first happen—in towns, cities, states, and so on? 8

- Why did people start wearing makeup? 6

- Where did the first language come from? If they couldn't communicate with each other, how could they tell people what they meant? 8

- Who was the first rock-and-roll group? 8

- How much do electric guitars cost these days? 7

- Who was the first farmer? 8

- Why are all these questions "who was"? 7

- How come most grown-ups never understand us kids? 7

- How come kids don't understand kids sometimes? 7

- How come when deep down I'm getting tired of someone, I lose their phone number, and I don't even mean to? 7

- How come there isn't life on other planets? 8

- How come it appears that we know so much about outer space when we really know so little? 7

- How is it possible that the universe is limited? It seems impossible. There's got to be some point at which it stops. 8

- How come people believe in different religions and have to be separated because of that? 7

- Who ever thought of having fun? 7

- Who has time to have fun now anyway? 7

That's all I can think of.

- *My Life as a Traveling Homeschooler* by Jenifer Goldman (Solomon Press, 1991)

Fruity Curriculum
Hope Ware, Peoria, Illinois

I designed this game to incorporate many areas of study for my kindergarten-aged son. Begin by having the child draw and cut out various fruits or vegetables from construction paper (art/small group motor skills). Introduce some that he's never tried before. How do these plants grow? Do we eat the fruit, stalk, or roots of this plant (vocabulary/science/nature)? Show and try a sample of some of them (snack time). Use your five senses to describe their taste and texture (science). What sound does the fruit begin with (phonics)? How many letters are in its name (arithmetic)? What is your favorite fruit or vegetable and why (making choices/narration)? List the names of the chosen fruits or vegetables on a piece of paper (penmanship). On the far right side of your list, assign a price for each fruit or vegetable (math). Place the correct fruit or vegetable picture next to its name and price on the paper (language).

Next, have mom or the child "go shopping." We always switch roles halfway through the game. I give him 45¢, all in pennies. He visits my "store" and buys as many of the fruits and vegetables as he can. Once the money is spent, we replenish his supply and begin again. As the game progresses, I say, "You have 15¢ left. You can buy two fruits or one vegetable. Look at the price list and see if you can figure out which ones you can purchase [math]."

After the game, we cut apart the names of the fruits and vegetables and separate them so my son can use his phonics skills to match the correct fruit or vegetable to the correct written name (language arts). They can be sorted, too, by price, type of plant, fruit or vegetable, part of the plant we eat, and so on (sorting/classification).

Boy Scout Merit Badge Books
Linda Dobson, Saranac Lake, New York

Your child doesn't have to be a Boy Scout in order for you to go to the local Boy Scout supply store and purchase any of the merit badge books that your child may be interested in. The subject matter spans the curriculum, and each small book is loaded with information about a specific topic, including related projects. Of course, if your child earns a merit badge at the same time, so much the better!

As Close to Testing as I Ever Got

With a deck of trivia cards, such as those with Brain Quest or another child's question-and-answer game, we would gather on my bed or on pillows somewhere, each with his pennies. They had to have some money to play. I had my big jar of pennies.

Each child would have a little target bowl or box. I asked questions in turn. If Kirby didn't know, Marty got second shot, and so on. Right answers got a penny, aimed at his bowl. If they really should have known the answer, I got a penny. If there was no reason they could have known and they missed, no penny changed hands.

I skipped things that were too hard. I rearranged questions (without them knowing) so Holly, younger than the oldest by five years, could answer some easily. We played until we were tired, usually late at night, and they always made a profit. For me, it was as close as I ever came to testing. It helped me know where the edge of their learning was, on geography or spelling or whatever. We'd often have a globe or map or dictionary close at hand, but as an aid, so they could count continents or something.

Our favorite part was finding questions that should have had more than one answer, or when we thought the "correct" answer was wrong. Once a card asked, "Which uses electricity: a bed, a lamp, or a chair?" We discussed for a *long* time oil lamps in different cultures, and gas lamps. We listed adjustable hospital beds, beds or recliners with vibrator-massage features, "*the* electric chair," and more. Other cards evoked similar discussions and much more learning than I had planned on, but I never complained.

— *Sandra Dodd, Albuquerque, New Mexico*

The Square Learning Tool

Cindy Allas, Fairfield, California

My children learn a great deal from television shows like *Assignment Discovery, Zoom, Nigel's Wild, Wild World, Zooboomafoo, Nova, Dora the Explorer, Magic School Bus,* and The History Channel.

Do You Get It?

Juleigh Howard-Hobson, Sacramento, California

For painless forays into every subject under the sun, we hit upon using a joke book. You need to know your stuff to get jokes like, "What do you call a monster comedian? Blob Hope," or "What do ghosts do in Congress? They listen to the spooker of the house."

They seem like dumb groaners, but each one has led to discussions about U.S. history, democracy, pop culture, and so on.

Children's Most Important Work, Play

Luz Shosie, Guilford, Connecticut

Play is children's most important activity. It's the way they figure out how the world works, what part they have in the world. Scientists play with materials and concepts, writers play with words and ideas, inventors play with materials and concepts, parents learn how to play again.

A Full Moon Curriculum

Diane Flynn Keith, adapted from *Carschooling: 500 Games and Activities to Turn Travel Time into Learning Time*

My kids were always fascinated by stories about the moon. They loved *Good Night Moon* and *Grandfather Twilight* by Barbara Berger when they were little, and as they got older, were captivated by *Walk When the Moon Is Full*, about a family that took monthly walks in the light of the full moon. The latter inspired us to organize a "Full Moon Walk" for a group of homeschooling families. We met at a heavily wooded park after dark on the night of a full moon. (Because the park officially closed at sunset, we got permission in advance from the park ranger to enter the park after hours.) We walked along a trail using just our night vision to see nocturnal creatures (an owl, opossum, bat, and raccoon). Then we came to a clearing—a meadow—and everyone played Moon Shadow Tag (whoever is "it" tries to step on the shadow of someone else). The full moon casts wonderful shadows, and the kids adored playing this game with the slower adults. After the game, we sat down for some hot cocoa and cookies and tried to identify a few constellations in the night sky.

The finale of the evening was that everyone was given a pack of WintOGreen LifeSavers. If you chew them in the dark with your mouth open, they let off sparks! This two-part phenomenon is called triboluminescence. When you crush sugar crystals with your teeth, they split apart with positive charges on one side and negative on the other, and emit an invisible ultraviolet light. It's very difficult to see the light with most sugar crystals. However, WintOGreen LifeSavers have another ingredient that makes the light brighter. Methyl salicylate, the flavor ingredient, absorbs the ultraviolet light and then emits it as visible light. We offered this explanation to the kids, who preferred to believe they had magically captured some moonlight in their mouths.

On the way home in the car, we sang moon tunes: *Moon River, Blue Moon, Moondance, By the Light of the Silvery Moon, Mr. Moonlight, Shine On Harvest Moon, Moonshadow, Moon Over Miami, Mississippi Moon,* and *That's Amore* ("When the moon hits your eye like a big pizza pie, that's *amore!*") It was a memorable, fun, and educational evening for everyone.

Let's Get Started

Lie in the grass together on a sunny day when you don't have any pressing engagements.

- *Goodnight Moon* by Margaret Wise Brown (HarperFestival, 1991)
- *Grandfather Twilight* by Barbara Helen Berger (Putnam Publishing Group Juvenile, 1984)

- *Walk When the Moon Is Full* by Frances Hamerstrom (Crossing Press, 1976)
- *Carschooling: 500 Games and Activities to Turn Travel Time into Learning Time* by Diane Flynn Keith (Prima Publishing, 2002)

Dinner Schooling
Jennifer Miller, Puyallup, Washington

Put a map, poster, periodic table of elements, or whatever you like on your dining room table and cover it with clear plastic vinyl. Dinner conversation is always interesting and educational.

Games
Cindy Allas, Fairfield, California

We play games: President's Rummy, Hive Alive, Carmen Sandiego, Lucky 13, Assignment Disc, Yahtzee, Count Dino, any games with numbers, Scrabble, UpWords, Battleship.

Games with a Twist
Jane Powell, Bowie, Maryland

Scrabble for Younger (Nonspelling) Folk

Ask that they tell you what the letter is, then place it on the board. Once they master the names of the letters, ask them to tell you the sound and the letter.

Trouble

Use it to teach your child number recognition and counting.

Uno

Played like Go Fish, it can help teach sorting, numbers, and letters.

We Love Noncompetitive Games!

Debbie Eaton, Rock Tavern, New York

A great Canadian company called Family Pastimes has wonderful games that emphasize cooperation and cover many aspects of a curriculum. We love them!

- Family Pastimes, R.R. #4, Perth, Ontario, Canada K7H 3C6; www.familypastimes.com

Leave 'Em Wanting to Know More

Jean Reed, Bridgewater, Maine, courtesy of *Home School Source Book*

Sometimes we sparked curiosity and learning by putting up wall posters of historical events or well-known people or quotations. At times we introduced the people, idea, or event and talked about it or read about it. At other times we found that if we just put up the posters, the children would get curious and do their own research, telling everyone else in the family about what they'd learned.

You can find posters in teacher supply catalogs and stores.

Don't Recycle—Learn!

Jane Powell, Bowie, Maryland

Here are just a few uses for old magazines, newspapers, and junk mail to learn:

Body Parts

Cut out eyes, ears, nose, mouth, and so on. Either have the child glue them to paper or do it yourself (on construction paper, newsprint, newspaper, etc.). Discuss what the names of the parts are and ask the child to tell you what they are.

Feelings

Cut out eyes, mouths, or any expressive body part. Glue them on paper and have the child tell you what feelings they are demonstrating. Ask the child to show you how he looks when he feels _____.

Number Order

Cut out numbers and have the child put them in sequential order. Could work with letters, too, in alphabetical order.

Number Recognition

Cut out numbers and have the child tell you what the numbers are. Could work with letters, too.

Create Theme Collages

Cut out a bunch of things and ask your child to create something. The theme could be nature, things with wheels, people, food, the letter ___, a given number of items, a country (import/exports, typical activities, sites, etc.), or a state. This is also a good way to introduce your next subject!

Toddler's Bank Diversion

Hope Ware, Peoria, Illinois

This is the *best* accidental idea I've ever had for keeping my toddler busy while his older brother and I work. One day he came to me with a small metal bank and begged to play with it. I was desperate, so I said yes.

He sat on the floor, joyfully removed the plastic stopper on the bottom of the bank, dumped the contents into a small bowl, then carefully placed each coin into the slot. He loved the plink of the coins as they hit the bottom of the metal bank, and was happily occupied for forty minutes! He was so fascinated with the game that I gave him *two* banks the next time.

Let's Get Started

Create a game that will help someone learn math, spelling, adjectives, new words, presidents, countries, direction, measurements.

Code Crash

Jerry Mintz, Alternative Education Resource Organization, Roslyn Heights, New York

For those interested in learning Morse code, I created a videotape on which two children learn the code in less than twenty minutes. The technique consists of associating the shape of the letter with its sound. "Dah" and "dit" are used for long and short. For example, the four shorts for the letter *H* are associated with the four corners of the letter. For the letter *B*, we think of the long line on the left as "dah," and the three lines going out for three "dits." Since people usually think of *M* for mother, it's easy to remember that *M* is "dah, dah." It's all reviewed and reinforced, and even the numbers are included.

- *Code Crash* videotape, AERO, 417 Roslyn Road, Roslyn Heights, New York 11577, or email jmintz@igc.apc.org.

Play Chess!
Linda Dobson, Saranac Lake, New York

If you know how to play chess, teach the kids. If you don't know how to play, learn with the kids. Your children will be learning much more than a thirteen-hundred-year-old game.

Research studies have shown that New York's inner-city children who learn to play chess show math score increases as high as 27 percent, in large part because the game increases the logical-mathematical intelligence, one of Howard Gardner's multiple intelligences.

Other enhancements are not as obvious. Visual-spatial intelligence gets a boost as your child improves her ability to think in pictures and visualize a future result from the moves she makes. Self-analysis after games improves intrapersonal intelligence. If playing as part of a team, social intelligence improves. Your child learns to relate to other people and work effectively with them.

Researchers have also found that an improvement in chess players' reading ability makes sense, as both activities involve decoding, comprehending, and analyzing toward making decisions.

Playing chess is also just a lot of fun!

Lego or Knex Challenge Cards
Bonnie Dolack, Philadelphia, Pennsylvania

When I wanted my eight year-old son to be a bit more inventive with the thousands of Lego and Knex pieces he already has, I decided to make up some idea cards for him. I use index cards and call them Lego/Knex Challenge cards.

Here are some examples. Build something as tall as yourself. Build something that spins. Build a musical instrument, play it, and make up a song. Build something that uses only one color of Legos. Build an amusement park ride. What is it called and how much does it cost to ride? Build a pyramid. Build something that will hold your weight if you sit on it. Build something that shows a repeating pattern.

These cards can be written according to your child's interests and age. My son spends hours working on these when the spirit moves him!

Special Interest
Lillian Jones, Sebastopol, California

The most learning-intensive activities are usually those that support the child's special interests. When a special interest exists, you can bet there's a lot of juice there; if you can facilitate that interest while staying out of the way (often the trickiest part), you never know where that interest may lead. It may lead to a career goal, a lifelong passion, or just a means toward learning simple skills that enhance other learning pursuits.

This can require a challenging amount of trust. We've been trained to think learning needs to be structured and methodical for effectiveness, but those who have been at homeschooling for a while see with our own eyes the wonders that emerge from unobtrusively supporting children in their interests. It might be something that seems world's apart from the "academic" subjects on which we place importance, but the seemingly unimportant things can become the most important in a child's future.

My son had an early interest in humor. He watched old cartoons with fascination, analyzing themes, the way characters responded to incidents, and what the writers felt would make people laugh. He did the same with old television shows like *Get Smart* and

Mary Tyler Moore. He looked up humor on the Internet to find out what psychologists have to say about the role humor plays in the human experience.

Now that he's in college, his humor impressed his English teachers, and I've a strong feeling it will somehow be an important part of his future career. Regardless, it will always be an important part of his private life, as it always has been.

People worry about whether their children properly learn a foreign language they may or may not ever use, but often overlook the vital importance of things that actually bear greater real importance in their children's lives. There's an old expression, "Take time to stop and smell the flowers." I think that same philosophy can be applied to "Take time to stop and listen to your child."

Audio Cassettes, Coloring Books, and Paper Dolls

Jean Reed, Bridgewater, Maine, from *Home School Source Book*

We stumbled into using cassette tapes by chancing upon an ad for old radio tapes that triggered a generational phenomenon. Five years can make a big different in perspective. I grew up watching television and can't remember the radio having any particular impact on me in any way. My husband, Donn, five years older, grew up when the radio was the major form of news and entertainment.

When Donn ordered the first old radio tapes, I thought we were throwing away our money for a one-time, thirty-minute buzz. Boy, was I wrong. With great dramatized literature and history on tape, we traveled back in time, around the world, and through our imaginations. Without giving it a thought, we learned about people and places we'd never heard of.

We always read to the kids, but at bedtime in particular they could frequently outlast our ability to stay awake and read coherently. Donn rewired the house to put speakers into the kid's room. They could then listen to stories, and we could have a little peace and quiet for ourselves.

We also used the tapes during the day. With the addition of historical coloring books or paper dolls to cut out and color, everyone had a good time. The CBS *You Are There* historical series prompted us to use maps and a globe. We also found that our kids particularly liked the paper dolls and would research historical figures, then write up biographies for "their people."

- Dover Publications (inexpensive coloring books and paper dolls): 11 East 2nd Street, Mineola, New York 11501; 800-223-3130; store.doverpublications.com

- Bellerophon Books (better for children ten years and up): P.O. Box 21307, Santa Barbara, California 93121; 800-253-9943; www.bellerophonbooks.com

- Brook Farm Books (historical coloring books, paper dolls, cassette tapes, and maps): P.O. Box 246, Bridgewater, Maine 04735 (request free brochure)

Modern Approach to the Oregon Trail— Take the Train

Pennie Rowland, Lake Oswego, Oregon

When we take family trips, we travel by train. We're modern-day Oregon Trail travelers, having moved to Oregon from New York City for a chance at a better life. Along the way, our daughter saw major cities, historical landmarks, and ghost towns, enabling her to use her imagination about all the places she visited. So far she has 18,000 miles of train travel under the belt, and many more to come.

Mealtime Alphabetical Quiz

Patty Roberts, Walnut Shade, Missouri

The quiz category is determined by what letter we are on. If the letter is *A*, for example, Dad or I might pick "animals" for the category. We don't tell the children what the category is.

Next we ask each child (ages two, seven, ten, and eleven) a skill-appropriate question. In the animal category, the two-year-old might be asked, "What do you call something that barks?" The seven-year-old might be asked to tell where moles sleep. Naming parts of an insect or three characteristics of mammals falls to the ten- and eleven-year-old. Somewhere along the way, the kids usually figure out the category, then anyone asks Dad and Mom questions. When all have answered a question, we move on to the next letter.

Sometimes we cover several letters at a meal; other times, one letter lasts the whole meal. We keep a world map on the dining room wall and a dictionary on the shelf for reference, if needed. Now, almost as soon as the food is blessed, one of the children calls out, "Quizzes, please!"

Find a Mentor

Athena Dalrymple, Columbia, Maryland

Using mentors is a great way to help a child learn. Here are some ways in which a child can find a mentor:

- Write to the author of a book on a topic in which the child is interested.

- Attend talks on a topic of interest at museums and elsewhere, and ask good questions of the speaker.

- Mingle with adults at parties and elsewhere to share areas of interest and find out what the adults do as careers and hobbies.

- Attend university open houses and ask for tours of the school's areas that might be of interest, such as a nuclear reactor, the AIDS research lab, and so on.

- Research the top names in the child's field of interest, then write to ask how they managed to become so successful and what advice they might offer a young student who wishes to succeed in the same field.

Models, Kits, and Mobiles

Jean Reed, Bridgewater, Maine, courtesy of *Home School Source Book*

We found that making models, kits, and mobiles that related to our history, science, geography, and other studies helped build in our children a stronger interest in what they were studying.

- Parkwest Publications, 451 Communipaw Ave., Jersey City, NJ 07304; 201-432-3257; www.parkwestpubs.com

Philosophy Room

Linda Dobson, Saranac Lake, New York

No, you don't need to build an extra room onto your home. In fact, you already have the perfect place for a "philosophy room," your bathroom!

Quite by accident, I discovered that by typesetting life-enhancing quotes and hanging them in the bathroom, even my youngest read and memorized them. It worked so well that I expanded the idea to include misspelled words, multiplication tables, and even maps showing the settings of books we were reading. It was amazing, actually.

Conversation Starters

- Take a walk through the busiest part of town.
- Stay up all night (or as long as your child is able), make pop-corn, leave the TV off, answer inevitable questions.
- What is your favorite season? Why?
- On last night's news there was a story about _____. How do you feel about this?
- How has using your imagination helped you solve problems?

Index

Sundial, human, 154–155
"Supporting Homeschooling Shut-Ins," 307–308
"Surrogate Grandchildren," 236
Symmetry, 209–210

T

"Tactile Letters," 89
"Take-Out Books," 104
Tambourine sticks, bottlecap, 220–221
Tangrams, 74–75
"Tasting Game," 137–138
Teaching Mathematics, 77
"Telephone Pole," 288–289
Television. *See* TV
Testing: authentic assessment vs., 29; learning and transfer evaluation and, 32; school mind and, 6; self-improvement vs., 15; trivia questions and, 321
"Test the Parent," 196
"Thank You Very Much," 115–116
"These Are a Few of My Favorite Things," 112
"Think Close to Home," 193
"This Old Magazine," 103
"Three Questions," 108
Tightwad Gazette, The, 159
Time: activity, 72; autonomous use of, 16–17; best times for field trips, 301–302; learning vs. busywork, 31
"Time Line Game," 195
Time lines, 170–171, 194–195
"*Time* Magazine as a Resource," 183–184
Tithing, 235–236
"Toddler's Bank Diversion," 327
"To Do Lists," 92
"To Fly," 162–163
"Tons, Tons, Tons of Information," 254–255
Tool use, 245
"Total Physical Response (TPR)," 126
Touch, children's need for, 12–13
"Track Food to Its Source," 247
"Tracking Mail or Phone Calls," 173
Traditions, creating, 287–288
Transcontinental railroad, 198
Transfer of learning, promoting, 31–32
Trapeze, flying, 233–234
"Traveling Times Tables," 57
Treasure hunts. *See* Scavenger and treasure hunts
Tree observations, 150
Trivia questions, 321
Trouble game, 324
"Try a New Sport Together," 241
"Turn a Pool into a Pond," 138
TV: closed captioning, 105; educational shows, 321; language arts and, 105, 123–124; limiting viewing of, 207; public access, 123–124; scientific news reports on, 129; Web sites, 254; *You Are There* historical series, 331
"26 Letter Pick-Up," 284
"Twisted Concentration," 55

U

Underground History of American Education, The, 21
Understanding Fractions, 77
"Unforgettable," 315–316
Unnecessary words, reminding about, 123
Uno card game, 325
"Up Close and Personal," 155–156
"Up on the Ceiling, It's the Alphabet!," 93
Urgent Action newsletter (Amnesty International), 188
"Use It, Don't Lose It," 122
"Use that Extra Check Transaction Booklet," 280–281

V

"Valediction Against Mourning, A," 107
"Veggie Geography," 181
"Velcro-Aided Graphs," 73–74
"Verbal Scavenger Hunt," 125
"Versatile Dominoes," 48
"Versatile Treasure Hunt," 141
Vexillogy (study of maps), 167–168, 171–176, 249
Videotaping: exercise routines, 240; music video, 225
"Visitors from Another Culture," 237
"Visual Square Number Patterns," 57–58
Vocabulary, 117–118, 120–122, 275
"Vocabulary Building Leads to Spelling Proficiency," 117–118
"Volunteer in Soup Kitchen," 236
Volunteer work. *See* Community service

W

"Wacky Cake Chemistry," 145–146
Walk When the Moon is Full, 322, 324
Wampum belts, 196–197
War card game, mathematics using, 52, 59–60, 68
"Watching Water Cycles," 139–140
"Wayne Kapit's Coloring Book," 179
"Weather Diary," 154
Weather (meteorology), 154–155
Web sites. *See* Internet resources
"Wednesday Cleanse Day," 296
"We Love Noncompetitive Games!," 325

About the Author

Linda Dobson is the author of six books about home education and is an international speaker on education issues. A former news analyst for a national magazine, she has provided scores of media interviews for radio talk shows and publications, such as *The Wall Street Journal, U.S. News & World Report, Reader's Digest,* and "Live Online" for the *Washington Post.* Media appearances include "Upfront Tonight" with Diane Diamond (CNBC) and "The News with Brian Williams" (MSNBC). Linda serves on her town council, is the early years' advisor for Homeschool.com, is a columnist, edits the Prima Publishing Home Learning Library series, and loves learning how to play golf. She lives on Mt. Pisgah in Saranac Lake, New York.